Deep Fusion of Computational
and Symbolic Processing

Studies in Fuzziness and Soft Computing

Editor-in-chief
Prof. Janusz Kacprzyk
Systems Research Institute
Polish Academy of Sciences
ul. Newelska 6
01-447 Warsaw, Poland
E-mail: kacprzyk@ibspan.waw.pl
http://www.springer.de/cgi-bin/search_book.pl?series = 2941

Vol. 3. A. Geyer-Schulz
*Fuzzy Rule-Based Expert Systems
and Genetic Machine Learning, 2nd ed. 1996*
ISBN 3-7908-0964-0

Vol. 4. T. Onisawa and J. Kacprzyk (Eds.)
*Reliability and Safety Analyses under Fuzziness,
1995*
ISBN 3-7908-0837-7

Vol. 5. P. Bosc and J. Kacprzyk (Eds.)
Fuzziness in Database Management Systems, 1995
ISBN 3-7908-0858-X

Vol. 6. E.S. Lee and Q. Zhu
Fuzzy and Evidence Reasoning, 1995
ISBN 3-7908-0880-6

Vol. 7. B.A. Juliano and W. Bandler
Tracing Chains-of-Thought, 1996
ISBN 3-7908-0922-5

Vol. 8. F. Herrera and J.L. Verdegay (Eds.)
Genetic Algorithms and Soft Computing, 1996
ISBN 3-7908-0956-X

Vol. 9. M. Sato et al.
Fuzzy Clustering Models and Applications, 1997
ISBN 3-7908-1026-6

Vol. 10. L.C. Jain (Ed.)
*Soft Computing Techniques in Knowledge-based
Intelligent Engineering Systems, 1997*
ISBN 3-7908-1035-5

Vol. 11. W. Mielczarski (Ed.)
Fuzzy Logic Techniques in Power Systems, 1998,
ISBN 3-7908-1044-4

Vol. 12. B. Bouchon-Meunier (Ed.)
*Aggregation and Fusion of Imperfect Information,
1998*
ISBN 3-7908-1048-7

Vol. 13. E. Orłowska (Ed.)
Incomplete Information: Rough Set Analysis, 1998
ISBN 3-7908-1049-5

Vol. 14. E. Hisdal
*Logical Structures for Representation of Knowledge
and Uncertainty, 1998*
ISBN 3-7908-1056-8

Vol. 15. G.J. Klir and M.J. Wierman
Uncertainty-Based Information, 2nd ed., 1999
ISBN 3-7908-1242-0

Vol. 16. D. Driankov and R. Palm (Eds.)
Advances in Fuzzy Control, 1998
ISBN 3-7908-1090-8

Vol. 17. L. Reznik, V. Dimitrov and J. Kacprzyk
(Eds.)
Fuzzy Systems Design, 1998
ISBN 3-7908-1118-1

Vol. 18. L. Polkowski and A. Skowron (Eds.)
Rough Sets in Knowledge Discovery 1, 1998
ISBN 3-7908-1119-X

Vol. 19. L. Polkowski and A. Skowron (Eds.)
Rough Sets in Knowledge Discovery 2, 1998
ISBN 3-7908-1120-3

Vol. 20. J.N. Mordeson and P.S. Nair
Fuzzy Mathematics, 1998
ISBN 3-7908-1121-1

Vol. 21. L.C. Jain and T. Fukuda (Eds.)
*Soft Computing for Intelligent Robotic Systems,
1998*
ISBN 3-7908-1147-5

Vol. 22. J. Cardoso and H. Camargo (Eds.)
Fuzziness in Petri Nets, 1999
ISBN 3-7908-1158-0

Vol. 23. P.S. Szczepaniak (Ed.)
Computational Intelligence and Applications, 1999
ISBN 3-7908-1161-0

Vol. 24. E. Orłowska (Ed.)
Logic at Work, 1999
ISBN 3-7908-1164-5

Vol. 25. J. Buckley and Th. Feuring
*Fuzzy and Neural: Interactions and Applications,
1999*
ISBN 3-7908-1170-X

continued on page 255

Takeshi Furuhashi
Shun'Ichi Tano
Hans-Arno Jacobsen
Editors

Deep Fusion
of Computational
and Symbolic Processing

With 145 Figures
and 13 Tables

Physica-Verlag

A Springer-Verlag Company

Dr. Takeshi Furuhashi
Nagoya University
Department of Information and Electronics
Furo-cho, Chikusa-ku
Nagoya 464-8603
Japan
furuhashi@nuee.nagoya-u.ac.jp

Dr. Shun'Ichi Tano
University of Electro-Communications
Graduate School of Information Systems
1-5-1 Choufugaoka
Choufu 182-8585
Japan
tano@is.uec.ac.jp

Dr. Hans-Arno Jacobsen
INRIA-Rocquencourt
Project CARAVEL
B.P. 105
78153 Le Chesnay Cedex
France
jacobsen@wiwi.hu-berlin.de
jacobsen@inria.fr

ISSN 1434-9922
ISBN 978-3-662-00373-2

Cataloging-in-Publication Data applied for
Die Deutsche Bibliothek – CIP-Einheitsaufnahme
Deep fusion of computational and symbolic processing: with 13 tables / Takeshi Furuhashi
... ed. – Heidelberg; New York: Physica-Verl., 2001
    (Studies in fuzziness and soft computing; Vol. 59)
    ISBN 978-3-662-00373-2   ISBN 978-3-7908-1837-6 (eBook)
    DOI 10.1007/978-3-7908-1837-6

Physica-Verlag Heidelberg New York
a member of BertelsmannSpringer Science+Business Media GmbH

© Physica-Verlag Heidelberg 2001

Softcover reprint of the hardcover 1st edition 2001

Hardcover Design: Erich Kirchner, Heidelberg

SPIN 10783082   88/2202-5 4 3 2 1 0 – Printed on acid-free paper

Foreword

"Deep Fusion of Computational and Symbolic Processing(DFCSP) is a bold effort to advance our ability to conceive, design and utilize systems which possess a much higher level of machine intelligence (MIQ) than those we have today.

Edited by T. Furuhashi, S. Tano and H-A. Jacobsen, DFCSP is a collection of original contributions by leading researchers in their fields. Authoritative and up-to-date, these contributions address a wide variety of issues and techniques which relate to the main theme of the volume: fusion of two fundamental modes of computer-based reasoning – symbolic and computational. These modes of reasoning had few bridges between them in the past.

The rapidly growing complexity and sophistication of modern information/intelligent systems makes it clear that achievement of success requires a marshalling of all of the methodologies and technologies which are in our possession. This is the genesis of the concept of soft computing, which is a consortium of fuzzy logic, neurocomputing, evolutionary computing, probabilistic computing, chaotic computing, machine learning and related methodologies. The same perception underlies the fusion of symbolic and computational methodologies in DFCSP.

Historically, symbol manipulation has been – and largely continues to be – the main province of AI. In recent years, however, it became increasingly clear that, by itself, symbolic processing is not powerful enough to deal with systems in which decision-relevant information is numerical rather than symbolic. Such is the case in robotics, computer vision, motion planning, diagnostics, and many other problem-areas in which machine intelligence plays an important role. The earlier, almost exclusive, commitment of mainstream AI to symbol manipulation has created separatist tendencies which led to the emergence of computation-oriented schools of thought which are embodied in computational intelligence, soft computing and what is referred to by some as New AI. In one way or another, the underlying idea in these schools of thought is that what is needed is a rapprochement between symbolic and computational paradigms in reasoning and information processing. It is this fundamental idea that is the leitmotif of DFCSP.

In examining the contents of DFCSP one sees an important trend that I should like to comment on in greater detail. Specifically what we see is a growing visibility of techniques in which natural language processing plays an essential role. This trend is a manifestation of realization that natural languages have a far greater expressive power than predicate-logic-based meaning-representation systems which lie at the center of AI.

To harness the power of natural languages what is needed is what may be called the computational theory of perceptions (CTP). This theory is inspired by the remarkable human capability to perform a wide variety of physical and mental tasks without any measurements and any computations. Everyday examples of such tasks are parking a car, driving in city traffic, playing golf, cooking a meal, deciphering sloppy handwriting and summarizing a story. Underlying this capability, is the brain's crucial ability to reason with perceptions – perceptions of time, distance, speed, force, direction, shape, intent, likelihood and truth, among others.

Perceptions are intrinsically imprecise. More specifically, most perceptions are both fuzzy and granular, or f-granular, for short. The fuzziness and granularity of perceptions is a concomitant of a fundamental limitation on the ability of sensory organs and, ultimately, the brain, to resolve detail and store information.

To be able to compute with perceptions it is necessary to have a way of representing their meaning in a computational-oriented framework. The f-granularity of perceptions places them well beyond the expressive power of conventional methods of meaning- representation. In the computational theory of perceptions, meaning representation is realized through the use of what is referred to as constraint-oriented semantics of natural languages (CSNL). A concept that plays a key role in CSNL is that of a generalized constraint. Basically, a generalized constraint is a family of constraints of various types which includes possibilistic constraints, veristic constraints, probabilistic constraints, random set constraints, Pawlak set constraints, usuality constraints and fuzzy graph constraints, among others. These constraints and their combinations serve to constrain the values which a variable can take. Thus, in CSNL the meaning of a perception, which is described by a proposition, p, in a natural language, is represented as a constraint on a variable – a variable which is implicit in p. The class of such representations constitutes what is called the generalized constraint language (GCL). In this framework, constraint-oriented semantics of natural languages may be viewed as a method of expressing the meaning of perceptions as expressions in GCL. Furthermore, computation and reasoning with perceptions is reduced to goal-directed constraint propagation from antecedent constraints to consequent constraints. The rules governing generalized constraint propagation coincide with the rules of inference in fuzzy logic.

The importance of the computational theory of perceptions derives from the fact that it provides a machinery for processing of information which is perception-based rather than measurement-based. Existing scientific theories, especially probability theory, utility theory, decision analysis and control do not have this capability. Thus, in existing theories perceptions are dealt with by converting them into measurements. The problem is that conversion of perceptions into measurements – which is traditionally viewed as a desideratum in science – is frequently infeasible, unrealistic or counterproductive. By adding the capability to compute with perceptions to existing theories, CTP lays the groundwork for a significant generalization of measurement-based theories – a generalization which in retrospect may be seen as a basic paradigm shift from computation with measurements to computation with perceptions.

Although DFCSP does not contain an exposition of the computational theory of perceptions, its main theme – the deep fusion of computation and symbolic processing – is essential to the development of CTP and, more generally, to an enlargement of the role of natural languages in the conception, design and utilization of high MIQ systems. Such systems are certain to play a major role in the evolving knowledge-based society which is now in its initial stages of gestation.

Viewed in this perspective, the issues addressed in DFCSP are of pivotal importance. The editors, the authors and the publisher have produced a text which is a must reading for anyone who is interested in latest advances in the realm of information/intelligent systems. Deep Fusion of Computational and Symbolic Processing is an outstanding work in all respects. Its creators deserve our thanks and congratulations.

Lotfi A. Zadeh

June 28, 2000

Introduction

Symbolic processing has limitations as highlighted by the symbol grounding problem. Computational processing methods, like fuzzy logic, neural networks, and statistical methods appear to have overcome some of these limitations. However, these methods also suffer from shortcomings in that, for example, multi-stage inference is difficult to realize. The deep fusion of symbolic and computational processing is expected to open up a new paradigm for building intelligent systems. In this paradigm, symbolic processing and computational processing should interact at all abstract and computational levels. For this undertaking, attempts to combine these processing techniques must be thoroughly investigated and the direction of novel integrated approaches must be clarified.

In this volume leading researches in the field show the current status of this approach and discuss future research directions. This volume intends to be a comprehensive coverage of recent developments in the study of soft computing methodologies for the deep fusion of symbolic and computational processing, including both theoretical, as well as, practical aspects. The individual chapters have been written by leading scholars and researchers from all parts of the world.

This book consists of three major parts: Integration of Computational and Symbolic Processing, Toward Deep Fusion of Computational and Symbolic Processing, and Knowledge Representation. Each part contains recent results of innovative and highly advanced studies.

In the first Chapter Sun and Peterson present a hybrid model that combines neural, symbolic, and reinforcement learning into one architecture. This model learns not only low-level skills but also high-level declarative knowledge. The high-level knowledge is acquired from an agent's experience interacting with the world through the mediation of low-level skills. Sun and Peterson distinguish (conceptual) declarative knowledge and (sub-conceptual) procedural skills through the difference in accessibility. Declarative knowledge is easily accessible and linguistically expressible, whereas procedural skills are not. The authors conjecture that symbols should be grounded, not only in sub-symbolic activities, but also in the direct interactions between the agent and the world. Concepts, represented by symbols, are not formed in isolation from the world. They are formed in relation to the life-world of agents, through the perceptual apparatuses of agents, linked to their goals, needs, and actions. The authors demonstrate that symbols can be grounded in this manner through their system, CLARION.

In the second Chapter, Ohsuga discusses integration of different information processing methods, such as procedural programming, declarative knowledge-based approaches, and neural network processing. Ohsuga concludes that only symbolic and declarative knowledge-based processing method are suited for an integrator to integrate any combination of the different processing methods. He clarifies a big gap existing between symbolic and non-symbolic information processing methods based on a mathematical formalization and proposes an extension of knowledge-based processing to expand upon the scope of integration.

In the third Chapter Tsukimoto presents a concept for the integration of symbols and patterns. The integration brings about the logical reasoning of patterns and the numerical computation of symbols. This is achieved by combining logical reasoning and neural network processing. Tsukimoto describes patterns with functions: three-layered feed-forward neural networks, regarded as function approximators, and neural networks, regarded as multi-linear functions. Multi-linear functions can be used to model propositions of intermediate logic. This forms the basis for a framework allowing to reason with patterns.

FYNESSE (Fuzzy-Neuro-System) is presented by Schoknecht et al. in Chapter 4. This system consists of a fuzzy controller that proposes possible control actions, and a neural critic that learns to select the optimal control action from the set of proposed actions. The fuzzy controller allows the incorporation of vague and uncertain a priori knowledge describing the control strategy. Schoknecht et al. compare FYNESSE with CLARION and point out several differences.

In Chapter 5, Takeuchi and Furuhashi present a new modeling scheme for dynamic systems by introducing fuzziness into symbolic dynamic system. This approach introduces topological nature into symbolic sequences, which allows an interpretation of the knowledge in a numerical manner.

In Chapter 6, Osorio et al. clarify four properties a hybrid symbolic-connectionist system should offer. Their hybrid system INSS (Incremental Neuro-Symbolic System) endows these properties. INSS is comprised of a constructive network that is able to develop its structure and its knowledge while maintaining the old knowledge intact. INSS performs an incremental rule extraction to analyze only the newly added units. Production rules are inserted in artificial neural network by the cascade-correlation learning algorithm, and fuzzy rules are extracted from the trained neural network.

In Chapter 7, Jacobsen classifies state-of-the-art intelligent systems into four classes: (1) single component systems, (2) fusion-based systems, (3) hierarchical systems, and (4) hybrid systems. He then focuses on hybrid systems. In these systems adaptive components are integrated in complementary fashion on a side-by-side basis. Jacobsen presents two original hybrid intelligent systems, one based on a reinforcement-driven fuzzy relation adaptation architecture and the other one based on an expert guided neural fuzzy system.

Tano proposes a new paradigm for the deep fusion of computational and symbolic processing in Chapter 8. His model consists of two layers: the lower layer is a neural network implementing Q-learning, and the upper layer watches for emerging symbols from the lower layer. The emerging symbols are generalized and embedded into the different position in the lower layer. This model realizes an autonomous interaction between computational and symbolic processing at all abstract and computational levels.

In Chapter 9, Takagi introduces Conceptual Fuzzy Sets (CFS) to represent meaning of concepts. The CFS represent meaning through the distribution of activation of labels that name a concept. The meaning of a concept is represented by the totality of its use. The CFS can represent various context dependent meanings. The CFS are realized using an associative memory, and a combination of symbolic and computational processing is achieved.

Hagiwara and Ikeda present a knowledge representation method referred to as area representation of knowledge and motivate an implementation of this scheme by neural networks in Chapter 10. The area representation can express hierarchical knowledge by employing a new inclusion relation in which an upper level concept includes its lower level concepts. This inclusion relation also solves the part/whole problem by representing the upper level concept by the whole area of the lower level concepts.

In the last chapter, Mukai et al. propose a method to extract elemental motion units from gesture motion images using a self-organizing network. They also present a gesture recognition method for a large vocabulary based on the recognition of elemental motion units. A gesture is a non-verbal symbol and is considered as a pattern. Their work addresses the mapping of patterns to symbols.

We are confident that this volume has successfully collected leading work in the field working towards deep fusion of computational and symbolic processing. We thank all the reviewers who devoted their precious time in improving the quality of the contributions and this volume.

Takeshi FURUHASHI
Shun-ichi TANO
Hans-Arno JACOBSEN

Contents

Foreword   V
L. A. Zadeh

Introduction   IX
T. Furuhashi, S. Tano and H.-A. Jacobsen

Part I. Integration of Computational and Symbolic Processing

A Subsymbolic and Symbolic Model for Learning Sequential
Decision Tasks   3
R. Sun, T. Peterson

Integration of Different Information Processing Methods   21
S. Ohsuga

Symbol Pattern Integration Using Multilinear Functions   41
H. Tsukimoto

Part II. Toward Deep Fusion of Computational and Symbolic Processing

Design of Autonomously Learning Controllers Using FYNESSE   73
R. Schocknecht, M. Spott, M. Riedmiller

Modeling for Dynamical Systems with Fuzzy Sequential Knowledge 104
I. Takeuchi, T. Furuhashi

Hybrid Machine Learning Tools: INSS - A Neuro-Symbolic System
for Constructive Machine Learning   121
F. Osorio, B. Amy, A. Cechin

A Generic Architecture for Hybrid Intelligent Systems   145
H.-A. Jacobsen

New Paradigm toward Deep Fusion of Computational
and Symbolic Processing   173
S. Tano

Part III. Knowledge Representation

Fusion of Symbolic and Quantitative Processing
by Conceptual Fuzzy Sets   201
T. Takagi

Novel Knowledge Representation (Area Representation)
and the Implementation by Neural Network   220
M. Hagiwara and N. Ikeda

A Symbol Grounding Problem of Gesture Motion through
a Self-organizing Network of Time-varying Motion Images   238
T. Mukai, T. Nishimura, T. Endo, R. Oka

Index   251

Part I

Integration of Computational and Symbolic Processing

A Subsymbolic and Symbolic Model for Learning Sequential Decision Tasks

Ron Sun, Todd Peterson

[1] NEC Research Institute, 4 Independence Way, Princeton, NJ 08540
[2] The University of Alabama, Tuscaloosa, AL 35487
{rsun, todd}@cs.ua.edu

Abstract: For dealing with reactive sequential decision tasks, a learning model CLARION was developed, which is a hybrid connectionist model consisting of both localist (symbolic) and distributed representations, based on the two-level approach proposed in Sun (1995). The model learns and utilizes procedural and declarative knowledge, tapping into the synergy of the two types of processes. It unifies neural, reinforcement, and symbolic methods to perform on-line, bottom-up learning (from subsymbolic to symbolic knowledge). Experiments in various situations shed light on the working of the model. Its theoretical implications in terms of symbol grounding are also discussed.

1.1 Introduction

We present here a hybrid model that unifies neural, symbolic, and reinforcement learning into an integrated architecture. It addresses the following three issues: (1) It deals with concurrent on-line learning: It allows a situated agent to learn continuously from on-going experience in the world, without the use of preconstructed data sets or preconceived concepts. (2) The model learns not only low-level specific skills but also high-level (declarative) knowledge (which is beyond traditional reinforcement learning algorithms as will be discussed later). (3) The learning is bottom-up: high-level knowledge is acquired from an agent's experience interacting with the world through the mediation of low-level skills. This differs from top-down learning in which low-level knowledge is acquired through "compiling" mostly externally given high-level knowledge (Anderson 1983). In this article, we will focus first on computational issues. We will then discuss its implications in terms of symbol grounding.

Reactive sequential decision tasks (see Bertsekas and Tsitsiklis 1996, Kaelbling et al 1996, and references cited therein) involve selecting and performing a sequence of actions, step by step, on the basis of the current state, or the moment-to-moment perceptual information (hence the term "reactive"). At certain points, the agent may receive *payoffs* or *reinforcements* for their actions performed at or prior to the current state. The agent may want to maximize the total payoffs. Thus, the agent may need to perform *credit assignment*, to attribute the payoffs/reinforcements to actions at various points in time (the temporal credit assignment problem), in accordance with various aspects of a state (the structural credit assignment problem). There is in general no teacher input. The agent starts with little or no a priori knowledge. One example involves learning to navigate through mines (see Figure 1.1).

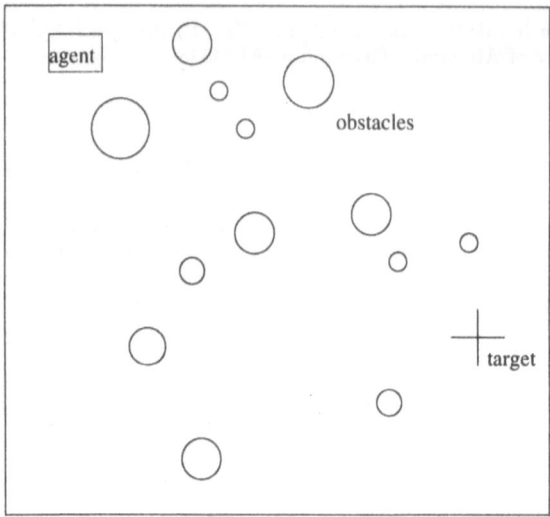

Fig. 1.1. Navigating through a minefield

To acquire low-level specific skills in these tasks, there are some existing methods available. Chief among them is the temporal difference method (Sutton 1990), a type of reinforcement learning algorithm that learns through exploiting the difference in evaluating actions in successive steps and thus handling sequences in an incremental manner. This approach has been applied to learning in mazes, navigation tasks, and robot control (Sutton 1990, Lin 1992). But they do not learn high-level knowledge (rules). This approach can be extended to dynamic programming and partially observable Markov decision process models (Bertsekas and Tsitsiklis 1996, Monohan 1982, and references cited therein); however, these models often require a domain model to begin with.

In terms of learning high-level declarative knowledge or rules for such tasks, however, the characteristics of the task render most existing rule learning algorithms inapplicable. This is because they require either preconstructed exemplar sets (thus learning is not online; Michalski 1983, Quinlan 1986), incrementally given *consistent* instances (Mitchell 1982, Fisher 1986, Utgoff 1989), or complex manipulations of learned structures when inconsistency is discovered (which is typically more complex than the limited time a reactive agent may have; Hirsh 1994). Non-stationary ("drifting") worlds are more than noise and inconsistency as considered by some learning algorithms because they involve changes over time and lead to radical changes in learned knowledge. This often requires extra dedicated mechanisms. Above all, most of the rule learning algorithms do not handle the learning of sequences which necessarily involves temporal credit assignment.

1.2 Hybrid Models

How can an agent develop a set of skills that are highly specific (geared towards particular situations) and thus highly efficient but, at the same time, acquire sufficiently general knowledge that can be readily applied to a variety of different situations and be communicated to others? Although humans seem to possess such abilities and be able to achieve an appropriate balance between the two sides, existing systems fall short. What appears to be missing is the duality and coexistence of both procedural and declarative knowledge. There has been a great deal of work demonstrating the difference between procedural knowledge and declarative knowledge: for example, Anderson (1983), Keil (1989), and Sun (1994) (see also Sun and Alexandre 1997 for more examples). It is believed that a balance between the two believed to be is essential to the development of complex cognitive agents. This is based on two lines of argument. First, there are ample psychological data that support the distinction between procedural and declarative knowledge and the need for both. Anderson (1983) initially proposed the distinction based on such data; Fitts and Posner (1967), Keil (1989), and Sun (1994) subsequently made similar points also based on psychological data. Second, there are many philosophical arguments for making this distinction and achieving an appropriate balance between the two. Dreyfus and Dreyfus (1987) proposed the distinction between analytical and intuitive thinking; Smolensky (1988) proposed the distinction between conceptual (publicly accessible) and subconceptual processing; in addition, the distinction between conscious and subconscious processes, although controversial, is well known (cf. James 1890). We are not aiming to capture all of the above dichotomies. Denoting more or less the same thing, these dichotomies serve as justifications for our main distinction, between (conceptual) declarative knowledge and (subconceptual) procedural skills, which is distinguished by the difference in accessibility (declarative knowledge is easily accessible and linguistically expressible, procedural skills are not; Anderson 1983, Sun 1995).

Declarative knowledge has some advantages which make it indispensable to a learning agent despite the fact that procedural skills are more efficient or easier to learn. These advantages are:

- It helps to guide the exploration of new situations, and reduces the time necessary to develop specific skills in new situations. In other words, it helps the transfer of learned skill (as shown psychologically by Willingham et al 1989).
- Declarative knowledge can help to speed up learning. If properly used, knowledge that is extracted on-line during skill learning can help to facilitate the learning process itself (Willingham et al 1989).

– Declarative knowledge can also help in communicating learned knowledge and skills to other agents.

A two-level hybrid model provides the needed framework for representing both types of knowledge. CLARION is similar to the model in Sun (1995) but is specifically designed for reactive sequential decision making. It consists of two levels: The bottom level contains procedural knowledge (Anderson 1983) and the top level contains declarative knowledge in the form of propositional rules. An overall pseudo-code algorithm that describes the operation of CLARION is as follows:

1. Observe the current state x.
2. Compute in the bottom level the Q-values of x associated with each of all the possible actions a_i's: $Q(x, a_1)$, $Q(x, a_2)$, ..., $Q(x, a_n)$.
3. Find out all the possible actions $(b_1, b_2, ..., b_m)$ at the top level, based on the input x and the rules in place.
4. Combine the values of a_i's with those of b_j's, and choose an appropriate action b
5. Perform the action b, and observe the next state y and (possibly) the reinforcement r.
6. Update the bottom level in accordance with *Q-Learning*.
7. Update the top level with *Rule-Extraction-Revision*.
8. Go back to Step 1.

1.2.1 The Bottom Level

Reinforcement Learning. A Q-value is an evaluation of the "quality" of an action in a given state: $Q(x, a)$ indicates how desirable action a is in state x (which consists of sensory input). To acquire the Q-values, we use the *Q-learning* algorithm (Watkins 1989; a temporal difference reinforcement learning algorithm). In the algorithm, $Q(x, a)$ estimates the maximum discounted cumulative reinforcement that the agent will receive from the current state x on. The updating of $Q(x, a)$ is based on minimizing $r + \gamma e(y) - Q(x, a)$, where γ is a discount factor, $e(y) = \max_a Q(y, a)$, and y is the new state resulting from action a. Thus, the updating is based on the *temporal difference* in evaluating the current state and the action chosen. Through successive updates of the Q function, the agent can learn to take into account future steps in longer and longer sequences notably without explicit planning (Watkins 1989).

Implementation. To implement Q-learning, we chose to use a four-layered network (see Figure 1.2), in which the first three layers form a backpropagation network for computing Q-values and the fourth layer (with only one node) performs stochastic decision making. The output of the third layer (i.e., the output layer of the backpropagation network) indicates the Q-value of each action (represented by an individual node), and the node in the fourth layer determines probabilistically the action to be performed based on a Boltzmann distribution (Watkins 1989). The lookup table implementation of Q-learning is out of question here because of the (likely) continuous

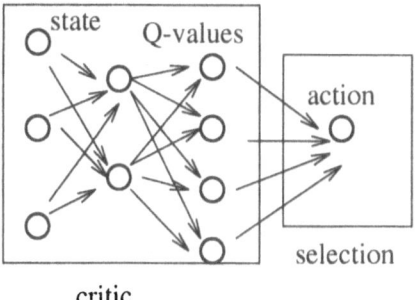

state   Q-values

action

selection

critic

Fig. 1.2. The Q-learning method

input space and when discretized, the resulting huge state space (e.g., in the navigation task there are more than 10^{12} states). Some kind of function approximator has to be used (Sutton 1990, Lin 1992, Tesauro 1992) and as a result the convergence of learning is not guaranteed.

1.2.2 The Top Level

Rule Encoding. Declarative knowledge is captured in a simple propositional rule form. Although we can directly use a symbolic rule representation, to facilitate correspondence with the bottom level and to encourage uniformity and integration, we chose to use a localist connectionist model instead. Basically, we connect the nodes representing the conditions of a rule to the node representing the conclusion (Sun 1992, Towell and Shavlik 1993). That is, we directly translate the structure of a rule set to that of a network. We will omit some rule encoding details here, because they are not essential for this model. For more complex rule forms including predicate rules and variable binding, see Sun (1992).

    Rule Learning. Here, we devised a novel rule learning algorithm, because of the differing characteristics of our tasks (that is, sequential decision tasks rather than classification or categorization tasks): concurrent (on-line) learning, reactivity, lack of teacher input and a priori knowledge, "drifting" environments, and requisite revisions (see Sun and Peterson 1998 for the discussion of these charactersitics present in sequential decision tasks). The basic idea is as follows: we perform rule learning (extraction and subsequent revision) at each step, which is associated with the following information: (x, y, r, a), where x is the state before action a is performed, y is the new state entered after an action a is performed, and r is the reinforcement received after action a. If some action decided by the bottom level is successful then the agent extracts a rule that corresponds to the decision and adds the rule to the rule network. Then, in subsequent interactions with the world, the agent verifies the extracted rule by considering the outcome of applying the rule: if the outcome is not successful, then the rule should be made more specific and exclusive of the current case; if the outcome is successful, the agent may try to generalize the rule to make it more universal. Rules are in the following form: *conditions* ⟶ *action*, where the lefthand side is a conjunction of individual conditions each of which refers to a primitive: a value range or a value in a dimension of the (sensory) input state.

Let us look into a refined version of the overall algorithm that fleshes out some rule learning details (in steps 8 and 9).

Do the following for each decision step:

1. Observe the current state x.

2. Calculate the Q-values of all the actions in the current state: $Q(x, a_1)$, $Q(x, a_2)$, ..., $Q(x, a_n)$

3. Find the set of rules that matches the current state. Choose a rule based on specificity (choose at random if more than one rule has the same highest specificity). (The action suggested by the chosen rule has an activation value 1.)

4. Combine the outcomes of the previous two steps: Based on the values of actions from the two levels, select an action b to be performed using either the *percentage combination* or the *stochastic combination*.

5. Perform the action b.

6. Enter the new state y resulting from the action. Possibly receive a reinforcement r.

7. Calculate all the Q-values for the new state: $Q(y, a_1), Q(y, a_2), ..., Q(y, a_n)$

8. Check the current criterion for rule extraction and revision. Update statistics (with respect to the action performed).

8.1. If the result is good according to the current criterion, and there is no rule matching that state and that action, then perform *extraction* of a new rule: state ⟶ action. Add the extracted rule to the rule network.

8.2. If the result is bad according to the current criterion, revise all the matching rules using *shrinking* and *deletion*.

8.2.1. Remove the matching rules from the rule network.

8.2.2. Add the revised versions of the rules into the rule network.

8.3. If the result is good according to the current criterion, then generalize the matching rules.

8.3.1. Create new rules using *expansion*.

8.3.2. Add the expanded rules to the rule network to replace the original rules.

9. Perform *merge* to combine existing rules.

At each step, we update the following statistics for each rule condition and each of its minor variations (i.e., the rule condition plus/minus one value), with regard to the action a performed: that is, PM_a (i.e., Positive Match) and NM_a (i.e., Negative Match). Here, positivity/negativity is determined by the following inequality: $\max_b Q(y, b) - Q(x, a) + r > threshold$, which indicates whether or not the action is reasonably good. Based on these statistics, we calculate the information gain measure; that is,

$$IG(A, B) = log_2 \frac{PM_a(A) + 1}{PM_a(A) + NM_a(A) + 2} - log_2 \frac{PM_a(B) + 1}{PM_a(B) + NM_a(B) + 2}$$

where A and B are two different conditions that lead to the same action a. The measure compares essentially the percentage of positive matches under different conditions A and B (with the Laplace estimator; Lavrac and Dze-roski 1994). If A can improve the percentage to a certain degree over B, then A is considered better than B. In the algorithm, if a rule is better compared with the match-all rule (i.e, the rule with the condition that matches all inputs), then the rule is considered successful (for the purpose of deciding on expansion or shrinking operations).

We decide on whether or not to extract a rule based on a simple success criterion which is fully determined by the current step (x, y, r, a):

– *Extraction*: if $r + \gamma e(y) - Q(x, a) > threshold$, where a is the action performed in state x and y is the resulting new state (that is, if the current step is successful), and if there is no rule that covers this step in the top level, set up a rule $C \longrightarrow a$, where C specifies the values of all the input dimensions exactly as in x.

The criterion for applying the *expansion* and *shrinking* operators, on the other hand, is based on the afore-mentioned statistical test. Expansion amounts to adding an additional value to one input dimension in the condition of a rule, so that the rule will have more opportunities of matching inputs, and shrinking amounts to removing one value from one input dimension in the condition of a rule, so that it will have less opportunities of matching inputs. Here are the detailed descriptions of these operators:

– *Expansion*: if $IG(C, all) > threshold1$ and $\max_{C'} IG(C', C) \geq 0$, where C is the current condition of a matching rule, *all* refers to no condition at all (with regard to the same action specified by the rule), and C' is a modified condition such that $C' = C$ plus one value (i.e., C' has one more value in one of the input dimensions) (that is, if the current rule is successful and the expanded condition is potentially better), then set $C'' = argmax_{C'} IG(C', C)$ as the new (expanded) condition of the rule. Reset all the rule statistics. Any rule covered by the expanded rule will be placed in its children list. [1]
– *Shrinking*: if $IG(C, all) < threshold2$ and $\max_{C'} IG(C', C) > 0$, where C is the current condition of a matching rule, *all* refers to no condition at all (with regard to the same action specified by the rule), and C' is a modified condition such that $C' = C$ minus one value (i.e., C' has one less value in one of the input dimensions) (that is, if the current rule is unsuccessful, but the shrunk condition is better), then set $C'' = argmax_{C'} IG(C', C)$ as the new (shrunk) condition of the rule. Reset all the rule statistics. Restore those rules in the children list of the original rule that are not covered by the shrunk rule. If shrinking the condition makes it impossible for a rule to match any input state, delete the rule.

---

[1] The children list of a rule is created to keep aside and make inactive those rules that are more specific (thus fully covered) by the current rule. It is useful because if later on the rule is deleted or shrunk, some or all of those rules on its children list may be reactivated if they are no longer covered.

– *Deletion*: The same as *Shrinking*.
– *Merge*: when the conditions of two rules are close enough, the two rules may be combined. If one rule is covered completely by another, it is put on the children list of the other. If one rule is covered by another except for one dimension, produce a new rule that covers both.

Note that although the accumulation of statistics is gradual, the acquisition and revision of rules is one-shot and all-or-nothing.

1.2.3 The Whole Model

In the overall algorithm, Step 4 is for making the final decision of which action to take by incorporating outcomes from both levels.

We combine the corresponding values for an action from the two levels by a weighted sum; that is, if the top level indicates that action a has an activation value v (which should be 0 or 1 as rules are binary) and the bottom level indicates that a has an activation value q (the Q-value), then the final outcome is $w_1 * v + w_2 * q$. Stochastic decision making with the Boltzmann distribution based on the weighted sums is then performed to select an action out of all the possible actions. Relative weights or percentages of the two levels are automatically set based on the relative performance of the two levels. That is, if the success rate of the decisions made by the top level is s_b and the success rate of the bottom level is s_t, then the weights are $s_t/(s_b + s_t)$ for the top level and $s_b/(s_b + s_t)$ for the bottom level.

1.2.4 Some Analyses

We can contrast the characteristics of the two levels. The top level is discrete, all-or-nothing, rigorously verified (through experience), and without random exploration, and it learns through trial-and-error in a one-shot fashion. The bottom level is continuous, graded, not rigorously verified, and with random exploration, and it learns in a gradual and cumulative fashion. Thus they complement each other. Note also that the generalization of rules complements the generalization in the bottom level: While the bottom level generalization is continuous/graded, rule generalization at the top level is discrete/crisp (in terms of results, not the process), thus capturing different kinds of regularities. Because they possess different characteristics, each level tends to learn differentially; thus a combination of the two, through stochastic "averaging", is likely to result in improved performance (similar in a way to "stacking" and "bagging"; Breiman 1996).

The temporal difference in Q-values that determines rule learning encourages the exploration of those steps (state/action pairs) that are worth exploring, i.e., leading to an improvement (a new state with a higher Q-value). The criterion encourages the increase of Q-values, since the action and the updating that are based on large temporal differences lead to the increase of the Q-value for the state and the action.

When learning is well under way, the actions leading to large temporal differences (≥ 0) tend to be the best or near best actions in given states, because a large temporal difference means a new state with an above average Q-value compared with other possible new states (each Q-value tends to be the average of all the possible outcomes from the corresponding action and is also "averaged" by neighboring Q-values due to network generalization/approximation).

1.3 Experiments

1.3.1 The Task Setting

We tested CLARION on the on-line simulated navigation task as shown in Figure 1.1. The agent has to navigate an underwater vessel through a minefield to reach a target location. The agent receives information only from a number of instruments. As shown in Figure 1.3, the sonar gauge shows how close the mines are in 7 equal areas that range from 45 degrees to the left of the agent to 45 degrees to the right. The fuel gauge shows how much time is left before fuel runs out. The bearing gauge shows the direction of the target from the present direction of the agent. The range gauge shows how far the target is from the current location. Based only on such information, the agent decides on (1) how to turn and (2) how fast to move. The time allotted to the agent for each episode is 200 steps. The agent, within an allotted time period, can either (1) reach the target (a success), (2) hit a mine (a failure), or (3) run out of time (a failure again). Each episode starts with the agent on one side of the minefield and the target on the other. An episode ends when (1) the target is reached, (2) time runs out (200 steps), or (3) the agent hits a mine. A random mine layout is generated for each episode. The mines are randomly placed between the starting point of the agent and the target. experiment. This setting is stochastic and non-Markovian. On-line, real-time simulation was used for navigation and learning.

1.3.2 The Model Setup

In CLARION, as input to the bottom level, each gauge was represented by a set of nodes. We tried both discrete and analog input values. In the case of discrete inputs, the following nodes are used for the inputs:

fuel	1 input node
range	2 inputs nodes
bearing	6 input nodes
sonar	4 X 7 input nodes

That is, one node is used for "fuel" (with two values: *a lot* and *a little*), six for "bearing" (including *far left, left, straight ahead, right, far right*, and *right behind*), four for each of the seven "sonars" (ranging from *very far* to *very close*), and one for "range" (with two values: *far* and *near*). There are 41 inputs and thus more than 10^{12} states.

We have to deal with the problem of high input dimensionality. A lookup table implementation for Q-learning at the bottom level is not possible, because of the high dimensionality (Tesauro 1992, Lin 1991). A function approximator, such as a backpropagation network, must be used (Bertsekas and Tsitsiklis 1996).

The action outputs in the bottom level consist of two clusters of nodes: one clusters of 5 nodes for 5 different values of "direction" (including *left, slightly left, straight, slightly right*, and *right*), and the other cluster of 5 nodes for 5 different values of "speed" (including *very fast, fast, normal, slow*, and *standstill*).

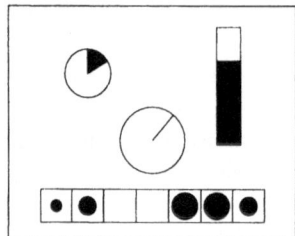

Fig. 1.3. The navigation input
The display at the upper left corner is the fuel gauge; the vertical one at the upper right corner is the range gauge; the round one in the middle is the bearing gauge; the 7 sonar gauges are at the bottom.

CLARION's internal parameters are set through trial-and-error optimization by hand. Seven hidden units are used in the backpropagation network, the momentum parameter is 0.7, network weights are randomly initialized between -0.01 and 0.01. The Q-value discount rate is 0.95. The temperature (randomness parameter) for stochastic decision making is set at 0.01. A schedule for the gradual lowering of learning rates is used: $\alpha := \alpha_0 * e^{c*s}$, where α is the current learning rate, $\alpha_0 = 0.03$ is the initial learning rate, $c = 6.0$ is a constant, and s is the success rate (the percentage of successful episodes during the previous block of 20 episodes).

The thresholds for rule extraction and revision are set as follows: *threshold* = 0.06, *threshold1* =1.5, and *threshold2* =0.5. To limit the number of rules at the top level, we instituted an upper limit of 100 rules. When more rules are created than allowed, we purge "old" existing rules, according to the rank ordering of rules on the basis of their ages, where the age of a rule is defined to be the number of steps occurred since the last application of the rule.

The reinforcements for an agent are produced from two sources. One is the gradient reward, which is proportional to the change in the "range" readings (i.e, the change in the distance to the target). [2] The other is the end reward,

---

[2] When the agent is going toward the target, the reinforcement is $gr = 1/c*((x_2 - x_1)/x)^4$, where $c = 7.5$, $x_2 - x_1$ is the distance traveled in the target direction

which is determined by how successful the agent is at the end of an episode. The end reward is 1 if the agent reaches the target within the allotted time, and is inversely proportional to the distance (from the target) if the agent runs out of time or gets blown up. [3] experiments,

1.3.3 Results

Learning Speed. Figures 1.4, 1.5, and 1.6 show the data of CLARION (using the analog inputs in the bottom level and the secondary features in the top level). In terms of learning effectiveness, which is measured by the number of successful episodes out of a total of 1000 episodes of training (averaged over 10 runs), the "training" columns of these figures show the difference between CLARION and the bottom level alone (trained with pure Q-learning).

It appears that at higher mine densities (that is, the more difficult settings), CLARION is significantly better compared with the bottom level alone. In the 30-mine and 60-mine cases, the superiority of CLARION (over the bottom level alone with Q-learning only) is statistically significant (with t tests, $p < 0.05$). However, the performance is statistically undifferentiable in the 10-mine case. Figure 1.7 shows the learning curves during the course of training, in which each data point is the average of the percentages of successful episodes in a 20-episode block.

Transfer. The right three blocks of Figures 1.4, 1.5, and 1.6 show the transfer data, where transfer is measured by the percentage of successful episodes in the new setting by the trained models (each trained model is applied to minefields that contain a *different* number of mines for a total of 20 episodes; the data is averaged over 10 runs). The data generally follows the pattern that the higher the mine density is, the lower the success rate is. mine density). Moreover, the performance of a model is generally better if it is trained at a higher mine density (probably because if it is trained at a high mine density, it tends to learn strategies that are more suitable for high-density minefields). As also indicated by the tables, CLARION outperforms the bottom level alone (trained with Q-learning) in transfer at higher mine densities; the higher the mine density, the more pronounced the difference. The differences are statistically significant in the 30-mine and 60-mine cases (using t tests, $p < 0.05$). Finally, comparing the transfer performance of the top level, the bottom level, and the whole system (after they are trained together), we notice that the whole system always performs much better than either level alone. There is definitely a synergy between the two levels (in the sense that the whole system performs better than either levels). Learning rules does help to improve the transfer performance.

---

in one step, and x is the maximum distance possible (which is 40). When the agent is going away from the target, the reinforcement is $gr' = -0.5gr$.

[3] When the agent runs out of time, the reinforcement is $er = 500/(500 + x) - 1$, where x is the distance to the target. When the agent gets blown up, the reinforcement is $er = 1/2 * 500/(500 + x) - 1$.

Mine Density During Training: 10

Model	Training 10	Both 10	Bottom 10	Top 10	Both 30	Bottom 30	Top 30	Both 60	Bottom 60	Top 60
CLARION	651.8	63.5	6.5	4.5	35.5	1.5	0.5	11.5	1.0	0.0
s.d.	31.3	34.4	4.5	6.9	21.0	2.3	1.5	9.5	2.0	0.0
Q	645.7		82.0			42.0			14.5	
s.d.	86.9		14.2			24.5			18.1	

Fig. 1.4. Learning and transfer from 10-mine minefields.
Q refers to the bottom level used alone with Q-learning as the sole learning method. *Training* indicates the total numbers of successful episodes during training. The next three blocks contain performance data (in percentage), in three different mine densities (10, 30, and 60) using the trained models with either the top level, the bottom level, or both together.

Mine Density During Training: 30

Model	Training 30	Both 10	Bottom 10	Top 10	Both 30	Bottom 30	Top 30	Both 60	Bottom 60	Top 60
CLARION	663.8	89.0	5.0	1.0	75.0	7.0	0.0	47.5	2.5	0.0
s.d.	48.4	26.5	3.2	2.0	23.6	5.6	0.0	24.9	2.5	0.0
Q	539.1		77.0			68.0			35.5	
s.d.	105.6		17.5			20.4			20.7	

Fig. 1.5. Learning and transfer from 30-mine minefields.
Q refers to the bottom level used alone with Q-learning as the sole learning method. *Training* indicates the total numbers of successful episodes during training. The next three blocks contain performance data in percentage, in three different mine densities (10, 30, and 60) using the trained models with either the top level, the bottom level, or both together.

Mine Density During Training: 60

Model	Training 60	Both 10	Bottom 10	Top 10	Both 30	Bottom 30	Top 30	Both 60	Bottom 60	Top 60
CLARION	581.4	99.5	9.5	2.0	96.0	8.5	0.0	76.0	6.0	0.0
s.d.	79.0	1.5	6.5	3.3	3.7	4.5	0.0	15.9	6.6	0.0
Q	495.8		71.5			67.5			47.5	
s.d.	137.9		11.6			16.8			24.3	

Fig. 1.6. Learning and transfer from 60-mine minefields.
Q refers to the bottom level used alone with Q-learning as the sole learning method. *Training* indicates the total numbers of successful episodes during training. The next three blocks contain performance data in percentage, in three different mine densities (10, 30, and 60) using the trained models with either the top level, the bottom level, or both together.

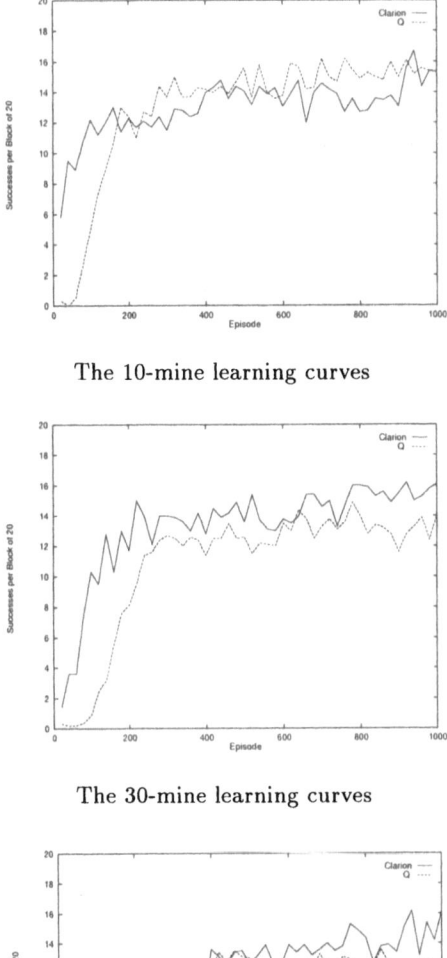

The 10-mine learning curves

The 30-mine learning curves

The 60-mine learning curves

Fig. 1.7. Learning curves for 10-mine, 30-mine, and 60-mine settings.

Trained Performance. The right three blocks of Figures 1.4, 1.5, and 1.6 also contain the trained performance data: The 10-mine block in Figure 1.4 shows the trained performance after training in 10-mine minefields. The 30-mine block in Figure 1.5 shows the trained performance after training in 30-mine minefields. The 60-mine block in Figure 1.6 shows the trained performance after training in 60-mine minefields. Trained performance is defined to be the percentage of successful episodes in the *same* setting as used in training by the trained models (each trained model is applied to the minefields for a total of 20 episodes; the data is averaged over 10 runs). At higher mine densities, we notice that the trained performance of CLARION is better than the bottom level alone (trained only with Q-learning). Comparing the performance of the whole system and the two levels separately after the two levels are trained together, we again notice that the whole system performs much better than the bottom level and the top level alone, which strongly suggests a synergy between the two levels. Q-learning only,

1.3.4 Experiments in Mazes

We have also done extensive experiments in a maze domain (see Sun and Peterson 1997 for details) and the same basic conclusions hold. Briefly, in the maze, the agent has sensory inputs regarding its immediate left, front and right side, indicating whether there is a wall, an opening, or the goal. As the maze has no location marker the agent has no knowledge of its location. It has no information about the goal location either. The agent can move forward, turn to the left, or turn to the right. It is to reach the goal through a sequence of such actions. A reward is given when the goal is reached. See Figure 1.8 for an example maze. Below, we will mention briefly our main findings in this domain (since Sun and Peterson 1997 contains complete details, we will not repeat them here).

Fig. 1.8. A maze.

Learning Speed. Learning speed was measured by the average number of moves in the first 60 episodes. When CLARION was compared with the bottom level alone (trained only with Q-learning), the differences in learning speed were statistically significant: CLARION learns faster than the bottom level alone by large margins.

Trained Performance. The average number of steps needed to reach the target in one episode after training were measured. CLARION outperformed the bottom level alone (trained only with Q-learning) by large margins. There was clearly a *synergy* between the top level and the bottom level: the whole CLARION model always performed better than the top level alone or the bottom level alone, after both were trained together as part of CLARION. Furthermore, rule learning not only improved the performance of the whole system, but it also improved the bottom level per se when it was trained as part of CLARION.

Transfer. We applied our trained models to a larger maze to assess transfer. We were mainly concerned with comparing the transfer of the bottom level alone (trained only with Q-learning) vs. that of CLARION. We found that CLARION transfered much better than the bottom level alone (trained only with Q-learning), in terms of the average number of steps taken to reach the goal in one episode. Furthermore, often learned rules alone performed better in transfer than either the bottom level (trained as part of CLARION) or the whole CLARION model.

1.4 Discussion of Symbol Grounding

Symbols should be grounded, as has been argued by many (Harnad 1990). But we insist that they should be grounded not only in subsymbolic activities, but also in the direct interactions between the agent and the world. The point is that concepts, which symbols represent, are not formed in isolation (from the world), in abstraction, or "objectively". They are formed in relation to the life-world of agents, through the perceptual/motor apparatuses of agents, linked to their goals, needs, and actions. What should be emphasized here is the primacy of direct, unmediated interactions between agents and the world. Symbolic representations and concepts are derived from such direct interactions, not prior to them. Precisely in this sense, can symbols really be grounded. We have showed here how this can be done through CLARION.

On this view, high-level conceptual, symbolic representations are rooted, or grounded, in low-level behavior (or comportment as termed by Heidegger) from which they obtain their meanings and for which they provide explanations. The rootedness/groundedness is guaranteed, in our view, by the way high-level representations are produced: They are, in the main, extracted out of low-level behavioral structures. Even culturally transmitted symbols have to be linked up, within the mind of an individual agent, with low-level processes in order to be effective.

It is worth noting that conceptual, symbolic representations so formed are in general formed in a functionally relevant way, in relations to everyday activities of agents. In other words, in general they must bear certain existential and/or biological significance to agents and be in the service of agents' activities. The world is of such a high (or even an infinitely high) dimensionality, and thus there can be no totally objective way of perceiving/conceiving it (due to complexity), except in relation to what an agent has to do with it in everyday activities (comportment). Learning symbolic representations on the basis of comportment provides agents with a viable way of basing their conceptual representations on their everyday activities in a functionally relevant way. [4]

On the other hand, the existence of explicit symbolic representations, or at least their importance, has been denied, or downplayed, by many advocates of (the strong forms of) situated cognition and interactivism. Here we emphasize that symbolic representations are important while maintaining that they are derived and mediated by direct comportment.

This approach boils down to the dual process theory (i.e., the *dual-level hypothesis*; Sun 1994). The following hypothesis was put forth in Sun (1994):

> It is assumed in this work that cognitive processes are carried out in two distinct levels with qualitatively different processing mechanisms. Each level encodes a fairly complete set of knowledge for its processing, and the coverage of the two sets of knowledge encoded by the two levels overlaps substantially.

This idea is closely related to some well-known dichotomies in cognitive science: The dichotomy of symbolic vs. subsymbolic processing (Rumelhart and McClelland 1986), the dichotomy of conceptual vs. subconceptual processing, the dichotomy of explicit vs. implicit learning, and the dichotomy of controlled vs. automatic processing. However, here, in addition to such dichotomies, we went one step further in positing separate and simultaneous existence of multiple levels (i.e., separate "processors"), each of which embodies one side of a dichotomy. Therefore, in this view, the two sides of a dichotomy are not simply two ends of a spectrum, or two levels of analysis of the same underlying system. But they are two separate, although closely connected, systems, one being derived from the other.

1.5 Concluding Remarks

In this work, we focused on a hybrid architecture as an example of what integration can do. Utilizing a principled dichotomy, CLARION was able, at least in some circumstances, to learn faster, perform better, and transfer more effectively than models that neglect such a dichotomy. Experiments in various different tasks demonstrated in the three aspects the potential for such advantages (some experiments in the navigation domain was presented).

---

[4] In addition, of course, the biological pre-endowment in agents (acquired through evolutionary processes) may also provide them with some ways of picking out useful and relevant information. The two aspects may interact closely in forming conceptual representation.

They suggested that the combination of the two types of knowledge can yield synergistic results.

Theoretically, the work points to a new way of looking at the declarative vs. the procedural (or the symbolic vs. the subsymbolic) dichotomy. We emphasize that the relationship between the two types of processes is that of the symbolic being derived from the subsymbolic. Furthermore, the subsymbolic process has direct interactions with the world. This leads to a better understanding of the genesis and grounding of symbols and symbolic representations.

Although we focus currently on a relatively simple architecture as an illustration of the ideas, there are many obvious ways to enhance the model for more complex settings. Future work should focus on developing more sophisticated rule extraction methods, for example, based on the relevance of features, and learning more sophisticated rule forms, such as those in first-order inductive logic programming systems. We may also investigate more complex combination methods for combining outcomes from the two levels.

Acknowledgements: This work is supported in part by Office of Naval Research grant N00014-95-1-0440. The simulator for the navigation task was provided by Naval Research Lab (D. Gordon, A. Schultz, and J. Ballas).

References

J. R. Anderson, (1983). *The Architecture of Cognition*, Harvard University Press, Cambridge, MA

D. Bertsekas and J. Tsitsiklis, (1996). *Neuro-Dynamic Programming*. Athena Scientific, Belmont, MA.

L. Breiman, (1996). Bagging predictors. *Machine Learning*, Vol.24, No.2, pp.123-140.

H. Dreyfus and S. Dreyfus, (1987). *Mind Over Machine*. The Free Press, New York, NY.

D. Fisher, (1987). Knowledge acquisition via incremental conceptual clustering. *Machine Learning*. 2, 139-172.

P. Fitts and M. Posner, (1967). *Human Performance*. Brooks/Cole, Monterey, CA.

S. Harnad, (1990). The symbol grounding problem. *Physica D*, 42, 335-346.

H. Hirsh, (1994). Generalizing version spaces. *Machine Learning*, 17, 5-46.

W. James, (1890). *The Principles of Psychology*. Dover, New York.

L. Kaelbling, M. Littman, and A. Moore, (1996). Reinforcement learning: A survey. *Journal of Artificial Intelligence Research*, 4, 237-285.

F. Keil, (1989). *Concepts, Kinds, and Cognitive Development*. MIT Press. Cambridge, MA.

N. Lavrac and S. Dzeroski, (1994). *Inductive Logic Programming*. Ellis Horword, New York.

L. Lin, (1992). Self-improving reactive agents based on reinforcement learning, planning, and teaching. *Machine Learning*. Vol.8, pp.293-321.

R. Michalski, (1983). A theory and methodology of inductive learning. *Artificial Intelligence*. Vol.20, pp.111-161.

T. Mitchell, (1982). Generalization as search. *Artificial Intelligence*, 18, 203-226.

G. Monohan, (1982). A survey of partially observable Markov decision processes: theory, models, and algorithms. *Management Science*, 28 (1), 1-16.

R. Quinlan, (1986). Inductive learning of decision trees. *Machine Learning*. 1, 81-106.

P. Rosenbloom, J. Laird, A. Newell, and R. McCarl, (1991). A preliminary analysis of the SOAR architecture as a basis for general intelligence. *Artificial Intelligence*. 47 (1-3), 289-325.

Technology. 213-225. U. of New Hampshire, Durham.

P. Smolensky, (1988). On the proper treatment of connectionism. *Behavioral and Brain Sciences*, 11(1):1–74.

R. Sun, (1992). On variable binding in connectionist networks, *Connection Science*, Vol.4, No.2, pp.93-124.

R. Sun, (1994). *Integrating Rules and Connectionism for Robust Commonsense Reasoning*. John Wiley and Sons, New York, NY.

R. Sun, (1995). Robust reasoning: integrating rule-based and similarity-based reasoning. *Artificial Intelligence*. 75, 2. 241-296.

R. Sun, (1997). Learning, action, and consciousness: a hybrid approach towards modeling consciousness. *Neural Networks*, special issue on consciousness. 10 (7), pp.1317-1331.

R. Sun and F. Alexandre, (eds.) (1997). *Connectionist Symbolic Integration*. Lawrence Erlbaum Associates, Hillsdale, NJ.

R. Sun and T. Peterson, (1995). A hybrid learning model of reactive sequential decision making. In: R. Sun and F. Alexandre, (eds.) *The Working Notes of The IJCAI Workshop on Connectionist-Symbolic Integration*.

R. Sun and T. Peterson, (1998). Some experiments with a hybrid model for learning sequential decision making. *Information Sciences*. Vol.111, pp.83-107.

R. Sutton, (1990). Integrated architectures for learning, planning, and reacting based on approximating dynamic programming. *Proc.of Seventh International Conference on Machine Learning*. Morgan Kaufmann. San Mateo, CA.

T. Tesauro, (1992). Practical issues in temporal difference learning. *Machine Learning*. Vol.8, 257-277.

G. Towell and J. Shavlik, (1993). Extracting Refined Rules from Knowledge-Based Neural Networks, *Machine Learning*. 13 (1), 71-101.

P. Utgoff (1989). Incremental induction of decision trees. *Machine Learning*. Vol.4, 161-186.

C. Watkins, (1989). *Learning with Delayed Rewards*. Ph.D Thesis, Cambridge University, Cambridge, UK.

D. Willingham, M. Nissen, and P. Bullemer, (1989). On the development of procedural knowledge. *Journal of Experimental Psychology: Learning, Memory, and Cognition*. 15, 1047-1060.

Integration of Different Information Processing Methods

Setsuo Ohsuga
Waseda University,
Department of Information and Computer Science,
3-4-1 OhkuboShinnjyuku-ku Tokyo, 169-8555, Japan
Ohsuga@ohsuga.info.waseda.ac.jp

Abstract: A way of integrating different information-processing methods is discussed. By analyzing various methods a possible way of integrating dynamically these methods is studied. A special processor to combine different methods is necessary for integration. It is called an integrator. Among various information-processing methods, only declarative knowledge-based method is suited for an integrator. Then the realistic way of developing the integrator is discussed. Even with this integrator however the scope of actual integration is limited because of a big gap existing between symbolic and non-symbolic methods of information processing. The difference between symbolic and non-symbolic methods is clarified by representing them by the same mathematical formula and based on this result a possible extension of knowledge-based processing is proposed in order to expand the scope of integration.

2.1 Introduction

There are different information-processing methods based on the different principles for representing and processing information. Ordinary procedural programming method, declarative knowledge-based method, neural network method are the typical examples. The first two methods are based on the symbolic representation while the last is computational one. There is a large difference between them. Each method has its own limitation when used in the real environment. Researches are being made on the way of integrating them [1]. But most of the research works are in the conceptual level.

At the implementation level, every method is reducible to the procedural form. But the different methods based on the different principles are interested in this paper. Each method has its own characteristics. Persons select different methods that are best suited for their purpose of problem solving. To select one method however means to lose chances to use advantages that the other methods offer. When problems that persons wish to solve get large, they cannot be coped with by a single method. Then there arises the need for combining different methods. What methods should be combined and how are these combined in order to satisfy the requirement of solving large-scale problem?

Actually each of these methods represents a framework in which various actual systems are developed as instances and what are combined are the instance systems. For example a neural network is developed in the general framework of the network-style method of information processing as a general concept. By combining the instances, the combination of the methods is achieved. In the following the term integration is used to mean to put the instances together in a new instance system. A term information-processing unit (hereafter IP-Unit for short) is used in order for denoting such an instance system. Two or more IP-Units can be integrated to form another (integrated) IP-Unit. In an integrated IP-Unit, the methods that the original IP-Units were based on are combined.

Every method as a framework based on which different IP-Units are generated has its own representation scheme and a processing mechanism. These representation scheme and processing mechanism are inherited to every IP-Unit in this framework. In addition, each IP-Unit is endowed its own characteristics. For example, every IP-Unit has its own scope of variables only in which the IP-Unit is valid. These characteristics specify the IP-Unit and decide the condition of integration with the other IP-units. Not necessarily every combination of IP-Units is possible for integration but there are some conditions for integration.

What is the condition of more-than-two IP-Units being able to be integrated? What is the measure of the effect of the integration?

These are the main issues that are discussed in this paper. That is, the objective of this paper is to discuss the possibility and the way of integrating the different IP-Units.

In the following integration is defined formally as an operation to integrate the different IP-units in order to obtain a new IP-unit with a larger scope than any of the old IP-units and construct a processing mechanism in the new scope. There are two approaches of integration. The first is to merge two or more different IP-units specifically in order to make a new IP-unit that has a larger functional capability including both functions of the original IP-units but without any specific problem to solve at the time of integration. This integration is called the static integration. The second is to integrate IP-units in real time in order to satisfy the necessity for solving a given problem as an application from outside. This is called the dynamic integration. The former is for providing the more powerful set of IP-units than those currently available while the latter is for solving given problem. The former is usually an ad hoc operation that has been performed manually by person. The person sometimes resolves the original IP-units into parts and rebuilds a new IP-unit. This is almost the same as making a new IP-unit from scratch. For example, two procedural programs with small scopes can be integrated to acquire the large scope such as the case of integrating image-processing program with acoustic processing program in order to acquire the program to deal with image and acoustic information at the same time. It is excluded from the following discussion. For the latter, on the other hand, it is required to perform integration automatically in a computer system. It is difficult to take such a procedure as to resolve the IP-Units into parts and rebuild them as taken by persons. In the sequel therefore, integration is limited only to using the original IP-units without resolving into parts. It is however allowed that some extra function(s) is added from outside to paste the IP-units. If the IP-Unit is the one that has been obtained by integration of the smaller IP-Units however, it can be resolved to the level of the original IP-Units. As will be shown below, a processor that is described explicitly is identified as an independent IP-Unit and is used for creating the other IP-Units by integration.

In this paper IP-Unit and integration of IP-Units are defined in section 2.2. In section 2.3 a possible method of integration is discussed. It is concluded through this discussion that symbolic, declarative knowledge-based method of processing is suited for an integrator to integrate any combination of the different methods. Realizing this integrator is discussed in section 2.4. In reality there is a big gap between symbolic and non-symbolic methods of information processing. Integration is limited because of this gap even with the integrator discussed above. The symbolic and non-symbolic methods are compared in order to clarify the difference in section 2.5. A possible extension of knowledge based processing is proposed also in this section. Section 2.6 is a conclusion.

2.2 Definition of IP-Unit and Integration

Every IP-unit is built on the basis of a specific representation method and its processing mechanism inherited from the method it originates. Every IP-unit has its own scope of representation as an inherent characteristic of the IP-Unit. If this scope cannot cover the information processing requests from outside given as problem, then the IP-Unit alone cannot solve this problem but needs to strengthen the capability with an expanded scope. If the expansion of the scope is difficult by modifying the original IP-Unit, then a new IP-Unit has to be developed. This was often the case in the ordinary software method. Integration of different IP-Units is an effort to expand the scope by still the other way so that the integrated IP-Unit has a larger scope to cover what is required. Thus from the viewpoint of integration, the scope of an IP-Unit, i.e. what information it can accept and process, is the primary importance. Integration of IP-Units is not restricted to the case of IP-Units with the different methods but those of the same method, for example two procedural programs, can also be the objects of integration.

2.2.1 Definition of IP-Unit

Every IP-unit receives input from the outside and generates an output. Let the input and the output be specified by a set of variables, $x = x1,x2,--,xm$ and $y = y1,y2,--,yn$ respectively. The scope of a variable is defined by 'type $\times$ domain'. Let the scope of the variable xi be Xi. Then the scope of the IP-Unit is defined as $X1 \times X2 \times -- \times Xm \times Y1 \times Y2 \times --\times Yn$. The function that the IP-Unit can achieve on the other hand is a mapping P from $X1 \times X2 \times -- \times Xm$ to $Y1 \times Y2 \times --\times Yn$. This is the external definition of the IP-Unit that is necessary and sufficient for discussing integration. The internal structure of this IP-Unit has to be specified to the detail for the purpose of implementation. It is not necessary for the discussion below. Thus an IP-Unit is represented formally as P(X1, X2,--, Xm ; Y1, Y2, --, Yn).

In some simple methods of information processing like a neural network, the processing mechanism defines the scope directly. In the more complex scheme, especially the information processing methods based on symbolic representation, syntax and semantics are defined first as the representation scheme and then a processing mechanism is defined based on the scheme. Procedural program processing, database processing and declarative knowledge processing are all in this class, but the actual representation schemes and processing mechanisms, and accordingly the possibility of integration of an IP-Unit with the other, are different by the methods.

2.2.2 Scope of IP-Unit

The scope of an IP-Unit is a sub-space $\prod_i Xi \times \prod_j Yj$ in a large open universe. It is decomposed as follows.

(1) Type ; There are types of different nature. Every variable has its own type and is classified by the type as follows: (i) Numerical variable with such types as 'real', 'integer' and so on. (ii) Logical variable to represent some entity in the universe, for example a variable xi represents some person of a type 'Person' as an abstract set of persons. This is dealt with as a type because it represents entities of a nature that is different from the similar but the other type, say 'Table', 'TV set', etc. (iii) Variable to represent a truth value of a proposition. Every variable has its own type. Let Txi and Tyj represent the types of variables xi and yj respectively. Then the type of the IP-Unit is $\prod_i Txi \times \prod_j Tyj$. The type (ii) above is defined by a classification structure of conceptual entities. In reality the type (i) is a part of the type (ii) because a numerical entity is also a conceptual entity. Figure 2.1 shows an example of the classification structure. Since this is a tree, there can be a close relation between two types. For example, Person > Boy where > denotes that the left side concept is upper to the right side. It is read 'greater-than' in the sequel.

(2) Domain ; every variable is specified a set of values that the variable can take in a type. It is called a domain. In case of numerical variable as (i) above, let the type be ' real number'. Then the domain may be a set of real value, for example, an interval like [a, b]. Similarly, in case of logical variable as (ii), the domain is specified in the type. It is a set of the individual entities, like persons, women, boys, etc. Sometimes the domain can be the set of all possible individuals and the same as the type. In case of truth value as (iii) above, the domain is either (0, 1) in the simple case or an interval [0, 1] including incompleteness of truth value.

(3) Granularity ; every variable has its own minimum distance between adjacent values in its domain depending on the syntax of language as representation scheme or the precision of processing mechanism. In principle, IP-Units with the different granularity cannot be integrated. Every IP-Unit P(X1, X2,--, Xm ; Y1, Y2, --, Yn) is endowed a logical value implicitly. It is either logically true if this

relation holds or false otherwise. An operation to obtain an output for the given input is to keep it true. In a neural network, on the other hand, the truth value of the relation between input and output is not always exactly one but can be any value between zero and one. This causes a difficulty in integrating symbolic system and non-symbolic system. This issue is discussed in section 2.5 and it is assumed for a while that every neural network generates only True or False.

The type of an IP-Unit represents a skeletal structure of its scope. The domain is specified as the detailed information on the scope.

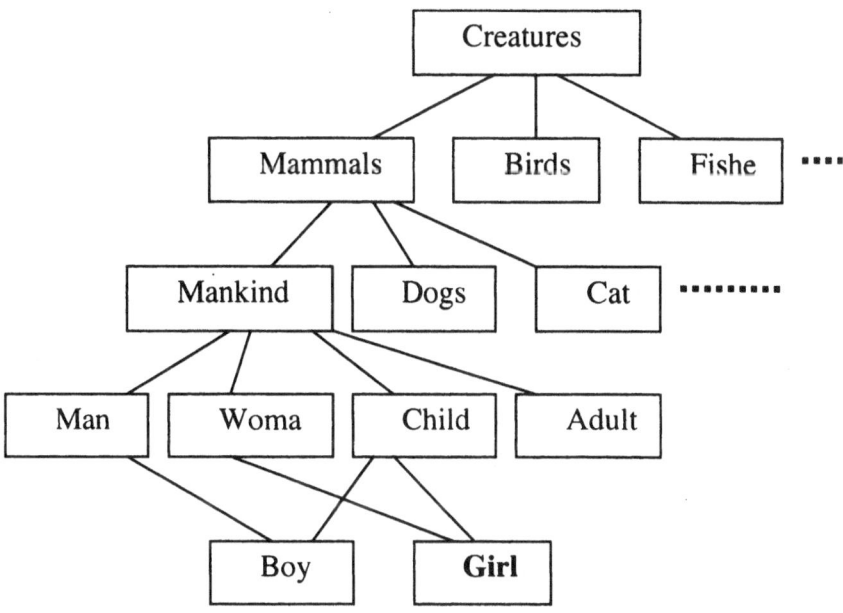

Fig. 2. 1. Hierarchy of conceptual entities

2.2.3 Representation of Integration in Terms of Scope of IP-Units

Integration is discussed in two steps. In the following, the first step, the possible cases of IP-Units being integrated without changing the contents, is discussed. The second step, the integration method, is discussed in section 2.3.

In the following, Tx ~ Ty denotes that the variable x and y are of the same type. Let x and y be of the type A and B respectively. If A > B, then Tx ~ Ty. There are the cases of integration as follows.

(1) Direct serial concatenation.

Two IP-unit, P1(X1, X2,--, Xm ; Y1, Y2, --, Yn) and P2(U1, U2,--, Up ; V1, V2, --, Vq) can be integrated to Q(X1', X2',--, Xm'; V1', V2', --, Vq') by concatenation, if n = p and Ty1 ~ Tu1, Ty2 ~ Tu2, --, Tyn ~ Tun.

$$
\begin{aligned}
&Q(X1', X2',--, Xm'; V1', V2', --, Vq') = \\
&\quad P1(X1', X2',--, Xm'; Z1, Z2, --, Zn) \\
&\quad @\ P2(Z1, Z2,--, Zn ; V1', V2', --, Vq').
\end{aligned}
\tag{1}
$$

$Zi = Yi \wedge Ui$, $(i = 1, 2, --, n)$, represents that Zi is a new scope of which the type is the common type of Tyi and Tui, and the domain is generated as the set-theoretical intersection of the domains of the variables yi and ui, @ denotes a concatenation operation, Xi', $(i = 1, 2, --, m)$, is a subset of the scope Xi of the variable xi that can map into reduced domain Zj, $(j = 1, 2, --, n)$, and Vi', $(i = 1, 2, --, q)$, is a subset of the scope Vi of the variable vi that can be mapped from the reduced domain Zj, $(j = 1, 2, --, n)$.

In this case two IP-Units are concatenated via the corresponding variables with the same type, Yi and Ui, $(I = 1,2,--,n)$. These variables are called the pivot variables. The subspaces defining the scopes of IP-Units are connected via the pivot variables. The intersection set of the domains of the corresponding pivot variables, Zi, replaces Yi and Ui in the expression and the domain of the other variables, Xi and Vi, are restricted to the smaller sets that have the mating elements in Zi. This manipulation must be done in all cases and abbreviated in the following.

If Txi ~ Tvi, $(i = 1, 2, --, q)$, instead of Tyi ~ Tui, $(i = 1, 2, --, q)$, then Q = P2 @ P1 are produced by the similar relation.

(2) Indirect serial integration

As the extension of the direct serial concatenation, there is a case in which two IP-units can be integrated serially by inserting an extra function E between them as follows.

$$
\begin{aligned}
&Q(X1, X2,--, Xm; V1, V2, --, Vq) = \\
&\quad P1(X1, X2,--, Xm ; Y1, Y2, --, Yn), \\
&\quad @\ E(\ Y1, Y2, --, Yn ; U1, U2,--, Up), \\
&\quad @\ P2(U1, U2,--, Up ; V1, V2, --, Vq),
\end{aligned}
\tag{2}
$$

This is an extended form of (1) connecting the different subspaces by the plural pivot variables. In more general case, a serial integration holds via any finite number of extra functions between integrated IP-Units, i.e., Q = P1 @ E1 @ -- @ En @ P2. The direct serial concatenation is the special case of n = 0.

(3) Parallel integration

Two IP-unit, P1(X1, X2,--, Xm ; Y1, Y2, --, Yn) and P2(U1, U2,--, Up ; V1, V2, --, Vq) are integrated in parallel to produce Q(R1, R2,--, Rm+p ; S1, S2,--, Sn+q) with an expanded scope by the following rules.

$$Q(R1, R2,--, Rm+p ; S1, S2,--,Sn+q) =$$
$$A (R1, R2, --, Rm, Rm+1, Rm+2, --, Rm+p)$$
$$@ [P1(X1, X2,--, Xm ; Y1, Y2, --, Yn)$$
$$\oplus P2(U1, U2,--, Up ; V1, V2, --, Vq)]$$
$$@ B(S1, S2, --, Sn,Sn+1,---, Sn+q).$$

(3)

Here $Ri \sim Xi$, $(i = 1,2,--, m)$, $Rm+i \sim Ui$, $(i = 1,2,--, p)$, $Yi \sim Si$, $(i = 1,2,--, n)$, $Vi \sim Sn+i$, $(i = 1,2,--, q)$, that is, all corresponding scopes of variables are of the same type. This is the case of expanding the subspaces of the IP-Units and a new IP-Unit with the expanded scope is generated by this integration. It is important that this integration enlarges the structure of the scope.

(4) Integration of alternative operations

Let an output of an IP-Unit, say D, be a set of truth-values of alternative propositions. Then an IP-Unit can corresponds to each proposition and is evoked when its truth-value is 1. Such an IP-Unit as D appears in computational processing like neural network. Let its output be a vector $(d1, d2, --, dk)$ and an IP-Unit Pi corresponds to di, $(i = 1, 2, --, k)$. An additional IP-Unit SELECT is inserted between D and a set of IP-Units Pi, $(i = 1, 2, --, k)$ in order to integrate them as follows. Moreover, if necessary, still another IP-Unit COLLECT is put at the end to collect the output of Pi's. The IP-Unit D has a set of input $(U1,--,Ua)$ and generate k outputs. Each Pi, $(i = 1, 2, --, k)$, requires its own pi inputs Xij, $(j = 1, 2, --, pi)$ and generates qi output Yij, $(i = 1, 2, --, qi)$.

$$Q(U1, U2, --, Ua; X11, X12,--, X1p1;--; Xa1, Xa2,--, Xapa;$$
$$Y11, Y12, --, Y1q1:--; Ya1, Ya2, --, Yaqa) =$$
$$D(U1, U2, --, Ua; d1, d2, --, dk)$$
$$@ SELECT(d1=1,P1; d2=1,P2; --, dk=1, Pk)$$
$$@ [P1(X11, X12,--, X1p1; Y11, Y12, --, Y1q1) \oplus -- \oplus Pa(Xa1,$$
$$Xa2,--, Xapa; Ya1, Ya2, --, Yaqa)]$$
$$@ COLLECT(Y11, Y12, --, Y1q1; --; Ya1, Ya2, --,Yaqa)$$

(4)

(5) Integration by inserting an IP-Unit into another IP-Unit

Assume that an IP-Unit has some incomplete operation and is completed by being inserted another IP-Unit there. An IP-Unit SUBSTITUTE connects these IP-Units.

$$Q(X1, X2,--, Xm; V1, V2, --, Vq) =$$
$$P1(X1, X2,--, Xm ; Y1, Y2, --, \underline{Yi}, --, Yn)$$
$$@ P2(X1, X2,--, Xm ;Yi) @ SUBSTITUTE(Yi, \underline{Yi})$$

(5)

where $\underline{Yi}$ included in P1 can not be obtained by P1. The other IP-Unit P2 can obtain it and SUBSTITUTE substitutes Yi into $\underline{Yi}$. This kind of integration holds when the IP-Unit P1 is defined incompletely as the relation among the scopes of variables without specifying the precise operation. Figure 2. 2 shows possible forms of integration.

2.3 Possible Method of Integration

To integrate the different IP-Units is to generate a new IP-Unit by any of the generation methods given in the last section. The objective is that the generated IP-Unit covers the scope of a given problem from outside. In order to apply the above rules a special processing system that have the capability to execute the following operations is necessary. It is called an integrator in this paper. Developing an integrator is an important objective of AI [3, 4].

(1) To decide what type of integration to achieve.

(2) To look for the suitable IP-Units for integration.

(3) To provide special IP-Unit(s), such as SELECT, for pasting the selected IP-Units.

(4) To generate a new IP-Unit by applying the selected rule of integration.

Seeing from the integrator, every IP-Unit is an object of integration. It must be clearly defined and represented explicitly by means of the representation scheme of the integrator so that the integrator can identify and manipulate it. However the integrator is itself an IP-Unit in the sense that it must use any one of the possible information processing methods, such as procedural programming method, declarative knowledge-based method, computational method, and so on. The necessary operation as above for integration must be achievable by processing mechanism of the integrator, that is, by the processing mechanism of the method used for implementing the integrator. Thus here is a problem of realizing the integrator by means of any of these methods. As the typical examples of methods currently available, the following three are taken into account.

(1) Neural Network (N), (2) Procedural Processing (P), (3) Knowledge Processing (K).

The last two are based on the symbolic representations while the first one is on the computational methods. There is a large difference between the symbolic processing method and the computational processing method. Each of the methods has its own limitation when used in the real environment.

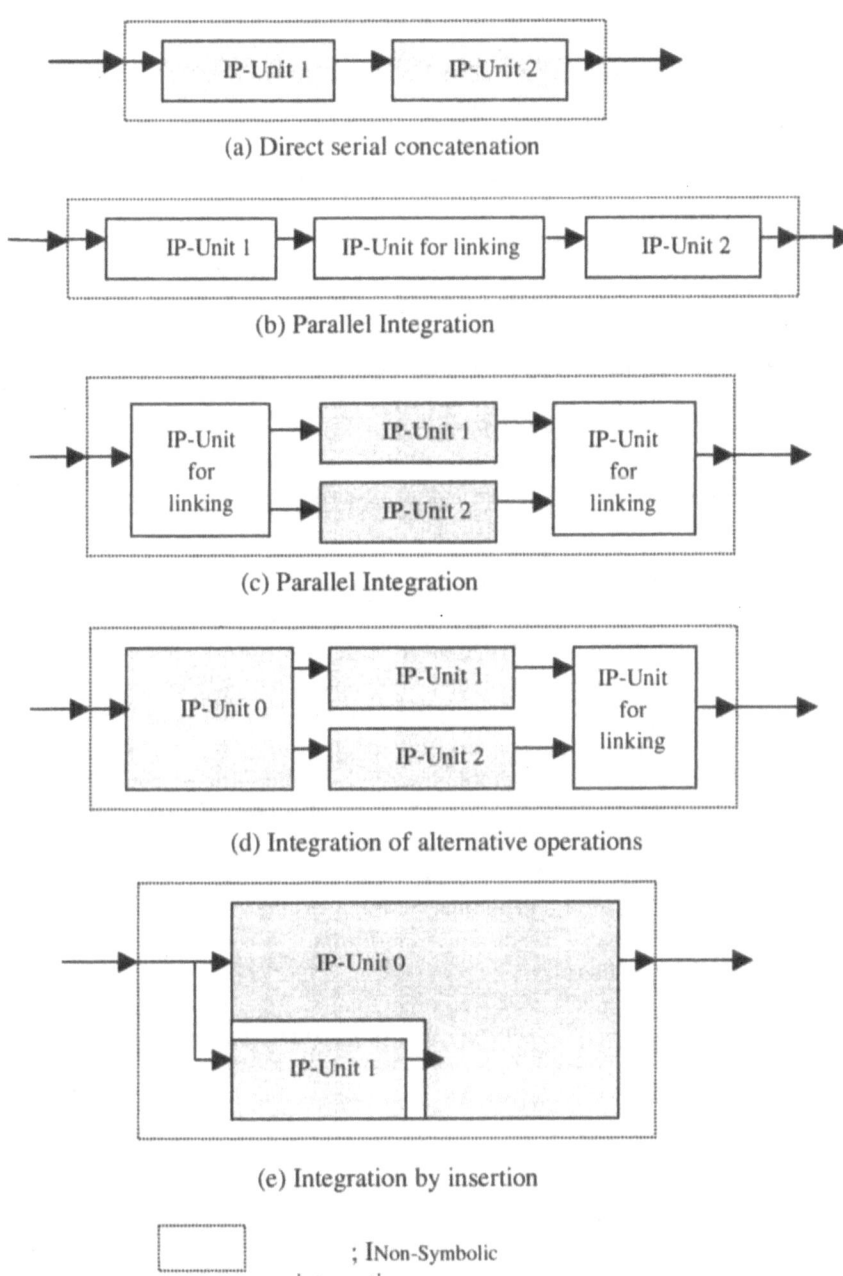

(a) Direct serial concatenation

(b) Parallel Integration

(c) Parallel Integration

(d) Integration of alternative operations

(e) Integration by insertion

; INon-Symbolic integration

Fig. 2.2. Various cases of integration

2.3.1 Computational Method and Symbol Processing Method

Computational method such as neural network can represent things to the very fine level in the restricted area. Its representation scheme is determined depending on its physical organization and, therefore, its power of expression is strongly limited. It cannot represent the integration rules formally by its representation scheme and consequently it cannot be an integrator.

Symbolic processing method on the other hand covers from the simple logic level at the bottom to the program level in a procedural form or knowledge processing level in a declarative form at the top. A physical organization and a representation scheme are separated and syntax as a software method of representation is defined in every symbolic method. It allows a very complex expression to be made in a constructive way. Accordingly, in principle, symbol processing ensures a larger scope of information processing than computational method. But there is still a big difference between a procedural program-based processing system and a declarative knowledge-based processing system.

2.3.2 Procedural Method and Declarative Method

The procedural processing method has been developed as a method of writing down a process of transforming an input to an output. To write a program is itself to define a problem. In other words, the same method is used for representing and solving problems. Or, in many interactive applications, the problem-solving method is defined in advance and problems are given later. The problems have to be presented in a form strictly specified according to the problem-solving method. In this regard, there is no difference between procedural method and computational one. This style of solving problems cannot deal with problems that need exploration in order to find solutions. Moreover, the scope of a program as an IP-Unit is fixed and it is difficult to expand it in the IP-Unit. It is inconvenient for realizing the integration rules.

On the other hand declarative representation as the base of knowledge processing can realize a very flexible ways of processing. Transformation from an input to an output is achieved by making a sequence of rules in the declarative form. It is not decided in advance but is constructed dynamically after given a problem.

2.3.3 Declarative Knowledge-based Method as Integrator

Let's think of a simple knowledge-based processing system. It is described in the logical form as follows.
(1) It is composed of a knowledge base containing
 (i) a set of rules represented in the form like $A(X, Y) \wedge B(Y, Z) \rightarrow C(X, Z)$, where X
      $= X1, X2, --, Xk, Y = Y1, Y2, --, Ym, Z = Z1, Z2, --, Zn,$

(ii) a set of facts such as A(X, Y), B(Y, Z).

(2) A deductive inference engine that deduces a conclusion based on the deduction rule to the given X. When a problem is presented in the form of C(X, Z) requiring to get the value of Z, the system tries to find a rule having C(X, Z) in the conclusion part (A backward reasoning is assumed here). If the inference engine finds the rule as shown above, then it deduces A(X, Y) ∧ B(Y, Z) as the new requirement to be satisfied. If all the predicates (A and B in this case) are matched with the facts, the process ends and a solution is gotten. If some or all predicates match with the other rules, then the predicates are further expanded by the body parts of the rules and thus a logical structure of facts are formed. The problem-solving process is thus to find a logical structure of facts and the value of variables that make the original problem logically true.

From integration's point of views, this has some important characteristics as follows.

(3) Not the rule but the facts decides finally whether a given logical expression is true or not. If all predicates in a given logical expression match with facts, then the logical expression is true. Usually the facts are in the knowledge base. But it can also be any IP-Unit. If, in this case, the scope of the IP-Unit match with the scope of the predicate in the logical expression being asked, then the IP-Unit is regarded as logically true and it is executed to obtain its output. This result is substituted into the corresponding variable in the predicate and the predicate is made logically true. Thus the fact can be put outside of the logical rule base as an independent IP-Unit, if the system is provided with the method to connect it with the predicates in the logical expression. This is to insert the IP-Unit in a knowledge-based processing embodying the integration by insertion. Let the IP-Unit be called an external fact in contrast to the ordinary fact in the knowledge base that is referred to an internal fact.

(4) The knowledge processing system looks for the logical structure of facts that meets the condition by a trial-and-error process. Rule is used to generate a tentative logical structure. If the structure fails to meet the condition, then the other rule is used in order to generate the other structure. Different rule makes the different structure and defines a different subspace including pivot variables.

(5) The more rules a knowledge-based system has, the larger number of the logical structures can be generated. Let the union set of all different variables included in a knowledge base be the subspace spanned by the knowledge base and is called the scope of the knowledge base. A logical structure connects some variables in this scope. One of these logical structures represents an actual method of problem solving. Thus the total number of the logical structures represents the potential capability of problem solving by a knowledge-based system. A set of logical structures can be gotten by applying deductive inference operations repeatedly to knowledge in the knowledge base until a new structure cannot be generated any more.

(6) It is possible to add a new rule or fact independently from those existing already in knowledge base. It expands the scope of the original knowledge base and increases the number of logical structure by the combination of this added

knowledge with knowledge that has already been there. This means that two separate knowledge bases can be merged with the least effect to the other parts of the system. It is to integrate two IP-Units of knowledge-based type. Actually some additional tasks are needed for integration when two knowledge bases are not homogeneous. It is shown in [3]. But this case is not included here.

With these characteristics a declarative knowledge-based method is suited for realizing an integrator. By using a proper language the rule of integration given in the last section can be represented. It is shown in Appendix. The other methods do not have these characteristics.

In order for a knowledge-based processing system being an integrator some condition as the followings must be met.

(c1) IP-Units that are to be integrated must be represented as the external facts by the representation language of knowledge-based system. This representation includes, (i) the scope and (ii) the function to be executed. This information is necessary for making a correct matching with the required predicate in the logical expression and the IP-Unit as an external fact. The information (ii) is usually the name of the function. When an IP-Unit is developed newly this condition can be met without difficulty. Otherwise it is sometimes not easy. For example, it is required to describe the scope and the function of a program in the form of knowledge. If the program is not new and no one knows its content precisely, it needs the reverse engineering.

(c2) Problems from outside must be accepted by the knowledge-based system. Since the main role of integrator is to satisfy the requirement asked by the problems by integrating the existing IP-Units, both the method which the integrator based on and the representation scheme which the problem is described concern the way of integration.

2.4 Realizing Integration

In order to integrate two or more IP-Units it is necessary that both the scope and the functions of the IP-units are made clear and stated explicitly by a representation scheme of an integrator. There can be the different cases by what IP-Unit accept problem from outside. It depends on the source of the problem. If a person brings a problem into the computer system, the problem representation is in the form familiar to the person. Usually it is in a symbolic expression. In many cases it can be in a declarative form even if a procedural program is used for solving the problem. This is a problem driven or a goal driven case. The other possibility is the case in which problems must be captured by a computational method such as the case in which an analog sensor catches a signal. This is an event driven case. Even in this case it can happen that symbol level processing is required. For example, a smell sensor in a system catches a signal, say of smoke, and the system reasons what happens and makes decision on what to do. It needs a rather complex decision and may require integration of some IP-Units. It is difficult to do in the computational processing but is necessary to ask the help of integrator.

Let two independently defined IP-Units A and B are to be integrated. A and B are any of Knowledge Processing (K) or Procedural Processing (P) or Neural Network (N). Database should be included but abbreviated here. There are such different combinations of IP-Units to be integrated as follows.

(1) K-($\underline{\underline{K}}$)-K, (2) K-($\underline{\underline{K}}$)-P, (3) K-($\underline{\underline{K}}$)-N, (3') K-(K)-$\underline{\underline{N}}$, (4) P-($\underline{\underline{K}}$)-P,

(5) P-($\underline{\underline{K}}$)-N, (5') P-(K)-$\underline{\underline{N}}$, (6) N-($\underline{\underline{K}}$)-N, (6') $\underline{\underline{N}}$-(K)-N

In these cases (K) means that the integrator is realized as knowledge-based processing and the term with the double underline denotes that this IP-Unit accept problem from outside world. If a problem is represented in a symbolic form, it can be translated into the representation language of knowledge-based processing, and the integrator accept it. ($\underline{\underline{K}}$) denotes it. If, on the other hand, the problem from the outside is captured in the non-symbolic form, a non-symbolic IP-Unit processes first the information. It may be a neural network or the other processor. $\underline{\underline{N}}$ denotes it. A method of calling the integrator from neural network is necessary.

2.4.1 The Case when Problem is Represented in a Symbolic form (The Cases 1, 2, 3, 4, 5, 6)

When a problem is represented in a symbolic form it is not difficult to translate it into a formal way of representation of knowledge-based processing. The integration of IP-Units for the cases (1), (2), (3), (4), (5) and (6) above is performed as follows.

(1) An actual integration of two IP-Units as knowledge-based processing system, when those are implemented in the different way, needs conversion between them at integration. However, it is possible in principle as has already been discussed. As the bases of integration for some other cases as shown below, a practical method of its realization including conversion must be developed. But it is out of the scope of this paper. The related topics are discussed in [3].

(2) If IP-Unit as program is recorded as an external fact to the integrator, then it is executed automatically.

(3) If IP-Unit as neural network is recorded as an external fact to the integrator, then it is executed automatically. This case is shown in [2] and the other papers.

(4) If each IP-Unit as program is registered as an external fact to the separate IP-Unit as knowledge-based processing, then integration is achieved by integrating the knowledge-based processing units. Assume that the programs A and B are integrated with the knowledge processing units Ka and Kb respectively by the method as shown in (2). Assume also that Ka and Kb be integrated as the case (1). Then A and B can be integrated by a set of integration, (i) A-(K)-Ka, (ii) Kb -(K)-B, (iii) Ka-(K)- Kb.

(5) In this case A and B are the IP-Units as program and as neural network respectively. This case is dealt with in the same way as (4).

(6) In this case both A and B are the IP-Units as neural network. This case is also dealt with in the same way as (4).

2.4.2 The Cases when Problem is Brought in the System in a Non-symbolic Form (The Case 3', 5' 6')

If a non-symbolic signal is captured by an IP-Unit, an event driven operation starts. Every signal processor is designed to activate some processor in order to perform a specific operation. The operation is dependent on the signal or, in other words, the IP-Unit that accept the signal, because for every non-symbolic IP-Unit the signal it accepts is decided in advance. Often it must be combined with the other IP-Units in order to decide the operation. For example, a smoke sensor is combined with the temperature sensor to judge that there is a fire and to issue a fire warning and/or to starts a fire fighting. In a more complex system like an intelligent robot, this decision making may be more complicated. Hence, except a very simple case in which an operation is directly evoked by the signal, a complex decision making is necessary requiring the integrated use of the other IP-Units or fusion of the sensors.

A method to ask the integrator to decide the operation is necessary. Different from the previous case where the problem is represented in a symbolic form and a problem-solving process starts from the top, the operation starts from the bottom. It goes up once and, through the operation in the integrator, the IP-Unit that accepts the signal is called again. Since integration is possible only in the symbolic processing level, this process is indispensable.

Every non-symbolic signal processor must be provided with a special function to ask the integrator the integration. It is to send a sensor-specific query in the symbolic form to the integrator like, analyzeSituation(IP-Unit name). This means to analyze the situation based on the signal caught by the IP-Unit. This IP-Unit can be a simple sensor or the more complex processor like neural network.

On the other hand, the integrator is provided with a rule to analyze the situation. For example, in the case of simple sensor,

analyzeSituation(smokeSensor) :-

equal(smokeSensor,1),equal(temperatureSensor,1), issueWarning(fireWarning),

+----

is provided. This rule says that if both smoke sensor and temperature sensor are on at the same time, then the warning is issued. If a neural network recognizes n patterns and needs a specific operation to each pattern, then a query decideOperation(neuralNetwork, y1, y2, --,yn) is sent and the following rule may be given to the integrator.

decideOperation(neuralNetwork, y1, y2, --,yn) :-

equal(y1, 1), operation1(--) + equal(y2, 1), operation2(--),--,+

equal(yn, 1),operationn(--) .

Figure 2.3 illustrates an actual form of integration.

2.5 Bridging the Gap between Symbolic and Non-Symbolic Processing

As has been mentioned in the last section there is a large gap between symbolic and non-symbolic processing. Because of this gap their integration is restricted to a special case. A way to reduce the gap is considered.

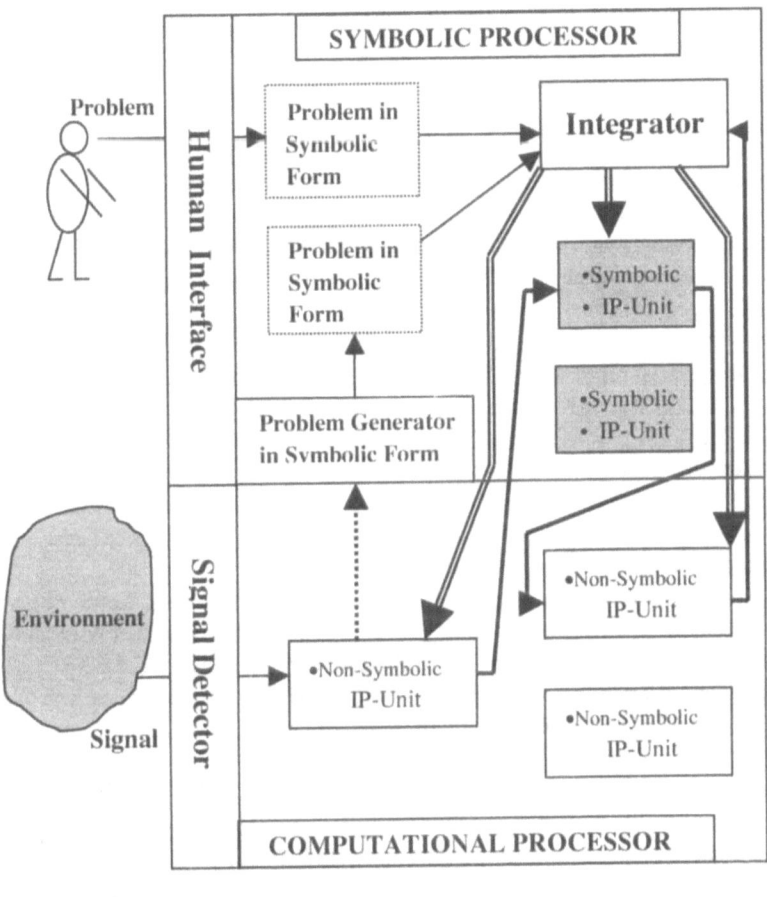

Fig. 2.3. Architecture and operation of system including integrator

2.5.1 Logical Inference by Non-Symbolic Processor

It has been assumed so far that a non-symbolic IP-Unit works completely in the sense that it generates output either one (true) or zero (false). It is not true. Many non-symbolic IP-Units work quite incompletely. The output of a non-symbolic IP-Unit spread in a range (0, 1). If one intends to describe a non-symbolic IP-Unit precisely in terms of the logical language, he/she may find it very difficult. Therefore the above discussion is rather a special case. This difficulty comes from the difference of granularity of the representation schemes between symbolic system and non-symbolic system. In order to clarify the difference, the author tried to represent a logical formula and a non-symbol processor in the same mathematical method in [4].

It starts from a very simple rule in the logical form $(\forall x/d)[F(x) \rightarrow G(x)]$, where x/d means d $\ni$ x. This formula shows that an implicative relation holds between F and G for a variable x defined on a set d = {a, b, c, --, z} as its domain. Here, a, b, c, --, z are the instances of x. Then a state of the set d with respect to F is defined as the combination of the state of every instance which is either F(a): True or F(a): False and so on for every other instance. For example, a vector (F(a), -F(b), -F(c), --, F(z)) represents a state of d such that F(a):True, F(b): False, F(c): False, --, F(z):True, and is represented (1,0,0,--,1). Let this vector be represented Sf_i (i =1,2,--, 2^n). The state covers the range from (0,0,--0) to (1,1,--1). Let the set of all states be Sf.

A state or a set of states corresponds to a logical expression. For example, (1,1,--,1) corresponds to $(\forall x/d)F(x)$ and a set of all states beside (0,0,--0) corresponds to $(\exists x/d)F(x)$ respectively. These are all possible logical expressions by the logical representation scheme usually used.

The state changes if some logical values of instances change. Let a system be in a state Sf_i with a probability Pf_i. A probability vector Pf is defined corresponding to the state vector Sf. In the same way the state vector Sg of d and corresponding probability vector Pg with respect to G is defined. Then it is shown that the deductive operation, $F \wedge [F \rightarrow G] \Rightarrow G$ is represented in the form of state transition using the same mathematical formula as a stochastic process with a transition matrix T, $Pg = Pf \times T$. T is defined such that the probability Pg_i of the state Sg_i can be obtained as $Pg_j = \Sigma i\, Pf_i \times t_{ij}$ where t_{ij} is (i,j)-th element of T. Since Pf_i and Pg_j corresponds to F and G, T correspond $[F \rightarrow G]$. In fact it is possible to make T in such a way that it is equivalent to a logical expression $(\forall x/d)[F(x) \rightarrow G(x)]$, i.e. generate the same result, according to the definition of the 'imply'. Figure 10.4 shows such a transition matrix.

This idea can be expanded to represent a formula of the form $(\forall x/d)[F1(x) \wedge F2(x) \rightarrow G(x)]$ by introducing the three dimensional matrix called a cubic matrix.

It should be noted here that $Pg_j = \Sigma i\, Pf_i \times t_{ij}$ represents the mathematical expression of a part of neural network with the input vector Pf_i, output Pg_i and the

37

	P_0	P_1	P_2	P_3	P_4	P_5	P_6	P_7	P_8	P_9	P_{10}	P_{11}	P_{12}	P_{13}	P_{14}	P_{15}
P_0	x	x	x	x	x	x	x	x	x	x	x	x	x	x	x	x
P_1	0	x	0	x	0	x	0	x	0	x	0	x	0	x	0	x
P_2	0	0	x	x	0	0	x	x	0	0	x	x	0	0	x	x
P_3	0	0	0	x	0	0	0	x	0	0	0	x	0	0	0	x
P_4	0	0	0	0	x	x	x	x	0	0	0	0	x	x	x	x
P_5	0	0	0	0	0	x	0	x	0	0	0	0	0	x	0	x
P_6	0	0	0	0	0	0	x	x	0	0	0	0	0	0	x	x
P_7	0	0	0	0	0	0	0	x	0	0	0	0	0	0	0	x
P_8	0	0	0	0	0	0	0	0	x	x	x	x	x	x	x	x
P_9	0	0	0	0	0	0	0	0	0	x	0	x	0	x	0	x
P_{10}	0	0	0	0	0	0	0	0	0	0	x	x	0	0	x	x
P_{11}	0	0	0	0	0	0	0	0	0	0	0	x	0	0	0	x
P_{12}	0	0	0	0	0	0	0	0	0	0	0	0	x	x	x	x
P_{13}	0	0	0	0	0	0	0	0	0	0	0	0	0	x	0	x
P_{14}	0	0	0	0	0	0	0	0	0	0	0	0	0	0	x	x
P_{15}	0	0	0	0	0	0	0	0	0	0	0	0	0	0	0	x

x ; non-zero positive value with row-sum =1

Fig. 2.4. Transition matrix to represent logical expression $(\forall x/d)[F(x) \to G(x)]$ $(d = \{a1, a2, a3, a4\})$

weight of the arc from the node i to j is tij. Though this is not exactly the same as the ordinary neural network but is included in the definition of neural network. Therefore it is said that non-symbol processor can represent input-and-output relations very finely including logical expressions as the special case in its scope. In other words, logical system cannot represent a non-symbol processor totally with the current representation scheme. Therefore integration discussed so far is not complete. It can involve only a part of non-symbolic representation in its scope.

It is possible to expand the framework of logical expression so that it can represent totally non-symbol processors. What is lacked in logical expression system is the quantitative measure of truthfulness of a logical expression. Let think of $(\forall x/d) F(x)$ again. If $d = \{a, b, c, --, z\}$ is a finite set, then this expression means that $F(a) \wedge F(b) \wedge -- \wedge F(z)$. Even if the probability of $F(x)$ being true is different by the cases of $x = a$ or $x = b$ or -- or $x = z$, it cannot be represented in the logical expression.

Let the expression be modified to $(\forall x/d)\{F(x), p(x)\}$ including $p(x)$ where $p(x)$ is the probability distribution of $F(x)$ for $x = a$, $x = b$, --, $x = z$. This expression is read, 'for all x in d, $F(x)$ with probability $p(x)$'. This corresponds to the fact representation and an input for a non-symbol processor as discussed above. The similar mathematical expression is used not only for the fact but also for the rule. That is, the expression of rules is shown like $(\forall x/d)\{[F(x) \to G(x)], T_{fg}(x,x)\}$ where

$T_{fg}(x,x)$ is the transition matrix corresponding to $[F(x) \rightarrow G(x)]$. By the inference operation $(\forall x/d)\{G(x), r(x)\}$ is deduced where $r(x) = p(x) \times T_{fg}(x,x)$.

In an ordinary logic system, every entity, for example a, b, c, d above, is considered independent. There is no cross effect of entities to the consequence of logical operation. This is the special case of the matrix $T_{fg}(x,x)$ being a diagonal matrix. It shows another exemplification of the fact that the logical representation deals with only a special case of computational method. In this case $T_{fg}(x,x)$ can be replaced by a function $q(x)$, and $r(x)$ is an inner product of $p(x)$ and $q(x)$. That is, the value of $r(x)$ is obtained separately for every entity x.

With this represenatatio, an IP-Unit like neural network can be represented, in a logical term. The basic form is $(\forall x/d)(\forall y/e)[F(x) \wedge H(x,y) \rightarrow G(y)]$ where $F(x)$ and $G(y)$ are input and output respectively, and $H(x,y)$ is a processor. In this case, the characteristics of input and output are different and therefore the different variables, x and y, are used with the ifferent domains, the set d and the set e. This logical expression says that if an input $F(x)$ is given to $H(x,y)$, then an output $G(y)$ is produced. In order to include the quantitative values, it is also expanded to, $(\forall x/d)(\forall y/e)[\{F(x), p(x)\} \wedge \{H(x,y), T_{fg}(x,y)\} \rightarrow \{G(y),r(y)\}]$ where $r(y) = p(x) \times T_{fg}(x,y)$.

With this expanded scheme of representation, the finer treaty of non-symbolic method at integration becomes possible. The other advantage of this expansion is the possibility of a logic system to learn from the data. By accumulating the data, the probability of a logical relation changes. It may change the logical expression finally. But the importance of integration is in the fact that the different IP-Units with different characteristics can be used in a system. What is necesary for the integrator from the integration's point of view therefor is the capability to represent various IP-Unit faithfully in order to use them as the external facts.

2.5.2 How Human Creatures could Evolve to Acquire Language?

The discussion hitherto was mainly on the practical way of integration in an information system. Symbolic language has been used even for the purpose of integrating non-symbolic information processing. Non-symbolic processing system has a limited scope and cannot work to integrate the other IP-Units. Therefore whatever many non-symbolic systems may have been developed, or whatever the new method to expand the scope of processor may be developed such as an emergent system, these cannot adapt to solve very complex problem that requires a combination of different information processing methods. By using symbolic processing these are integrated.

But here is a very academic interest. Every creature starts from amino acid and evolved to acquire a very complex organization. Among them human creatures acquired language with which we could develop high level culture. During while these creature had to integrate the different functions in order to adapt the changing environment and evolve further. How they could integrate without symbolic system? One of the answer to this question may be as follows. Output ports of neural systems are connected to input ports of the other neural systems randomly as the biological growth of the neural network. Most of them were irrational and these creatures have died by natural selection but some few connections were rational. If number of trials is large, the number of success increases to a significant level. This is another method of integration. But even though it is possible, it cannot be used actually.

But how to answer the next question, how human creatures could acquire language in the evolution process without any symbol processor ? Of course no one can answer this question today. But before the concept of symbolic language could be acquired and a language had been defined, logical operations had to be possible by means of non-symbolic processors in the creature. The author hopes that the way of executing logical deduction by means of neural network as discussed in the last section becomes a cue to answer this question.

2.6 Conclusion

A way of integrating different methods of information processing was discussed. Very often the term 'integration' means a special method to put two specific programs together in an ad hoc manner. There is no view to define a general way of integrating any pair of information processing methods. To find such a general way was the main issue in this paper.

First, by classifying the various information-processing methods a possible way of integration and a way of realizing this integration were discussed. Among various methods of information processing, only the declarative knowledge-based system is suited for being used as an integrator. On the other hand, there is a big gap between symbolic and non-symbolic methods of information processing and, because of this gap, even with the method of integration discussed above the real integration is limited. The symbolic and non-symbolic methods were compared in order to clarify the difference and a possible extension of knowledge-based processing was proposed.

References

[1] V. Honavar and L. Uhr (eds.) ; Artificial Intelligence and Neural Networks, Steps toward Principled Integration, Academic press, 1994.
[2] L. Monostori, Cs. Egresits, and B. Kadar ; Hybrid AI Solution and their Application in Manufacturing, Proc.Ninth International Conference on Industrial and Engineering Applications of Artificial Intelligence and Expert Systems, Gordon and Breach Publishers, 1996.
[3] S. Ohsuga ; Toward Truly Intelligent Information Systems - From Expert Systems to Automatic Programming, Knowledge-Based Systems, Vol. 10, 363-396, 1998.
[4] F. Hays-Ross ; Artificial Intelligence, What Works and What Doesn't ? AI Magazine, Volume 18, No.2, 1997

[5] S. Ohsuga ; Symbol processing by Non-Symbol Processor, Proc. 4th Pacific Rim International Conference on Artificial Intelligence, 1996, Cairns, Australia.

Appendix

The logical expressions are given for the definition of integration shown in section 2.2.2. The logical expressions are simpler than the definition as above because some parts of definition are executed implicitly as the deductive operation of logic system. This is a proof of the suitability of the declarative knowledge-based processing as the integrator.

(1) Direct serial concatenation.

$Q(X1', X2',--, Xm'; V1', V2', --, Vq')$:-

$P1(X1', X2',--, Xm'; Z1, Z2, --, Zn), P2(Z1, Z2,--, Zn ; V1', V2', --, Vq'),$

(2) Indirect serial integration

$Q(X1, X2,--, Xm; V1, V2, --, Vq)$:-

$P1(X1, X2,--, Xm ; Y1, Y2, --, Yn), E(Y1, Y2, --, Yn ; U1, U2,--, Up),$

$P2(U1, U2,--, Up ; V1, V2, --, Vq),$

(3) Parallel integration

$Q(R1, R2,--, Rm+p ; S1, S2,--,Sn+q)$:-

$P1(X1, X2,--, Xm ; Y1, Y2, --, Yn), P2(U1, U2,--, Up ; V1, V2, --, Vq),$

(4) Integration of alternative operations

$Q(U1, U2, --, Ua; X11, X12,--, X1p1;--; Xa1, Xa2,--, Xapa;$

$Y11, Y12, --, Y1q1;--;Ya1, Ya2, --, Yaqa)$:-

$D(U1, U2, --, Ua; d1, d2, --, dk) , SELECT(d1=1,P1; d2=1,P2; --, dk=1, Pk) ,$

$[P1(X11, X12,--, X1p1; Y11, Y12, --, Y1q1) \oplus -- \oplus$

$Pa(Xa1, Xa2,--, Xapa; Ya1, Ya2, --, Yaqa)],$

(5) Integration by inserting an IP-Unit into another IP-Unit

$Q(X1, X2,--, Xm; Y1, Y2, --, Yn)$:-

$P1(X1, X2,--, Xm ; Y1, Y2, --, \underline{Yi}, --, Yn) , P2(X1, X2,--, Xm ;Yi) .$

Symbol Pattern Integration Using Multilinear Functions

Pattern Reasoning

Hiroshi Tsukimoto

RWC Theoretical Foundation Toshiba Laboratory

Abstract: This paper presents an approach for the integration of symbols and patterns. The typical symbol processing is classical logic, where symbols are dealt with by logical reasoning. The typical pattern processing is neural networks, where patterns are dealt with by numerical computation. The integration of symbols and patterns means numerical computation of symbols and logical reasoning of patterns, that is, pattern reasoning . The key is the multilinear function space, which is an extension of Boolean algebra of Boolean functions and basically includes neural networks. The space is an algebraic model of several nonclassical logics. The above two integrations can be realized by the multilinear function space.

3.1 Introduction

The typical symbol processing is classical logic, where symbols are dealt with by logical reasoning. The typical pattern processing is neural networks, where patterns are dealt with by numerical computation. See Fig.3.1.

The integration of symbols and patterns means the following two integrations.

1. numerical computation of symbols
2. logical reasoning of patterns

See Fig. 3.2. For the numerical computation of symbols, it is shown that logics can be represented by linear algebra. For the logical reasoning of patterns, it is shown that patterns can be logically reasoned, which is based on the linear algebra representation of logics.

An example of pattern reasoning is presented. For example, expert doctors diagnose using a lot of images like brain images, electrocardiograms and so on, which can be formalized as follows:

Rule 1: If a brain image is a pattern, then an electrocardiogram is a pattern.
Rule 2: If an electrocardiogram is a pattern, then an electromyogram is a pattern.
Using the above two rules, we can reason
If a brain image is a pattern, then an electromyogram is a pattern.
This is a pattern reasoning. Symbols can be regarded as special cases of patterns. For example, let a rule be
If a brain image is a pattern, then a subject has a disease.

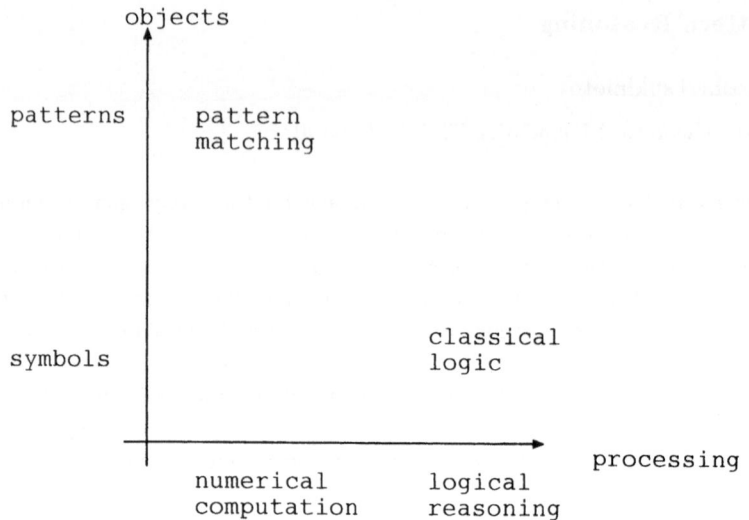

Fig. 3.1. Symbols and patterns

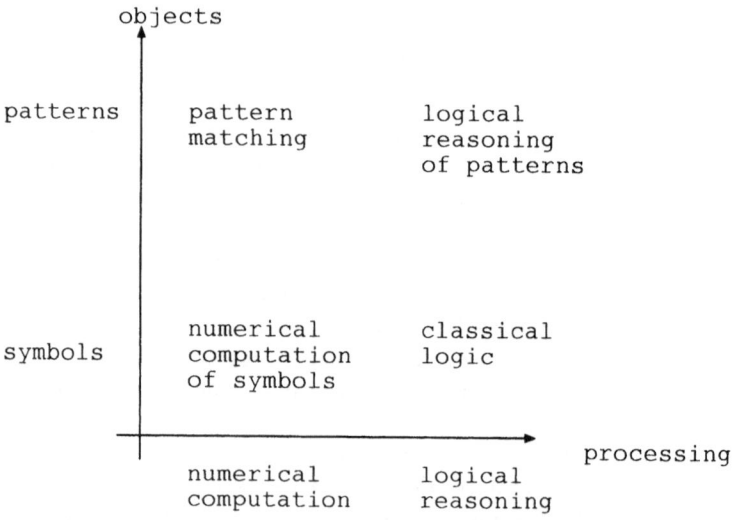

Fig. 3.2. Symbol pattern integration

The right side of the rule is a symbol. The rule can be regarded as a special case of pattern reasoning.

The pattern reasoning is a new solution for knowledge acquisition problem. The explanation is as follows. Since it is important to simulate human experts by computer software, expert systems have been studied to simulate human experts by computer software. Many expert systems are based on classical logic or something like classical logic (Hereinafter " classical logic" is used for simplification).

Knowledge acquisition is necessary, because the obscure knowledge of human experts cannot be reasoned by classical logic, while linguistic rules can be reasoned by classical logic. Knowledge acquisition means the conversion from obscure knowledge of human experts to linguistic rules. Knowledge acquisition has been studied by many researchers, but the results have not been successful, that is, the results show that knowledge acquisition is very difficult.

Generally speaking, a processing consists of a method and an object. For example, logical reasoning consists of the reasoning as the method and the symbols as the object. The methods of the processings by human experts are a kind of reasoning, which are different from the reasoning by classical logic. The objects of the processings by human experts are patterns (and symbols). That is, a lot of the processings by human experts can be regarded as the pattern reasonings.

Therefore, the pattern reasoning is a solution for the knowledge acquisition problem based on conversion of the knowledge acquisition to a completely different problem. However, readers may think that it is impossible to reason patterns. This paper shows that patterns can be reasoned by non-classical logics.

There are several possible definitions for patterns. Patterns such as images can be basically represented as functions. For example, two-dimensional images can be represented as the functions of two variables. Patterns are functions. Since it is desirable to be able to deal with any function, 3-layer feedforward neural networks, which can basically approximate any function[6], are studied.

Therefore, pattern reasonings are realized as logical reasonings of neural networks. However, classical logic cannot reason neural networks, while a few non-classical logics can reason neural networks. For example, intermediate logic LC[5], product logic[5], and Lukasiewicz logic[5] can reason neural networks. The reason why the above three logics can reason neural networks is as follows: Neural networks can be basically regarded as multilinear functions and the three logics are complete for multilinear function space, therefore, the three logics can reason neural networks.

The key is the multilinear function space. In the domain $\{0, 1\}$, the multilinear function space is an extension of Boolean algebra of Boolean functions. The space is the linear space expanded by the atoms of Boolean algebra of

Boolean functions and can be made into a Euclidean space. Logical operations are represented as vector operations, which are numerical computations. In the domain [0,1], continuous Boolean functions can be obtained. Roughly speaking, continuous Boolean functions consist of conjunction, disjunction, direct proportion and inverse proportion. The multilinear function space of the domain [0,1] is the linear space of the atoms of Boolean algebra of continuous Boolean functions and can be made into a Euclidean space.

As explained above, multilinear function space is a model of three logics, but due to space limitations, intermediate logic LC(Hereinafter, LC for short) is explained in this paper. The multilinear function space is an algebraic model of intuitionistic logic, but intuitionistic logic is not complete for the space. For intuitionistic logic, refer to [2]. LC, which is stronger than intuitionistic logic and weaker than classical logic, is complete for the space. Therefore, multilinear functions can be regarded as propositions of LC. Neural networks which can be basically regarded as multilinear functions, can also be regarded as propositions of LC. Therefore, neural networks can be logically reasoned.

The domain can be divided into the discrete domain and the continuous domain. The discrete domain can be reduced to $\{0,1\}$ by dummy variables. The continuous domain can be normalized to [0,1] by some normalization. Therefore, the domain $\{0,1\}$ and the domain [0,1] are discussed.

8.2 explains the space of multilinear functions of the domain $\{0,1\}$. 8.3 explains continuous Boolean functions. 8.4 describes multilinear functions of the domain [0,1]. 8.5 explains LC. 8.6 explains logical reasoning of neural networks by LC. 8.7 gives remarks on pattern reasoning. The following notations are used. $x, y, ..$ stand for variables. $f, g, ..$ stand for functions.

3.2 Multilinear Function Space of the Domain $\{0; 1\}$

Fig. 3.3 shows the Hasse diagram of the Boolean algebra of 2 variables. The diagram can be regarded as the projection of a hypercube of 4 dimensions to 2 dimensions. It can be intuitively understood from Fig. 3.3 that the atoms of Boolean algebra,

$$XY, X\bar{Y}, \bar{X}Y, \bar{X}\bar{Y}$$

correspond to the unit orthogonal vectorst[10].

The section explains that the atoms are the unit orthogonal vectors, that is, the multilinear function space of the domain $\{0,1\}$ is a Euclidean space. First, the multiliner functions are explained. Second, it is shown that the multilinear function space is the linear space spanned by the atoms of Boolean algebra of Boolean functions. Third, it is explained that the space can be made into a Euclidean space. Fourth, the vector representations are explained. Fifth, it is explained that neural networks are multilinear functions. Finally, approximation of multilinear functions by Boolean function is explained.

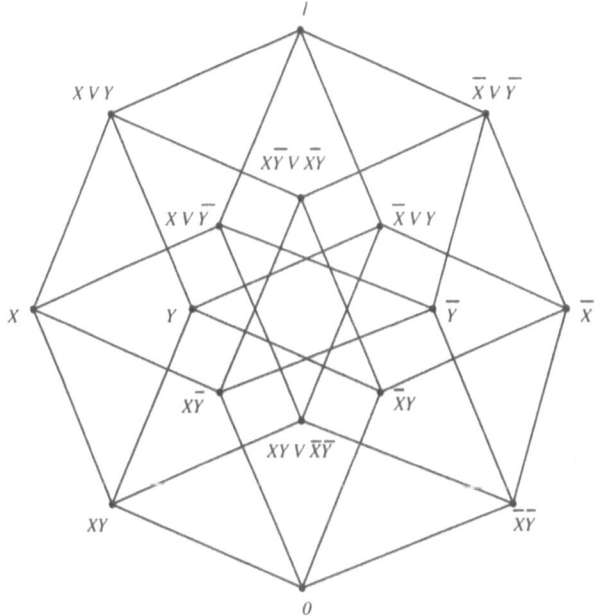

Fig. 3.3. Hasse diagram

3.2.1 Multilinear Functions

Definition 1. Multilinear functions of n variables are as follows[14]:

$$\sum_{i=1}^{2^n} a_i x_1^{e_{i1}} \cdots x_n^{e_{in}},$$

where a_i is real, x_i is a variable, and e_i is 0 or 1.

In this paper, n stands for the number of variables.
Example Multilinear functions of 2 variables are as follows:

$$axy + bx + cy + d.$$

Multilinear functions do not contain any terms such as

$$x_1^{k_1} x_2^{k_2} \cdots x_n^{k_n}, \tag{3.1}$$

where $k_i \geq 2$. A function

$$f : \{0, 1\}^n \to \mathbf{R}$$

is a multilinear function, because $x_i^{k_i} = x_i$ holds in $\{0, 1\}$ and so there is no term like (3.2.1) in the functions. In other words, multilinear functions are functions which are linear when only one variable is considered and the other variables are regarded as parameters.

3.2.2 Multilinear Function Space of the Domain $\{0;1\}$ is the Linear Space Spanned by the Atoms of Boolean Algebra of Boolean Functions

Definition 2. The atoms of Boolean algebra of Boolean functions of n variables are as follows:

$$\phi_i = \prod_{j=1}^{n} e(x_j) \; (i = 1, ..., 2^n), \tag{3.2}$$

where $e(x_j) = \overline{x_j}$ or x_j.

Example The atoms of Boolean algebra of Boolean functions o f 2 variables are as follows:

$$x \wedge y, \quad x \wedge \overline{y}, \quad \overline{x} \wedge y, \quad \overline{x} \wedge \overline{y}.$$

Theorem 1. The space of multilinear functions $(\{0,1\}^n \to \mathbf{R})$ is the linear space spanned by the atoms of Boolean algebra of Boolean functions.

Proof Any Boolean function can be represented as the linear combination of the atoms, that is,

$$\sum_{i=1}^{2^n} c_i \phi_i, \tag{3.3}$$

where ϕ_i in (3.3) is an atom, c_i is 0 or 1, and $\sum$ means logical disjunction.

Let logical conjunction, logical disjunction and negation be represented by elementary algebra. In the domain of $\{0,1\}$, logical conjunction $x \wedge y$ equals xy, which is the product of elementary algebra, and negation $\overline{x}$ equals $1-x$ of elementary algebra. Logical disjunction is calculated using de Morgan's law

$$x \vee y = \overline{\overline{x \vee y}} = \overline{\overline{x} \wedge \overline{y}}.$$

The representation of logical disjunction by elementary algebra is as follow s:

$$1 - (1-x)(1-y) = 1 - (1 - x - y + xy) = x + y - xy.$$

Table 3.1 shows the elementary algebra representations of logical operat ions.

Table 3.1. Elementary algebra representations of logical operations

	conjunction	disjunction	negation
logical operation	$x \wedge y$	$x \vee y$	$\overline{x}$
elementary algebra representation	xy	$x + y - xy$	$1 - x$

$$\phi_i \vee \phi_j$$

is represented as

$$\phi_i + \phi_j - \phi_i\phi_j.$$

However, the logical conjunction of different atoms is 0, that is,

$$\phi_i\phi_j = 0,$$

therefore,

$$\phi_i + \phi_j - \phi_i\phi_j = \phi_i + \phi_j.$$

Table 3.2. Elementary algebra representations of logical operations of atoms

	conjunction	disjunction	negation
logical operation	$\phi_i \wedge \phi_j$	$\phi_i \vee \phi_j$	$\bar{\phi_i}$
elementary algebra representation	$\phi_i\phi_j$	$\phi_i + \phi_j$	$1 - \phi_i$

Table 3.2 shows the elementary algebra representations of logical operations of atoms. The representation of (3.3) by elementary algebra is the same as (3.3) when $\prod$ in (3.2) is interpreted as the product of elementary algebra, $\sum$ is interpreted as the sum of elementary algebra, and $\bar{x}$ is interpreted as $1 - x$.

By extending the coefficients c_i in (3.3) from $\{0, 1\}$ to real, the functions become real linear functions as follows:

$$\sum_{i=1}^{2^n} a_i\phi_i, \tag{3.4}$$

where a_i is real and $\sum$ means the sum of elementary algebra.

The functions in (3.4) are the multilinear functions (of variables), because a function in (3.4), that is, a linear function of the atoms of Boolean algebra of Boolean functions can be developed to multilinear function uniquely, and a multilinear function can be expanded by the atoms uniquely.

Example A linear function of the atoms of 2 variables is

$$axy + bx\bar{y} + c\bar{x}y + d\bar{x}\bar{y}.$$

This function is transformed to the following:

$$pxy + qx + ry + s,$$

where

$$p = a - b - c + d, \quad q = b - d, \quad r = c - d, \quad s = d.$$

A multilinear function

$$pxy + qx + ry + s$$

can be transformed into

$$axy + bx\bar{y} + c\bar{x}y + d\bar{x}\bar{y},$$

where

$$a = p + q + r + s, \quad b = q + s, \quad c = r + s, \quad d = s.$$

Now, it has been shown that the multilinear function space of the domain $\{0, 1\}$ is the linear space spanned by the atoms of Boolean algebra of Boolean functions. The dimension of the space is 2^n. Next, it is shown that multilinear function space is made into a Euclidean space.

3.2.3 Multilinear Function Space of the Domain $\{0; 1\}$ is a Euclidean Space

Definition 3. The inner product is defined as follows:

$$< f, g >= \sum_{\{0,1\}^n} fg.$$

The sum in the above formula is done over the whole domain.
Example In the case of two variables,

$$
\begin{aligned}
< f, g > &= \sum_{\{0,1\}^2} fg \\
&= f(0,0)g(0,0) + f(0,1)g(0,1) + f(1,0)g(1,0) + f(1,1)g(1,1).
\end{aligned}
$$

Theorem 2. Atoms ϕ_is have unitarity and orthogonality

$$
\begin{aligned}
< \phi_i, \phi_i > &= 1 \text{ unitarity} \\
< \phi_i, \phi_j > &= 0 (i \neq j) \text{ orthogonality}
\end{aligned}
$$

Proof Unitarity can be easily verified from the fact that any ϕ_i is 1 at one point and is 0 at the other $2^n - 1$ points in the domain. Orthogonality can be easily verified from the fact that any $< \phi_i, \phi_j > (i \neq j)$ contains $x_k \bar{x}_k$, and $x_k \bar{x}_k = 0$
Example An example of unitarity and orthogonality of two variables is as follows:

$$
\begin{aligned}
< x\bar{y}, x\bar{y} > &= \sum_{\{0,1\}^2} x\bar{y}x\bar{y} = \sum_{\{0,1\}^2} x^2 \text{a} ry^2 = \sum_{\{0,1\}^2} x\bar{y} \\
&= 1 \cdot \bar{1} + 1 \cdot \bar{0} + 0 \cdot \bar{1} + 0 \cdot \bar{0} = 1 \cdot 0 + 1 \cdot 1 + 0 \cdot 0 + 0 \cdot 1 = 1.
\end{aligned}
$$

(The domain is $\{0, 1\}$, and so $x^2 = x, \bar{y}^2 = \bar{y}$.)

$$< xy, x\bar{y} >= \sum_{\{0,1\}^2} xyx\bar{y} = \sum_{\{0,1\}^2} x^2 y\bar{y} = 0.$$

Definition 4. Norm is defined as follows:

$$|f| = \sqrt{<f,f>} = \sqrt{\sum_{\{0,1\}^n} f^2}.$$

Example

$$|x\bar{y}| = \sqrt{<x\bar{y}, x\bar{y}>} = 1$$

From the above discussion, the space becomes a finite-dimensional inner product space, namely a Euclidean space.

Theorem 3. The multilinear function space is a Euclidean space. The above discussion is the proof.

Multilinear functions are divided into Boolean functions and the others. The others can be regarded as logical functions, which will be explained later. The vector representations of logical functions are called logical vectors. $\mathbf{f}((f_i)), \mathbf{g}((g_i)), ..$ stand for logical vectors. Note that f stands for a function, while f_i stands for an component of a logical vector $\mathbf{f}$.

3.2.4 Vector Representations

A few examples of vector representations are given.
Example

$$f(x,y) = x \vee y(= x + y - xy)$$

is transformed to

$$1xy + 1x(1-y) + 1(1-x)y + 0(1-x)(1-y),$$

that is, the logical vector is

$$(1,1,1,0).$$

Example

$$f(x,y) = 0.6x - 1.1y + 0.3 \tag{3.5}$$

is transformed to

$$-0.2xy + 0.9x(1-y) - 0.8(1-x)y + 0.3(1-x)(1-y),$$

that is, the logical vector is

$$(-0.2, 0.9, -0.8, 0.3).$$

Note that the above vectors are

$$(f(1,1), f(1,0), f(0,1), f(0,0)).$$

As easily seen from Table 3.1, vector representations of logical operations are as follows:

$$\mathbf{f} \wedge \mathbf{g} = (f_i g_i)$$
$$\mathbf{f} \vee \mathbf{g} = (f_i + g_i - f_i g_i)$$
$$\bar{\mathbf{f}} = (1 - f_i)$$

The above representations are the same as the representations below when multilinear functions are Boolean functions, that is, f_i and g_i are $\{0, 1\}$.

$$\mathbf{f} \wedge \mathbf{g} = (Min(f_i, g_i))$$
$$\mathbf{f} \vee \mathbf{g} = (Max(f_i, g_i))$$
$$\bar{\mathbf{f}} = (1 - f_i)$$

The latter representations will be found in 8.5.

Example Let f be $x \vee y$ and let g be $\bar{x} \wedge \bar{y}$. The logical conjunction of f and g is as follows:

$$(x \vee y) \wedge (\bar{x} \wedge \bar{y}) = (x \wedge \bar{x} \wedge \bar{y}) \ vee (y \wedge \bar{x} \wedge \bar{y}) = 0$$

The logical vectors of f and g, that is, $\mathbf{f}$ and $\mathbf{g}$ are as follows:

$$\mathbf{f} = (1, 1, 1, 0), \quad \mathbf{g} = (0, 0, 0, 1),$$

where the bases are

$$x \wedge y = (1, 0, 0, 0), x \wedge \bar{y} = (0, 1, 0, 0), \bar{x} \wedge y = (0, 0, 1, 0) \text{ and } \bar{x} \wedge \bar{y} = (0, 0, 0, 1).$$

The logical conjunction of $\mathbf{f}$ and $\mathbf{g}$ is as follows using the above definition.

$$\mathbf{f} \wedge \mathbf{g} = (Min(f_i, g_i))$$
$$= (Min(1, 0), Min(1, 0), Min(1, 0), Min(0, 1))$$
$$= (0, 0, 0, 0)$$
$$= 0$$

3.2.5 Neural Networks are Multilinear Functions

Pattern reasoning is realized as the logical reasoning of neural networks. The logical reasoning is based on that neural networks are multilinear functions.

Theorem 4. When the domain is $\{0, 1\}$, neural networks are multilinear functions.

Proof As described in 8.2.1, a function whose domain is $\{0, 1\}$ is a multilinear function. Therefore, when the domain is $\{0, 1\}$, neural networks, that i s, the functions which neural networks learn are multilinear functions.

3.2.6 Approximation of Multilinear Functions by Boolean Functions

Approximating multilinear functions by Boolean functions is useful for understanding what the multilinear functions mean. The approximation is applied to rule extraction from prediction models such as linear regression formulas, neural networks and so on, which enables the prediction models understandable to humans [11], [8]. In this paper, the approximation is necessary later, therefore, in this subsection, the basic method is briefly explained.

Consider that a logical vector is approximated by the nearest Boolean vector. Let (f_i) be a logical vector. Let $(g_i)(g_i = 0$ or $1)$ be a Boolean vector. The approximation method is as follows:

$$g_i = \begin{cases} 1(f_i \geq 0.5), \\ 0(f_i < 0.5). \end{cases}$$

Proof The nearest Boolean vector minimizes

$$\sum_{i=1}^{2^n}(f_i - g_i)^2.$$

Each term can be minimized independently, and $g_i = 1$ or 0. Therefore, the above approximation method is obtained.

Example An example of a linear function is given. The logical vector of (3.5) is

$$(-0.2, 0.9, -0.8, 0.3).$$

The above logical vector is approximated to

$$(0, 1, 0, 0),$$

which represents

$$x(1 - y).$$

Thus, (3.5) is approximated to

$$x(1 - y), \text{ that is, } x \wedge \bar{y}.$$

Example An example of a neural network is given. Fig. 3.4 shows a case of two variables. Crosses stand for the values of a unit of a neural network($f(x, y)$) and circles stand for the values of the nearest Boolean function($g(x, y)$). $00, 01, 10$ and 11 stand for the domains, for example, 00 stands for $x = 0, y = 0$. Note that the outputs of neural networks are $[0,1]$. The nearest Boolean function($g(x, y)$) is as follows:

$$\begin{aligned} g(x, y) &= 1\bar{x}\bar{y} + 1\bar{x}y + 0x\bar{y} + 0xy, \\ g(x, y) &= \bar{x}\bar{y} + \bar{x}y, \\ g(x, y) &= \bar{x}. \end{aligned}$$

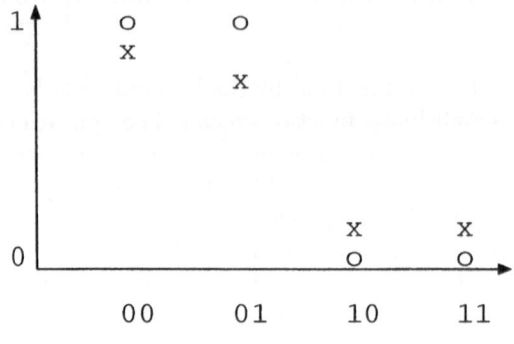

Fig. 3.4. Approximation

The approximation method can be regarded as a pseudo maximum likelihood method [11]. The computational complexity of the approximation method is exponential, therefore the method is unrealistic. A polynomial method has been presented in [15].

3.3 Continuous Boolean Functions

The multilinear function space of the domain [0,1] can be made into a Euclidean space, whose bases are continuous Boolean functions. This section describes continuous Boolean functions[12].

Continuous Boolean functions are generated by direct proportion, inverse proportion, conjunction and disjunction. Fig. 3.5 shows the direct proportion and the inverse proportion. The inverse proportion ($y = 1 - x$) is a little different from the conventional one ($y = -x$), because $y = 1 - x$ is the natural extension of the negation in Boolean functions. The conjunction is xy, which is a natural extension of the classical logical conjunction $x \wedge y$, The disjunction is $x + y - xy$, which is a natural extension of the classical logical disjunction $x \vee y$. See Table 3.1. The functions generated by direct proportion, inverse proportion, conjunction and disjunction are called continuous Boolean functions, because they satisfy the axioms of Boolean algebra, which will be explained later.

First, an elementary algebra model for classical logic is presented. Second, the domain of the model is extended to [0,1]. Third, it is shown that the extended model satisfies the all axioms of Boolean algebra. For the comparison with fuzzy logic[16], refer to [12].

3.3.1 An Elementary Algebra Model for Classical Logic

3.3.1.1 τ.

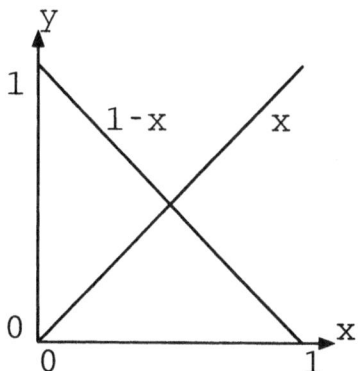

Fig. 3.5. Direct proportion and inverse proportion

Definition 5. Let $f(x)$ be a real polynomial function. Consider the following formula:

$$f(x) = p(x)(x - x^2) + q(x),$$

where $q(x) = ax + b$ (a and b are real). That is, $q(x)$ is the remainder. τ_x is defined as follows:

$$\tau_x : f(x) \to q(x).$$

The above definition implies the following property:

$$\tau_x(x^n) = x(n \geq 2).$$

The following formulas hold:

$$\tau_x(f(x) \pm g(x)) = \tau_x(f(x)) \pm \tau_x(g(x)).$$
$$\tau_x(f(x)g(x)) = \tau_x(f(x)(\tau_x(g(x)))).$$
$$\tau_x(\tau_y(f(x,y))) = \tau_y(\tau_x(f(x,y))).$$

The above formulas can be easily verified.

Definition 6. In the case of n variables, τ is defined as follows:

$$\tau = \prod_{i=1}^{n} \tau_{x_i}.$$

Example

$$\tau(x^2 y^3 + xy + 2y - 1) = xy + xy + 2y - 1 = 2xy + 2y - 1.$$

The following formulas hold:

$$\tau\left(\prod_{i=1}^{n} \tau(f_i)\right) = \tau\left(\prod_{i=1}^{n} f_i\right), \tag{3.6}$$

$$\tau\left(\sum_{i=1}^{n} f_i\right) = \sum_{i=1}^{n} \tau(f_i). \tag{3.7}$$

The above formulas can be easily verified.

3.3.1.2 Definition of L_1.

Definition 7. L_1 is inductively defined as follows:

1. Variables are in L_1.
2. If f and g are in L_1, then $\tau(fg)$, $\tau(f + g - fg)$ and $\tau(1 - f)$ are in L_1. (We call these three calculations τ *calculation*.)
3. L_1 consists of all functions finitely generated by the (repeated) use of 1. and 2.

Note that f in L_1 satisfies $\tau(f) = f$.

3.3.1.3 A New Model for Classical Logic.
Let the correspondence between Boolean algebra and τ calculation be a s follows:

$$
\begin{aligned}
F \wedge G &\Leftrightarrow \tau(fg), \\
F \vee G &\Leftrightarrow \tau(f + g - fg), \\
\overline{F} &\Leftrightarrow \tau(1 - f).
\end{aligned}
$$

Then $(L_1, \tau$ calculation$)$ is a model for classical logic; that is, L_1 and τ calculation satisfy the axioms for Bool ean algebra. The proof will be found in the next subsection.

Example

$$(X \vee Y) \wedge (X \vee Y) = X \vee Y,$$

is calculated as follows:

$$
\begin{aligned}
\tau((x + y - xy)(x + y - xy)) &= \tau(x^2 + y^2 + x^2 y^2 + 2xy - 2x^2 y - 2xy^2) \\
&= x + y + xy + 2xy - 2xy - 2xy \\
&= x + y - xy.
\end{aligned}
$$

3.3.2 Extension of the Domain

The domain is extended to $[0,1]$. $f : [0, 1]^n \to \mathbf{R}$. With this extension, we have a continuously-valued logic, which satisfies all axioms of classical logic. However, since this logic does not have a Boolean structure, what "satisfy" means in this paper is a little different from the conventional usage by logicians.

3.3.3 The Continuously-valued Logic Satisfies all Axioms of Classical Logic

Let us now see how the continuously-valued logic satisfies all axioms of classical logic (Boolean algebra).

3.3.3.1 The Axioms of Boolean Algebra. The axioms of Boolean algebra are as follows[1]. F, G and H stand for propositions. I stands for the maximum element and O stands for the minimum element.

1. $F \wedge F = F, F \vee F = F$.

2. $F \vee G = G \vee F, F \wedge G = G \wedge F$.

3. $F \wedge (G \wedge H) = (F \wedge G) \wedge H$, $F \vee (G \vee H) = (F \vee G) \, vee H$.

4. $F \wedge (F \vee G) = F, F \vee (F \wedge G) = F$.

5. $F \wedge (G \vee (F \wedge H)) = (F \wedge G) \vee (F \wedge H)$, $F \vee (G \wedge (F \vee H)) = (F \vee G) \wedge (F \vee H)$.

6. $F \wedge (G \vee H)) = (F \wedge G) \vee (F \wedge H)$, $F \vee (G \wedge H) = (F \vee G) \wedge (F \vee H)$.

7. $F \wedge O = O, F \vee O = F$, $F \wedge I = F, F \vee I = I$.

8. $F \wedge \overline{F} = O, F \vee \overline{F} = I$.

9. $\overline{\overline{F}} = F$.

10. $\overline{F \wedge G} = \overline{F} \vee \overline{G}$, $\overline{F \vee G} = \overline{F} \wedge \overline{G}$.

$2, 3, 7, 9$, and 10 can be easily verified from the definition. The others can be proved with $\tau(f^2) = f$, which holds in L_1. Due to space limitations, we will prove $\tau(f^2) = f$ and complements $(F \wedge \overline{F} = O, F \vee \overline{F} = I)$.

3.3.3.2 Proof of τ $(f^2) = f$.
Proof Variables x and y satisfy

$$\tau(f^2) = f,$$

which is obvious from the definition of τ. Since the functions in L_1 are inductively generated by

$$\tau(fg), \tau(f + g - fg) \text{ and } \tau(1 - f),$$

we only have to prove that

$$\tau((\tau(fg))^2) = \tau(fg),$$
$$\tau((\tau(f + g - fg))^2) = \tau(f + g - fg)$$

and
$$\tau((\tau(1-f))^2) = \tau(1-f)$$

with the assumption of
$$\tau(f^2) = f \text{ and } \tau(g^2) = g,$$

using (3.6) and (3.7).

$$
\begin{aligned}
\tau((\tau(fg))^2) &= \tau(\tau(fg)\tau(fg)) \\
&= \tau(fgfg) \\
&= \tau(f^2g^2) \\
&= \tau(\tau(f^2)\tau(g^2)) \\
&= \tau(fg). \\
\tau((\tau(f+g-fg))^2) &= \tau(\tau(f+g-fg)\tau(f+g-fg)) \\
&= \tau((f+g-fg)(f+g-fg)) \\
&= \tau(f^2 + g^2 + f^2g^2 + 2fg - 2f^2g - 2fg^2) \\
&= \tau(f^2) + \tau(g^2) + \tau(f^2g^2) + \tau(2fg) \\
&\quad -\tau(2f^2g) - \tau(2fg^2)) \\
&= \tau(f) + \tau(g) + \tau(fg) + \tau(2fg) - \tau(2fg) - \tau(2fg) \\
&= \tau(f+g+fg+2fg-2fg-2fg) \\
&= \tau(f+g-fg). \\
\tau((\tau(1-f))^2) &= \tau(\tau(1-f)\tau(1-f)) \\
&= \tau((1-f)(1-f)) \\
&= \tau(1-2f+f^2) \\
&= \tau(1) - \tau(2f) + \tau(f^2) \\
&= \tau(1) - \tau(2f) + \tau(f) \\
&= \tau(1-2f+f) \\
&= \tau(1-f).
\end{aligned}
$$

Thus,
$$\tau(f^2) = f$$

has been proved.

3.3.3.3 Proof of Complements.
Proof

$$F \wedge \overline{F} = O$$

can be easily proved, so the proof is omitted.

$$F \vee \overline{F} = I$$

is represented as

$$\tau(f + (1 - f) - f(1 - f)) = 1.$$

The left side of the equation is calculated as follows:

$$
\begin{aligned}
\tau(f + (1 - f) - f(1 - f)) &= \tau(f + 1 - f - f + f^2) \\
&= \tau(1 - f + f^2) \\
&= \tau(1) - \tau(f) + \tau(f^2) \\
&= 1 - f + \tau(f^2) \\
&= 1 - f + f \\
&= 1.
\end{aligned}
$$

Thus,

$$\tau(f + (1 - f) - f(1 - f)) = 1$$

has been proved, that is,

$$F \vee \overline{F} = I$$

has been proved.

3.4 Multilinear Function Space of the Domain [0,1]

Theorem 5. When the domain is [0,1], multilinear function space is a linear space whose bases are continuous Boolean functions. This theorem is obvious, because continuous Boolean functions are the same a s the elementary algebra representations of Boolean functions when the domai ns are ignored.

3.4.1 Euclidean Space

The multilinear function space can be made into a Euclidean space[10]. The multilinear function space is denoted by L for simplification.

3.4.1.1 Inner Product.

Definition 8. An inner product is defined as follows:

$$< f, g > = 2^n \int_0^1 \tau(fg)dx,$$

where f and g are in L, and the integral is generally a multiple integral.

Theorem 6. This inner product has the following properties:

1. $< f, f > \geq 0, < f, f > = 0 \Leftrightarrow f = 0$.

2. $< af, g >= a < f, g >$, where a is a real number.

3. $< f + g, h >=< f, h > + < g, h >$.

Proof Property 2 and 3 can be easily verified. Property 1 is proved in the case of one variable as follows. Let

$$f = f_1 x + f_0(1 - x).$$

$$
\begin{aligned}
< f, f > &= 2^1 \int_0^1 \tau(ff)dx \\
&= 2^1 \int_0^1 (f_0^2(1 - x) + f_1^2 x)dx \\
&= f_0^2 + f_1^2 \geq 0
\end{aligned}
$$

and

$$< f, f >= 0 \leftrightarrow f_0^2 + f_1^2 = 0 \leftrightarrow f = 0.$$

$f_0^2 + f_1^2 = 0 \leftrightarrow f = 0$, because $f \in L$. This property is also proved in the same manner in the case of many variables.

3.4.1.2 Norm.

Definition 9. A norm is defined as follows:

$$|f| = \sqrt{< f, f >}.$$

Theorem 7. This norm has the following properties:

1. $|f| \geq 0, |f| = 0 \Leftrightarrow f = 0$.

2. $|af| = |a||f|$.

3. $|f + g| \leq |f| + |g|$.

The above properties can be easily verified, therefore, the proof is omitted.

h dep
L becomes an inner product space with the above norm. The dimension of this space is finite, because L consists of multilinear functions of n variables, where n is finite. Therefore, L becomes a finite-dimensional inner product space, namely a Euclidean space.

The distance between functions is roughly measured by the norm. For example, function A in Fig. 3.6, which stands for $x^k (k \geq 2)$, is different from x. However, by the norm, the distance between the two functions is 0, because τ in the norm

$$\sqrt{< f, g >} = \sqrt{2^n \int_0^1 \tau(fg)dx}$$

identifies $x^k (k \geq 2)$ with x. Therefore, the two functions are identified as being the same one in the norm. The norm can be regarded as a qualitative norm, because, roughly speaking, the norm identifies increasing functions as direct proportions and identifies decreasing functions as inverse proportions, and the norm ignores the function values in the intermediate domain between 0 and 1.

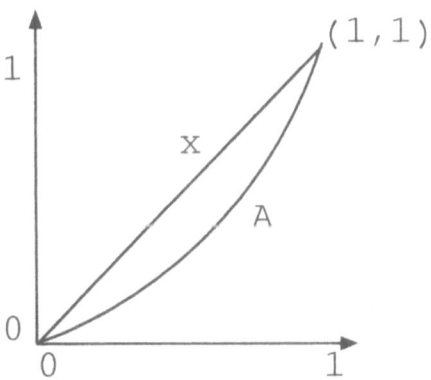

Fig. 3.6. Norm

3.4.1.3 Orthonormal System. The orthonormal system is as follows:

$$\phi_i = \prod_{j=1}^{n} e(x_j) \ (i = 1 \sim 2^n, j = 1 \sim n),$$

where $e(x_j) = 1 - x_j$ or x_j. It is easily understood that these orthonormal systems are the expansion of atoms in Boolean algebra. In addition, it can easily be verified that the orthonormal system satisfies the following properties:

$$
\begin{aligned}
< \phi_i, \phi_j > &= 0 (i \neq j), \\
&= 1 (i = j),
\end{aligned}
$$

$$f = \sum_{i=1}^{2^n} < f, \phi_i > \phi_i.$$

Example The vector representation of $x + y - xy$ of two variables (dimension 4) is as f ollows:

$$< f, xy > \quad = \quad 2^2 \int_0^1 \int_0^1 \tau(x + y - xy)xy \, dx \, dy = 1,$$
$$< f, x(1 - y) > \quad = \quad 2^2 \int_0^1 \int_0^1 \tau(x + y - xy)x(1 - y)dx \, dy = 1,$$
$$< f, (1 - x)y > \quad = \quad 2^2 \int_0^1 \int_0^1 \tau(x + y - xy)(1 - x)y \, dx \, dy = 1,$$
$$< f, (1 - x)(1 - y) > \quad = \quad 2^2 \int_0^1 \int_0^1 \tau(x + y - xy)(1 - x)(1 - y)dx \, dy = 0.$$

Therefore,

$$f = 1 \cdot xy + 1 \cdot x(1 - y) + 1 \cdot (1 - x)y + 0 \cdot (1 - x)(1 - y)$$

and the vector representation is

$$(1, 1, 1, 0),$$

where the bases are

$$xy = (1, 0, 0, 0), x(1 - y) = (0, 1, 0, 0),$$
$$(1 - x)y = (0, 0, 1, 0) \quad \text{and} \quad (1 - x)(1 - y) = (0, 0, 0, 1).$$

The space of the functions of n variables is 2^n-dimensional.

3.4.2 Vector Representation of Logical Operations

The multilinear function space of the domain $[0,1]$ has been made into a Eucl idean space, which is the same as the Euclidean space in the domain $\{0, 1\}$. Therefore, the vector representations of logical operations are the same as those in the domain $\{0, 1\}$. See 8.2.4.

3.4.3 Neural Networks are Approximately Multilinear Functions

When the domain is $[0,1]$, neural networks are approximately mult ilinear functions with the following:

$$x^k = \begin{cases} x(k \le a) \\ 0(k > a), \end{cases}$$

where a is a natural number. When $a = 1$, the above approximation is the linear approximation.

3.5 Intermediate Logic LC

3.5.1 Nonclassical Logics Complete for the Interval [0,1]

As stated in the preceding sections, multilinear function space is a linear space spanned by the atoms of Boolean algebra of (continuous) Boolean functions. The subset $[0, 1]^m$ of the space, where m is the dimension, is considered.

The logics which are complete for the interval $[0, 1]$ are also complete for the direct product of the interval $[0, 1][7]$, that is, $[0, 1]^m$. Therefore, logics which are complete for the interval $[0, 1]$ are studied. The logics are continuously valued logics. There are three logics which are complete for the interval, that is, intermediate logic LC (LC for short), Lukasiewicz logic and product logic.

Logical conjunctions and logical implications are defined as follows [5].

1. LC

$$\text{conjunction} \quad : \quad x \wedge y = \min(x, y)$$
$$\text{implication} \quad : \quad x \to y = \begin{cases} 1 & x \le y \\ y & \text{otherwise} \end{cases}$$

2. Lukasiewicz logic

$$\text{conjunction} \quad : \quad x \wedge y = \max(0, x + y - 1)$$
$$\text{implication} \quad : \quad x \to y = \min(1, 1 - x + y)$$

3. product logic

$$\text{conjunction} \quad : \quad x \wedge y = xy$$
$$\text{implication} \quad : \quad x \to y = \begin{cases} 1 & x \le y \\ y/x & \text{otherwise} \end{cases}$$

In sequent calculus, there are three structure rules as follows:

$$\text{contraction} \quad \frac{x, x \to y}{x \to y}, \qquad \text{weakening} \quad \frac{x \to y}{x, z \to y}, \qquad \text{exchange} \quad \frac{x, y \to z}{y, x \to z}.$$

Logics which do not have some of the above rules are called substructural logics. Pattern reasoning is related to probability calculus, which does not satisfy contraction[9]. Therefore, the probability calculus can be regarded as a logic without the contraction rule. In terms of contraction, LC satisfies contraction, Lukasiewicz logic and product logic do not satisfy contraction.

Due to space limitations, all three logics cannot be explained. Only LC is briefly explained. Similar explanations hold for Lukasiewicz logic and product logic.

3.5.2 LC and Multilinear Function Space

Intermediate logics are weaker than classical logic and stronger than intuitionistic logic. The explanation of intermediate logics can be found in [2]. LC is an intermediate logic, which was presented by Dummett[3]. The logic is defined as follows[2].

$$\text{LC=intuitionistic logic} + (\varphi \to \psi) \vee (\psi \to \varphi),$$

where φ and ψ are logical formulas. LC stands for Logic of Chain, which comes from the fact that the model of th e logic is a chain, that is, a linearly ordered set.

For the algebraic model of LC, since LC is intuitionistic logic plus an axiom, it is first explained that an interval [0,1] is an algebraic model of intuitionistic logic. Second, it is explained that intuitionistic logic is not complete for the model, that is, intuitionistic logic cannot prove the relation below

$$(\varphi \to \psi) \vee (\psi \to \varphi), \tag{3.8}$$

which corresponds to the following formula which holds in any interval:

$$(x \le y) \vee (y \le x),$$

where x and y are points in the interval, while LC has the axiom (3.8) and so LC is complete for the interval. The proof for the completeness of LC for the interval cannot be described due to space limitations, and so an intuitive explanation is given. Third, it is explained that the multilinear function space is an algebraic model of LC in the way that if an interval is an algebraic model, then the direct sum of the interval is also an algebraic model[7], and a subset $[0, 1]^m$ of the multilinear function space is a model of LC. Finally, a few examples of logical reasoning of multilinear functions by LC are given.

3.5.3 Heyting Algebra

Heyting algebra, which is the algebraic model of intuitionistic logic, is de fined as follows [2].

Definition 10. A Heyting algebra is a structure $< A, \wedge, \vee, \supset, \top, \perp >$ s uch that

1. it is a distributive lattice with respect to $\wedge, \vee$ and with $\top$ and $\perp$,

2. $f \wedge (f \supset g) = f \wedge g$,

3. $(f \supset g) \wedge g = g$,

4. $(f \supset g) \wedge (f \supset h) = f \supset (g \wedge h)$,

5. $\perp \wedge f = \perp$,

6. $\perp \supset \perp = \top$.

Complement f' is defined by $f' = f \supset \perp$.

Theorem 8. Interval $[0, 1]$ is a Heyting algebra.

Proof Interval $[0,1]$ is a Heyting algebra with the following definitions:

$x \wedge y = Min(x,y),$

$x \vee y = Max(x,y),$

$x \supset y = \left\{ \begin{array}{l} 1(x \leq y) \\ y(x > y), \end{array} \right.$

$\top = 1, \quad \perp = 0.$

Note that x and y are used instead of f and g, because x and y stand for real numbers.

3.5.4 An Intuitive Explanation for LC

An interval $[0,1]$ is an algebraic model of intuitionistic logic. Let φ and ψ stand for two points, then

$$(\varphi \leq \psi) \vee (\psi \leq \varphi)$$

holds. Roughly speaking, by replacing $\leq$ in the above formula by $\rightarrow$, the following formula is obtained.

$$(\varphi \rightarrow \psi) \vee (\psi \rightarrow \varphi),$$

where φ and ψ are propositions. The above formula does not hold in intuitionistic logic. In other words, intuitionistic logic is not complete for an interval $[0,1]$.

If the above formula is added to intuitionistic logic, a logic which is complete for an interval $[0,1]$ is obtained. The logic is LC.

$$(\varphi \rightarrow \psi) \vee (\psi \rightarrow \varphi),$$

holds in LC, therefore, LC is complete for an interval $[0,1]$.

The completeness of LC for an interval $[0,1]$ can be proved using the fact that LC is complete for linearly ordered Kripke models[2] and the correspondence between Kripke models and algebraic models [4]. The proof is omitted due to space limitations.

An interval $[0,1]$ is an algebraic model of intuitionistic logic and LC. LC , which is complete for the interval $[0,1]$, is better than intuitionistic logic, which is not complete for the interval $[0,1]$. Therefore, hereinafter, LC is discussed.

3.5.5 The Multilinear Function Space is an Algebraic Model of LC

It is explained that the multilinear function space is an algebraic model of LC as follows[13].

1. If an interval is a model of a logic, the direct sum of the intervals is also a model of the logic[7]. The logical operations are done c omponentwise. Therefore, since an interval [0,1] is an algebraic model of LC, a direct sum of intervals $[0, 1]^m$ (m is dimension) is also an algebraic model of LC.
2. The multilinear function space is a linear space, therefore, a subset $[0, 1]^m$ is a direct sum of intervals [0,1].
3. From item 1 and 2, the subset $[0, 1]^m$ of the multilinear function sp ace is an algebraic model of LC.

Theorem 9. LC is complete for the hypercube $[0, 1]^m$ of the space. The definitions, which are the same as in Heyting algebra (Theorem 8), are as fo llows:

$$\mathbf{f} \leq \mathbf{g} = \forall i (f_i \leq g_i),$$

$$\mathbf{f} \wedge \mathbf{g} = (Min(f_i, g_i)),$$

$$\mathbf{f} \vee \mathbf{g} = (Max(f_i, g_i)),$$

$$\mathbf{f} \supset \mathbf{g} = (f_i \supset g_i)$$

$$f_i \supset g_i = \left\{ \begin{array}{l} 1 (f_i \leq g_i) \\ g_i (f_i > g_i), \end{array} \right.$$

where $\mathbf{f}$ and $\mathbf{g}$ stand for logical vectors. This theorem is understood from the above discussions.

3.5.6 Examples

Example 1
$$f = 0.6xy + 0.1x + 0.1y + 0.1$$

is transformed to

$$0.9xy + 0.2x\bar{y} + 0.2\bar{x}y + 0.1\bar{x}\bar{y},$$

therefore

$$\mathbf{f} = (0.9, 0.2, 0.2, 0.1).$$

In the same way,

$$\bar{\mathbf{f}} = (f_i \supset 0) = (0.9 \supset 0, 0.2 \supset 0, 0.2 \supset 0, 0.1 \supset 0) = (0, 0, 0, 0).$$

Therefore, from Theorem 10,

$$f \vee \bar{f} = (0.9, 0.2, 0.2, 0.1),$$

which means

$$f \vee \bar{f} \neq 1$$

This example shows that the law of excluded middle

$$f \vee \bar{f} = 1,$$

which holds in classical logic, does not holds in LC. If f is limited to Boolean functions, the law of excluded middle holds. For example, let f be xy, that is,

$$f = 1.0xy + 0.0x + 0.0y + 0.0 = 1.0xy + 0.0x\bar{y} + 0.0\bar{x}y + 0.0\overline{xy},$$

then

$$f = (1, 0, 0, 0),$$

$$\bar{f} = (f_i \supset 0) = (1 \supset 0, 0 \supset 0, 0 \supset 0, 0 \supset 0) = (0, 1, 1, 1).$$

Therefore

$$f \vee \bar{f} = (1, 1, 1, 1),$$

that is,

$$f \vee \bar{f} = 1$$

Example 2

$$f \supset g$$

is calculated. Let f and g be as follows:

$$f = 0.6xy + 0.1x + 0.1y + 0.1$$

and

$$g = 0.1xy + 0.6x + 0.0y + 0.2,$$

then

$$f = (0.9, 0.2, 0.2, 0.1)$$

and

$$g = (0.9, 0.8, 0.2, 0.2).$$

From Theorem 10,

$$f \supset g = (1, 1, 1, 1),$$

that is,

$$f \supset g = 1$$

f and g are approximated to the nearest Boolean functions f' and g' as follows. As for the approximation method, see 8.2.6.

$$f' = (1, 0, 0, 0)$$

$$g' = (1, 1, 0, 0)$$
$$f' \supset g' = (1, 1, 1, 1),$$

that is,

$$f' \supset g' = 1.$$
$$f' = 1xy + 0x\bar{y} + 0\bar{x}y + 0\bar{x}\bar{y} = xy$$
$$g' = 1xy + 1x\bar{y} + 0\bar{x}y + 0\bar{x}\bar{y} = xy + x\bar{y} = x$$

Therefore,

$$f' \supset g' = (1, 1, 1, 1)$$

means

$$xy \supset x = 1$$

This example shows that $f \supset g$ in LC is equal to logical implication in classical logic, when multilinear functions are limited to Boolean functions.

3.6 Logical Reasoning of Neural Networks by LC

Neural networks are multilinear functions in the domain $\{0,1\}$ and approximately multilinear functions in the domain $[0,1]$. The multilinear function space is an algebraic model of LC. Therefore, neural networks can be reasoned by LC. Let he domain be $\{0,1\}^n$, where n is the number of variables.

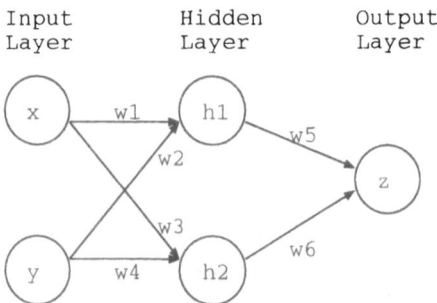

Fig. 3.7. Neural network

Let N_1 and N_2 be two trained neural networks, which have 3 layers, two inputs x and y, two hidden units, and one output. The output function of each unit is sigmoid function. Table 3.3 shows the training results of weight parameters and biases of N_1. Table 3.4 shows the training results of weight parameters and bias of N_2.

N_1 is as follows:

Table 3.3. Training results 1

unit	w1(w3, w5)	w2(w4,w6)	bias
hidden unit 1	-4.87	-4.86	-6.70
hidden unit 2	-2.86	-2.88	3.50
output unit	7.61	-3.83	4.50

Table 3.4. Training results 2

unit	w1(w3, w5)	w2(w4,w6)	bias
hidden unit 1	4.80	4.72	-2.31
hidden unit 2	-3.49	-3.56	1.67
output unit	5.81	-4.62	-0.42

$$S(7.61S(-4.87x - 4.86y - 6.70) - 3.83S(-2.86x - 2.88y + 3.50) + 4.50).$$

From the above formula, the logical vector is calculated as follows:

$$(0.98, 0.01, 0.01, 0.00),$$

For the calculation method, see 8.2.4. The logical vector of N_2 is calculated in the same way as follows:

$$(0.02, 0.98, 0.98, 0.99).$$

The logical conjunction of the two logical vectors is as follows:

$$(0.02, 0.01, 0.01, 0.00),$$

which is nearly equal to 0.

The multilinear function is as follows:

$$0.02xy + 0.01x(1 - y) + 0.01(1 - x)y + 0.00$$

$$= 0.01x + 0.01y,$$

The function is nearly equal to 0. The above result shows that the logical conjunction of two trained neural ne tworks is almost false, which cannot seen from the training results of neura l networks. N_1 has been trained using $x \wedge y$ and N_2 has been trained using the negation of $x \wedge y$. Therefore, the logical conjunction of N_1 and N_2 is as follows:

$$N_1 \wedge N_2 \simeq (x \wedge y) \wedge \overline{(x \wedge y)} = 0.$$

As seen in the above example, the logical reasoning of neural networks show the logical relations among neural networks. If the components of logical vectors are 0 or 1, the calculation can be done by Boolean algebra, that is, classical logic. However, even if the training targets are Boolean functions, the training results of neural networks are not 0 or 1, but are the values like 0.01 or 0.98. These numbers cannot be calculated by Boolean algebra, but can be calculated by LC. In the above example, the training targets are Boolean functions for simplification. However, any function can be the training target of neural networks and any trained neural network can be reasoned by LC. More examples cannot be explained due to space limitations. They will be presented in another paper.

3.7 Remarks on Pattern Reasoning

Patterns can be regarded as functions and the functions can be approximated by neural networks. Neural networks can be reasoned by a few logics such as LC, Lukasiewicz logic and product logic. Therefore, pattern reasoning can be realized by logical reasoning of neural networks. However, there are a lot of open problems for pattern reasoning to be applied to real data.

3.7.1 Computational Complexity

A basic algorithm of logical operations for pattern reasoning is exponential in computational complexity, therefore, a polynomial algorithm is needed. A polynomial algorithm for a unit in a neural network has been presented. For networks, an algorithm which uses only big weight parameters has been presented. Due to space limitations, the algorithms will be explained in another paper. The reduction of computational complexity is included in future work.

3.7.2 Appropriate Logics for Pattern Reasoning

It is desired that patterns can be reasoned naturally. Therefore, appropriate logics for pattern reasoning should be able to reason patterns naturally. What is "reason naturally"? It is very difficult to define "reason naturally". However, there is a hint, that is, probability calculus. Probability calculus is similar to pattern reasoning, although it does not have the formal system. Probability calculus does not satisfy the contraction rule. Therefore, appropriate logics for pattern reasoning should not satisfy the contraction rule. From this viewpoint, Lukasiewicz logic and product logic, which do not satisfy the contraction rule, are more appropriate than LC, which satisfies the contraction rule. It is desired that probability calculus be formalized logically, but this is very difficult. We are investigating appropriate logics for pattern reasoning.

3.7.3 Typical Patterns

There are countless patterns, and some patterns are appropriate for pattern reasoning, while other patterns are inappropriate. Therefore a dictionary of patterns is necessary. The patterns included in the dictionary are typical patterns, which cannot be described linguistically. The typical patterns can be gathered by various methods, but we do not have to be seriously concerned with gathering typical patterns, because pattern reasoning is flexible as explained in the next item. However, gathering typical patterns are important for efficient pattern reasoning.

3.7.4 A Difference between Pattern Reasoning and Symbol Reasoning in the Reasoning Mechanism

In symbol reasoning, when the left side of a rule is not matched, the rule does not work, while, in pattern reasoning, even when the left side of a rule is not matched, the rule works. For example, let a rule be $a \rightarrow b$ and the left side of the rule be a'. If a is very similar to a', the truth value of the rule is almost 1. On the other hand, if a is very different from a', the truth value of the rule is almost 0. Pattern reasoning works like this, because the pattern reasoning makes use of continuously valued logics. There are several other methods which deal with matching degrees of the left sides of rules. However, the methods are basically arbitrary, whereas the pattern reasoning presented in this paper includes the matching degrees in the system.

3.7.5 Formal System

In pattern reasoning, for example, a question like "Is this pattern logically deduced from the set of rules of patterns?" should be answered. Therefore, formal systems are needed for pattern reasoning.

3.7.6 Incompleteness

In mathematical logic, completeness is important. In reality, humans cannot reason or prove true things, that is, humans are incomplete. Therefore, pattern reasoning should deal with incompleteness.

3.7.7 The Relationship with Probability Theory

Probability calculus deals with continuous values, but probability events are not continuous, that is, the objects of probability theory are not continuous, while the objects of pattern reasoning are continuous. Therefore, pattern reasoning can be regarded as an extension of probability calculus.

3.7.8 Experimental Study

The most typical patterns are images, therefore the final target is the reasoning of images. We have to begin experiments with simple examples. We have tried to realize pattern reasoning for one-dimensional data, for example, time series data, by logical reasoning of neural networks using LC, Lukasiewicz logic or product logic. The results show that the logical reasoning of neural networks works well, which will be reported in another paper.

3.8 Conclusions

This paper has presented an approach for the integration of symbols and patterns. The integration of symbols and patterns means numerical computation of symbols and logical reasoning of patterns, that is, pattern reasoning. For the numerical computation of symbols, it has been shown that logics can be represented by linear algebra. For pattern reasoning, it has been explained that neural networks can be reasoned by a few nonclassical logics such as intermediate logic LC, which is based on the linear algebra representation of logics. The above integrations have been realized by the multilinear function space. There are a lot of open problems, therefore the author strongly encourages the readers to join the research field.

References

1. G. Birkhoff and T.C. Bartee: *Modern Applied Alge bra*, McGraw–Hill, 1970.
2. D.V. Dalen: Intuitionistic Logic, *Handbook of Philo sophical Logic III, D. Gab-bay and F.Guenthner eds.*, pp.225-339, D.Reidel, 1 984.
3. M. Dummett: A Propositional Calculus with Denumerable Matrix, *The Journal of Symbolic Logic*, Vol.24, No.2, pp.97-106, 1959.
4. M. C. Fitting: *Intuitionistic Logic-Model Theory and Forcing*, North Holland, 1969.
5. P. Hájek: *Metamathematics of Fuzzy Logic*, Kluwer, 1998.
6. K.Hornik: Multilayer Feedforward Networks are Universal Approximators, *Neural Networks*, Vol.2 pp.359-266, 1989.
7. T. Hosoi and H. Ono:Intermediate Propositional Logics(A Sur vey),*Journal of Tsuda College*, Vol.5, pp.67-82, 1973.
8. C. Morita and Hiroshi Tsukimoto: Knowledge discovery from numerical data, *Knowledge-based Systems*, Vol.10, No.7, pp. 413-419, 1998.
9. H. Ono and Y. Komori: Logics without the contraction rule, *J. Symbolic Logic* 50, pp.169-201, 1985.
10. H. Tsukimoto and C. Morita: The discovery of propos itions in noisy data, *Machine Intelligence 13*, pp.143-167, Oxford Univ ersity Press, 1994 .
11. H. Tsukimoto: The discovery of logical propositions in numerical data, *AAAI'94 Workshop on Knowledge Discovery in Database s*, pp.205-216, 1994.
12. H. Tsukimoto: Continuously Valued Logical Function Satisfying All Axioms of Classical Logic, *Systems and Computers in Japa n*, Vol.25, No.12, pp.33-41, SCRIPTA TECHNICA, INC., 1995.
13. H. Tsukimoto: The space of multi-linear functions as models of logics and its applications, *Proceedings of the 2nd Workshop on Non-Standard Logic and Logical Aspects of Computer Science*, 1995.
14. H. Tsukimoto and Chie Morita: Efficient algorithms for inductive learning-An application of multi-linear functions to inductive learning, *Machine Intelligence 14*, pp.427-449, Oxford University Press, 1995.
15. H. Tsukimoto: Extracting Propositions from Trained Neural Networks, *Proceedings of IJCAI-97*, pp.1098-1105, 1997.
16. L. A. Zadeh: Fuzzy Algorithms, *Information and Control* , Vol.12, pp.94-102, 1968.

Part II

Toward Deep Fusion of Computational and Symbolic Processing

Part II

Design of Autonomously Learning Controllers Using FYNESSE

Ralf Schoknecht[1], Martin Spott[2], Martin Riedmiller[1]

[1] Institut für Logik, Komplexität und Deduktionssysteme
[2] Institut für Programmstrukturen und Datenorganisation
   Universität Karlsruhe, Postfach 6980, D-76128 Karlsruhe

Abstract: With the growing number and difficulty of control problems there is an increasing demand for design methods that are easy to use. FYNESSE fulfils this requirement: without knowledge of a process model the system learns a control policy. Optimization goals like time-optimal or energy-optimal control as well as restrictions of allowed manipulated variables or system states can be defined in a simple and flexible way. FYNESSE only learns on basis of success and failure of former control interactions and, thus, learning can be carried out directly at the real process. A priori knowledge about the control policy as, for example, a fuzzy or linear control law considerably improves the learning process. Moreover, the learned policy can be interpreted as fuzzy control law which allows for easily checking the plausibility.

4.1 Introduction

As the degree of automation and the number and complexity of control applications are constantly rising, the limit of classic control design is reached more and more often. Especially nonlinear control problems require experts, because the design method varies with the class of the process (linear, nonlinear, single/multiple input/output, ...). Long development times increase the costs and provoke the danger of being too late for the market. The solution is often a compromise between costs and quality: simplified models are used for the processes that only roughly approximate reality. Furthermore, the adaptation of classic controllers to changing environmental parameters proves to be difficult. For these reasons, it is desirable that the design method

1. is independent from the class of the process;
2. does not require a model of the process;
3. allows a flexible definition of the desirable control behaviour;
4. allows adaptive control.

Our approach FYNESSE is a learning system that fulfils these requirements. In the **Fuzzy-Neuro-System** FYNESSE, controller design is mapped onto a dynamic optimization problem. The goal of optimization (e.g. time- or energy-optimal control) is transformed into a local cost function. No knowledge about the process is necessary for this procedure. Restrictions for the controlled and manipulated variables can be incorporated as well. Based on this specification, a global cost function is optimized by repeatedly controlling the real system (or a simulation).

Due to the fact that, theoretically, the system cannot cope with situations it has never seen before, the learning task is very complex, especially for high-dimensional problems. This is one of the reasons that we use a neural network to approximate the cost function. The experiments show that the network generalizes very well from situations it has already learned to situations it has never seen before.

The complete control architecture FYNESSE is shown in Figure 4.1. It consists of a fuzzy controller that proposes possible control actions, and the neural critic that learns to select the optimal control action from the proposed set. The fuzzy controller allows the integration of vague and uncertain a priori knowledge about the control strategy. Crisp control laws like classic linear controllers or control characteristics can be used as a priori knowledge as well. We experimented with different levels of a priori knowledge and observed that even low levels increase the stability of learning considerably. In contrast, without a priori knowledge, the system sometimes forgets successful control strategies. Stable learning is indispensable in adaptive systems. The lohaviour of the controlled process.

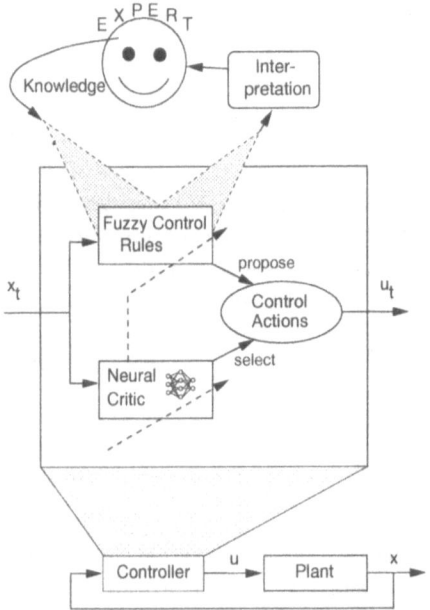

Fig. 4.1. The FYNESSE control architecture.

Since misbehaviour must be detected before a real process is driven into intolerable states, FYNESSE allows the interpretation of the learned strategy in terms of fuzzy control rules. Especially in combination with visualizations of classic control characteristics, fuzzy rules give a good overview of the global and local behaviour. Therefore, fundamental defects can easily be found.

With respect to its goals and architecture, FYNESSE can be compared to well known systems like GARIC [4] and CLARION [24]. All three systems realize autonomous learning and integrate symbolic and subsymbolic control knowledge. GARIC and many other architectures allow only the formulation of a negative control goal, i.e. the avoidance of intolerable states of the system. In CLARION and FYNESSE a positive control goal can be defined additionally, i.e. states the system must reach. A considerable advantage of FYNESSE is the flexibility and straightforwardness of defining an optimization criterion (time-optimality, energy-optimality, etc). This is essential for the practical relevance of an autonomously learning controller. Furthermore, FYNESSE offers the possibility to integrate different kinds of a priori knowledge (fuzzy control laws, control characteristics, etc). This is more difficult in GARIC and CLARION because of their special representation of symbolic knowledge.

This article is organized as follows. In Section 4.2, the cart pole balancing problem is introduced as our benchmark problem. The design of fuzzy controllers is discussed in Section 4.3 It is shown that the fuzzy methodology, a symbolic control approach, allows quick design of controllers. On the other hand, their quality is very often far from being optimal, sometimes even too bad for successful control. Section 4.4 explains our approach for the optimization of controllers, including the basics of dynamic programming. The actual design process with FYNESSE is demonstrated in Section 4.5 Results are shown in Section 4.6, they prove the high quality of the learned controllers and the advantages of using a priori knowledge. In Section 4.7, we introduce an alternative approach for the integration of imprecise a priori knowledge about the control strategy. Furthermore, a concept for the adaptation of the fuzzy controller is explained. Two important ways of interpreting the learned strategy are demonstrated in Section 4.8: classic control characteristics and fuzzy control rules. These interpretations are used for checking the plausibility of the learned controller. The conclusions summarize the controller design algorithm of FYNESSE and its results.

4.2 Control Task

The performance of the FYNESSE approach is demonstrated with the cart pole balancer which is depicted in Figure 4.2. A rotating pole mounted on a moving cart is to be balanced by suitably pushing the cart back and forth. The system state can be uniquely characterized by the vector $(s, \dot{s}, \theta, \dot{\theta})$. s, $\dot{s}$ denote the cart position and cart velocity, θ, $\dot{\theta}$ denote the pole angle and the angular velocity. s and θ are the controlled variables. The system can be manipulated by the force F used to accelerate the cart.

This unstable nonlinear four-dimensional system has been used as benchmark for various approaches to learning control (e.g. [2],[12],[15]). However, the control task presented here is considerably more complex than in many other approaches. In [2],[12], for example, the control goal only consists in preventing the pole from falling down and the cart from hitting the track

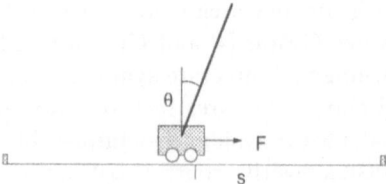

Fig. 4.2. The control task for the cart pole balancer consists in balancing a rotating pole mounted on a cart into upright position while the cart is brought to middle of the track. Constraints are posed by the boundaries of the track.

boundaries. This means that the specification of the control objective is only stated in terms of what situations should be avoided. In [15] an explicit control goal is specified, the cart is to be driven to a specific position on the track and the pole is to be balanced approximately to an upright position. However, it is assumed that the control task is finished when this control target is reached. Thus, the learned controller might not be able to stabilize the system and permanently keep it within the specified target region. In a standard control application, however, this is an essential requirement. Therefore, the control goal in FYNESSE consists in reaching an explicitly specified target region *and* stabilizing the system in that region. In comparison to the two other control tasks, this specification is much harder to fulfil but also much more natural. In FYNESSE, the control objective is formulated as an optimization problem. The optimization goal can be chosen very flexibly by the designer. It is, for example, possible to specify time-optimal or energy-optimal control. Additionally, the constraint of not exceeding the given track boundaries can also be formulated in the controller design framework FYNESSE. Thus, the specified control task fully comprises the control tasks used in the approaches mentioned above.

Our approach for autonomous learning of controllers has also been applied to other control problems. In [17], for example, a temperature regulation was learned. The main characteristic of this nonlinear system was the long dead time. As shown in [20] our approach is also applicable to nonlinear multiple input multiple output systems. We obtained a successful controller for the throttle valve angle and the fuel injection duration of a combustion engine.

4.3 Symbolic Control Rules

In most control applications, we have intuitive, qualitative knowledge about the control strategy. In case of the cart pole balancer, for example, we push the cart to the left if the pole falls to the left. It is fairly easy to write down a number of such rules that describe vague control actions for vague states of the system. The question is how a *vague* statement like "if the pole falls to the left", as well as the if-then-rule, can be formulated mathematically and how these rules will be used to calculate a control action from a given system state. In a nutshell, we search for a numerical method that implements symbolic fuzzy rules and approximate reasoning.

4.3.1 Technique

For formal reasons we translate the rule above into "if the angle x of the pole is *negative*[1] then apply a *negative* force u", or even shorter: "x is *negative* $\longrightarrow u$ is *negative*". In standard fuzzy systems like the popular MAMDANI-controller a vague concept like *negative angle* is modeled by a fuzzy set on the set of possible angles $\mathcal{X}_\theta$. Figure 4.3 shows fuzzy sets *positive, negative* and *zero*. The shape of these fuzzy sets is often very simple: triangulars like *zero* mean "around zero" or "approximately zero", border functions like *positive* mean "around the border value or bigger".

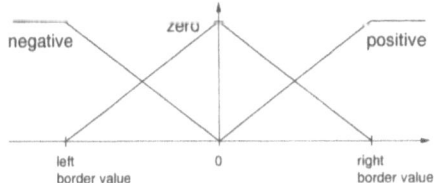

Fig. 4.3. Fuzzy partitioning of an interval on .

There are several possibilities to model and interpret rules, e.g. fuzzi-fied logic models, possibility theory, similarity based reasoning, interpolation schemes etc. The decision for one of these fuzzy models should be based on the semantics of the rules. In possibility theory [28, 9, 10, 22], for example, we deal with *negative information*, i.e. we exclude impossible statements. The MAMDANI-controller, on the other hand, can be interpreted as a set of pos-itive rules [27]; we actively support statements. Additionally, the reasoning behaviour must be considered.

In most control applications, positive rules are formulated and interpolat-ing behaviour is expected. For this reason, we focus on a classic interpolation scheme in this paper. It can be interpreted as a fuzzy system in the following way. As stated above, the fuzzy sets used in control applications are in most cases fuzzy numbers, i.e. they mean "*around x_0*" with a real value x_0. Then the rules read "x is *around x_i* $\longrightarrow u$ is *around u_i*". We base reasoning on the requirements

1. $x = x_i$ results in $u = u_i$;
2. x is similar to x_i results in u is similar to u_i.

In the second case, generally, x will be similar to several different x_i, so u must be similar to all respective u_i. If we deal with crisp inputs and out-puts, interpolation turns out to be a simple and efficient implementation

---

[1] Mathematically positive.

of the reasoning mechanism. It naturally fulfils both requirements and is mathematically well understood. The key idea in our approach is the use of B-spline-systems [6, 29, 21]. A B-spline is a function on that is positive in an interval and zero outside [8, 11]. For example, a linear B-spline is simply a triangular function, higher order B-splines look more like Gaussian functions. In this way they represent membership functions of local fuzzy sets. For reasons of simplicity, we use linear B-splines in this application. The antecedents "*around* x_i" and consequents "*around* u_i" of the rules are then given by triangular functions $\mu_{x_i}(x)$ and $\mu_{u_i}(u)$. A rule is a relation between states x and control actions u, $\mu_{R_i}(x, u) := \mu_{x_i}(x) \cdot \mu_{u_i}(u)$. Again, there are several possibilities to motivate this connection of antecedent and consequent as a rule, e.g. a fuzzy implementation of a conjunction or a fuzzy point on the control mapping. We definitely prefer the interpretation as a fuzzy point. The aggregation of all rules, the *meta-rule*, is defined by

$$\mu_R(x, u) := \sum_i \mu_{R_i}(x, u) = \sum_i \mu_{x_i}(x) \cdot \mu_{u_i}(u) , \qquad (4.1)$$

in analogy to the *max-min-composition* in classic fuzzy systems. Given a state x' as input, we obtain as output of the system the fuzzy state $\tilde{u}'$:

$$\mu_{u'}(u) = \mu_R(x', u) = \sum_i \mu_{x_i}(x') \cdot \mu_{u_i}(u) . \qquad (4.2)$$

The interpretation in the sense of the two requirements formulated above is simple: $\mu_{x_i}(x')$ measures the similarity between x_i and x'; the respective consequents are weighted with the similarity and aggregated by addition. In this way, the similarity of input and antecedents is transported to the consequents. The fuzzy output will then be defuzzified by the standard method *center of area*. In this special configuration (all membership functions are linear B-splines that are congruent and symmetric in the output dimension, COA-defuzzification), it can be shown that reasoning is identical to linear[2] interpolation between the points (x_i, u_i).

In the case of multidimensional input, the interpolation scheme must be extended. For a two-dimensional input $(\theta', \dot{\theta}')$ and one-dimensional output F, for example, we obtain

$$\mu_{F'}(f) = \sum_i \mu_{\theta_i}(\theta') \cdot \mu_{\dot{\theta}_i}(\dot{\theta}') \cdot \mu_{F_i}(f) \qquad (4.3)$$

for the fuzzy output $\tilde{F}'$.

Multistage reasoning is also possible with this approach. We developed a two-stage-controller for the cart pole balancer (Figure 4.4). In the first stage angle θ and angular velocity $\dot{\theta}$ are mapped onto a desired force F_d. The second stage maps the desired force together with position s and velocity $\dot{s}$ of the

---

[2] In case of multidimensional rule systems, we obtain a multi-linear interpolation.

cart onto the final force F. In this case, the consequents for the desired force in the first stage are identical to the antecedents of the second stage. An input to the first stage weighs the consequents (eq. 4.2). We then use these weights to weigh the respective antecedents of the second stage. Altogether, multistage reasoning is reduced to the propagation of similarities through a network. The reasoning mechanism is described in [21] in detail. It soundly embeds classic function approximation in approximate reasoning.

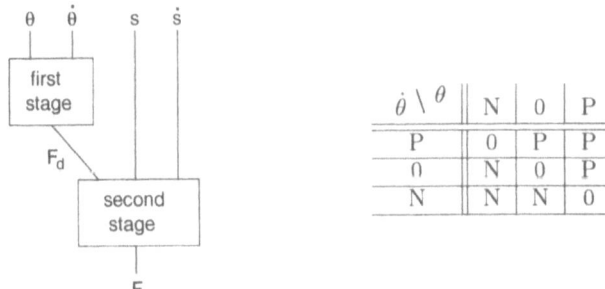

$\dot{\theta} \setminus \theta$	N	0	P
P	0	P	P
0	N	0	P
N	N	N	0

Fig. 4.4. The two-stage fuzzy controller for the cart pole balancer and the rule matrix of the first stage.

F_d	N			0			P		
$\dot{s} \setminus s$	N	0	P	N	0	P	N	0	P
P	N	N	N	N	P	P	P	P	P
0	N	N	N	N	0	P	P	P	P
N	N	N	N	N	N	P	P	P	P

Fig. 4.5. The rule matrix of the second stage of the fuzzy controller.

4.3.2 Design of the Fuzzy Controller

When the process variables have been found and the reasoning mechanism is determined the main design steps are

1. determination of the number of rule stages
2. definition of vague values (fuzzy areas) for the process variables;
3. definition of rules for the controller;
4. optimization of the vague values and possibly the rules.

As already described, we decided to use a two-stage-system. The rules are simpler because the dimension of the antecedents is smaller. On the other hand, we lose the possibility to formulate rules with certain combinations of antecedents. The reason is that multidimensional systems can generally not be decomposed due to dependencies between the variables. Therefore, the *hidden* variables (here: F_d) must be chosen carefully in order to preserve at least a good approximation of dependencies.

The domains of all process variables, s, $\dot{s}$, θ, $\dot{\theta}$, F and the hidden variable F_d, are divided into three fuzzy areas: *positive* (P), *around zero* (Z) and *negative* (N); this is point two. It must be clearly stated that these partitions are of a qualitative nature. They define some kind of fuzzy ordinal scale on the domains; the exact location and size of the fuzzy areas will be determined later. The number of fuzzy areas, i.e. the granularity of the partitions, reflect the granularity of our knowledge about the control strategy. Rough knowledge results in only a few fuzzy areas, more precise knowledge in fine-grained partitions. Based on the vague values for the process variables, we write down rules for the system. Figures 4.4 and 4.5 show the rules of the first and the second stage of the controller. The matrices mean, for example, "θ is *negative* and $\dot{\theta}$ is *positive* $\longrightarrow$ F_d is *zero*" in the first rule matrix (fig. 4.4) or "F_d is *zero* and s is *zero* and $\dot{s}$ is *positive* $\longrightarrow$ F is *positive*" in the second rule matrix (fig. 4.5). The number of rules is seven in each stage.[3]

The last point, the optimization of the vague values, is the most crucial one. We are able to formulate rules that are based on the ordinal scale we defined with the partitions of the domains, but we initially have no idea of the location of our vague values. We are not aware, for example, of the transition point between *positive* or *zero* angle θ or if the fuzzy angle *zero* is only a small or a wide area around $\theta = 0$. Possible sources of information are

1. experts, who are familiar with the process;
2. measurements or observation of the process.

Both sources of information lead to data our fuzzy system should fit. In most cases, we obtain crisp data which may be uncertain. The uncertainty is modeled by our fuzzy partitions. Obviously, this adaptation procedure of the fuzzy model in order to fit data is not trivial. Very often, interactive approaches are realized: the designer defines the vague partitions of the domains that can be adapted via a set of parameters. These will be optimized according to existing data. Due to the fact that all information we used for the controller design up here is vague or uncertain and sometimes even sparse, we cannot expect a very good controller. That is, the controller (or its parameters) must be optimized in direct interaction with the process. To a certain degree, this can be done by hand.

The fuzzy controller for the cart pole balancer is parameterized in the following way: the vague values *negative*, *zero* and *positive* uniformly cover

---

[3] Not every field in the rule matrices corresponds to one rule. We combine neighbouring antecedents that have the same conclusion like in KV-diagrams for boolean logic. For example, the left matrix in Figure 4.5 can obviously be reduced to one rule: "F_d is *negative* $\longrightarrow$ F is *negative*".

the domains, the only parameter is the border value in each dimension (cf fig. 4.3). Due to the symmetry of the problem, the absolute values of left and right border are identical. The inputs s, $\dot{s}$, θ and $\dot{\theta}$ are restricted by the border values: $input' := \max(border_{left}, \min(border_{right}, input))$, i.e. an input greater than the border value is simply substituted by the border value. In this way, it is possible to overcome the limitation to triangular fuzzy sets in linear B-spline-systems. Thus, the shape of *positive* and *negative* in Figure 4.3 can be constructed. The sensitive area of the controller lies in-between the border values.

We adjusted the border values on the basis of several test runs. The control trajectories of the system were examined and the parameters adjusted accordingly. The adjustments were purely based on qualitative knowledge of the process. The complete design process for a simple controller took an expert about two hours. The quality of this simple controller is not very good with respect to the optimization goal. The reason is that the chosen hierarchy of the controller does not allow the formulation of all rules that are known (formally speaking: $(s, \dot{s})$ and $(\theta, \dot{\theta})$ are not *separable* due to their dependency). Consequently, we constructed a second, more elaborate controller with one rule layer. The result are 59 rules, the expert's design time was about 20 hours and the quality is much better (cf Section 4.6).

As already pointed out, an optimal controller cannot be expected when we follow the design steps above. The final optimization requires more powerful techniques. In FYNESSE, we use the initial controllers as a priori knowledge for an optimization process that is based on dynamic programming. The resulting controllers are much better than the initial ones. It is also shown that even the simple controller as a priori knowledge improves the optimization procedure considerably in comparison to the controller learned without a priori knowledge.

4.4 Learning Control

In the following, we describe how the control law can be optimized in a reinforcement learning framework. This approach, which is implemented in the neural critic, is generally applicable with and without a priori knowledge.

The approach of *learning* the control law in interaction with the process is an alternative to designing a controller conventionally. This is attractive, because no knowledge about the process is required. The learning system determines which interdependencies of the system variables are relevant for control and uses this information for knowledge acquisition.

4.4.1 Problem Description

A dynamic system can be abstractly described in the time-discrete state space representation

$$x_{t+1} = f(x_t, u_t) \tag{4.4}$$

where u is the system input and x denotes the system state. The system is uniquely characterized by the state transition function f.

The control task consists in determining a control policy

$$\pi : \mathcal{X} \to \mathcal{U}, \quad u_t := \pi(x_t)$$

mapping every state $x \in \mathcal{X}$ onto a control action $u \in \mathcal{U}$ so that, from a certain time t_0 on, state x is kept within a tolerance limit T around x^{target}. Written formally, this means

$$||x_t - x^{target}|| < T, \quad \forall t > t_0.$$

Such a problem description is frequently found when using classical controller design methods. Unlike a classical approach, the design method described here does not need an analytical system model f. Instead, the control policy can be learned in direct interaction with the process. Alternatively, learning can be carried out using a 'black-box simulation model' of the process that has a similar input-output characteristic. What exactly happens on the physical level is completely irrelevant; thus, a costly analytical modeling of the plant with differential equations is not necessary.

4.4.2 Dynamic Programming

This section describes the transformation of the control problem in a dynamic optimization problem which can be solved with the methods of dynamic programming.

The controller for the dynamic system in equation (4.4) can make control decisions in discrete time steps where the difference between two control interactions is denoted as control interval Δt. The idea is to judge the quality of a control interaction by introducing a *local cost function*

$$r : \mathcal{X} \times \mathcal{U} \to , \quad r_t := r(x_t, u_t)$$

that denotes the costs incurred in state x_t by action u_t. Accumulated along whole control trajectories a *global cost function*

$$J^\pi(x_0) := \sum_{t=0}^{N} r(x_t, \pi(x_t)) \tag{4.5}$$

is derived that denotes the future costs that are incurred when applying policy π in state x_0. Often, especially in the field of reinforcement learning, J is also called *value function* which will be the term we use in the following. The number of steps N is called *horizon*. The notion of assigning costs to the different states is motivated by the desire of being able to judge the quality of the policy π in x_0. Depending on what quality measure is to be implemented the costs reflect, for example, time or energy. The objective is to find an optimal policy, i.e. a policy with minimal accumulated costs

$$J^*(x_0) = \min_{\pi \in \Pi} J^\pi(x_0). \tag{4.6}$$

In order to obtain an optimal policy, the whole control trajectory has to be taken into account, i.e. a decision taken because of low local costs can incur high future costs. So it can be useful to accept high local costs if the future course of the control trajectory is more favourable.

This situation is typical for problems of *dynamic optimization*. They can be solved with the methods of *dynamic programming* that are based on the *principle of optimality* established by Bellman [3]:

$$J^*(x) := \min_{u \in \mathcal{U}}\{r(x, u) + J^*(f(x, u))\}. \tag{4.7}$$

The costs of one state must equal the sum of the local costs and the future costs when acting according to the corresponding optimal policy π^*. This is the basis for the *value iteration method* to be described.

The principle of optimality only states a condition the optimal cost function has to fulfil. However, what we are looking for is a possibility to compute this optimal value function. The principle of optimality can be used to derive an iteration law for the value function

$$\forall x \in \mathcal{X} : J_{k+1}(x) := \min_{u \in \mathcal{U}}\{r(x, u) + J_k(f(x, u))\}. \tag{4.8}$$

Starting with an initial value function J_0 this yields a sequence $(J_0, J_1, \ldots)$ that converges against the optimal cost function J^* under certain assumptions. For a more detailed discussion on the convergence criteria see [5] and [16].

The value function J^* implicitly represents control knowledge. However, what we are looking for is a policy π^* that assigns every state x an optimal action u. This policy can be computed by the *greedy evaluation*

$$\pi^*(x) := arg \min_{u \in \mathcal{U}}\{r(x, u) + J^*(f(x, u))\}, \tag{4.9}$$

i.e., that action u is chosen that minimizes the sum of local costs and future costs incurred upon application of u.

The general form of the value iteration method as stated in (4.8) updates the value function for every state x of the whole state space $\mathcal{X}$. In practice, this is only applicable for a finite state space. When controlling real technical processes, however, the state space is often continuous. Thus, the iteration law has to be modified. Since there are infinitely many states, the cost function cannot be recomputed for all of them. Instead, the current control knowledge is greedily evaluated in order to determine an optimal action that transforms the system in a new state. The value function is then only updated for states on such real control trajectories. This approach is known as *real-time dynamic programming (RTDP)* [1].

As an absorbing terminal state, i.e. a state that is not left any more no matter what control action is selected, does not exist for most control tasks with continuous state space, the *fixed horizon algorithm* [18] is used. This algorithm allows for learning control laws for real control tasks like that posed in Section 4.2. As described in that section, many other approaches are only suited for solving much simpler control problems.

When using the current control knowledge to compute the optimal action that is applied to the system, equation (4.9) has to be used. However, this assumes that a system model f is available to test the effects of every action $u \in \mathcal{U}$ on the system, i.e. compute the next state $x_{t+1} = f(x_t, u)$ and evaluate $J(x_{t+1})$. After each such *single step prediction*, the system would have to be set back until the optimal action is determined. If learning should be carried out in direct interaction with the system, this is not possible, obviously. Thus, the action has to be selected without using f.

The key idea for modifying the action selection was proposed in [26] and consists in changing the representation of the value function. Instead of only evaluating the states, an evaluation of state-action pairs is learned. The new function

$$Q : \mathcal{X} \times \mathcal{U} \rightarrow$$

describes the global costs incurred in state x when applying action u. The relation between J and Q is given by

$$Q(x_t, u) = r(x_t, u) + J(f(x_t, u)). \qquad (4.10)$$

The modified value iteration method called *Q-learning* is described in the following:

– Action selection on basis of the current value function Q_k

$$u_t = arg \min_{u \in \mathcal{U}(x_t)} \{Q_k(x_t, u)\} \qquad (4.11)$$

– Application of the action to the plant

$$x_{t+1} = f(x_t, u_t) \qquad (4.12)$$

– Adaptation of the value function

$$Q_{k+1}(x_t, u_t) := r(x_t, u_t) + \min_{u \in \mathcal{U}(x_{t+1})} \{Q_k(x_{t+1}, u)\} \qquad (4.13)$$

The selected action can be directly applied to the real plant which 'computes' the next state that is only observed by the controller. Thus, learning can be carried out in direct interaction with the real process.

4.4.3 Learning the Value Function

After describing the algorithmic principle of computing the optimal value function Q^*, the question is how Q is represented. In case of finite state and action spaces that are not too big, a lookup-table representation would be possible where every state-action pair is saved with its corresponding costs. When dealing with the continuous and, hence, infinite state space of real systems, often a discretization approach is used. This, however, is only feasible for low dimensional problems. Otherwise, the number of states quickly gets intractable for a tabular representation. This is known as the *curse of dimensionality*. Therefore, in case of large scale problems it seems reasonable to use a function approximator for representing the value function. In the following, we use a multi-layer-perceptron that computes for every state-action pair (x, u) at the input the accumulated global costs $Q(x, u)$ at the output. The nonlinearities of the value function can be approximated by using a hidden layer. Generalization effects of the neural network lead to a good approximation of the cost values of states that have not yet been visited.

The parameters of the function approximator, i.e. the weights of the neural network, are adapted using a learning rule that has been derived from the update step of the Q-learning algorithm (4.13).

Basically, the weight update is carried out using

$$\mathbf{w}_{k+1} := \mathbf{w}_k + \alpha \Delta \mathbf{w}_k$$

where $\mathbf{w}_k$ is the weight vector corresponding to value function Q_k and α is the learning rate.

The weight change $\Delta \mathbf{w}_k$ depends on the difference between the current estimate $Q_k(x_t, u_t)$ and the following estimate $r(x_t, u_t) + Q_k(x_{t+1}, u_{t+1})$. For that reason, the concept is called *temporal difference (TD) learning* [25] which belongs to the field of *reinforcement learning*. Here the TD(0) learning rule is used which yields

$$\Delta \mathbf{w}_k = - \sum_{t=0}^{N-1} (Q_k(x_t, u_t, \mathbf{w}_k) - (r(x_t, u_t) + Q_k(x_{t+1}, u_{t+1}, \mathbf{w}_k))) \frac{\partial Q_k(x_t, u_t, \mathbf{w}_k)}{\partial \mathbf{w}_k}.$$

It can be implemented using the *backpropagation algorithm* for adapting the weights of the neural network.

In the next section, we show how the described concepts for learning control are integrated in the control architecture FYNESSE.

4.5 Controller Design

4.5.1 Specification of the Control Target

For the controller design in the FYNESSE framework, knowledge about the dynamic behaviour of the plant in form of an analytical process model is *not* necessary; hence, the user can fully concentrate on the specification of the controller without carrying out a costly modeling. First, the control target is specified. For the cart pole balancer the task consists in balancing the pole ($\theta = \dot{\theta} = 0$) and bringing the cart to the middle of the track ($s = \dot{s} = 0$) where s describes the cart position and θ the pole angle to the vertical. Since this state can never be reached without deviation, the user specifies a tolerance limit, which defines a target region $\mathcal{X}^+$. Determining a tolerance limit is a trade-off between high precision of the controller and increasing learning complexity of the control task. Here $\mathcal{X}_s^+ = [-0.05m, 0.05m]$ and $\mathcal{X}_\theta^+ = [-2.3°, 2.3°]$ are chosen. That yields an overall target region $\mathcal{X}^+ = \mathcal{X}_s^+ \times \mathcal{X}_\theta^+$.

Additionally, the specification of undesired or forbidden process states (*constraints*) is possible. These are described by $\mathcal{X}^-$. Here, for example, the length of the track is limited, i.e. $\mathcal{X}_s^- = \{s | s \leq -1.0m\} \cup \{s | s \geq 1.0m\}$. The angle of the pole is confined to a working range between $-40°$ and $40°$. This results in $\mathcal{X}_\theta^- = \{\theta | \theta \leq -40°\} \cup \{\theta | \theta \geq 40°\}$ which yields an overall forbidden region of $\mathcal{X}^- = \{(s, \theta) | s \in \mathcal{X}_s^- \vee \theta \in \mathcal{X}_\theta^-\}$.

These requirements are explicitly transformed in a *local cost function* $r(x, u)$. In order to create an incentive for reaching the target region, the costs within $\mathcal{X}^+$ are set to zero. The costs inside the forbidden region $\mathcal{X}^-$ should be chosen in order to create a 'repulsion effect', i.e. the controller tends to avoid this region. Actually, one would set the local costs within $\mathcal{X}^-$ to ∞. This choice is not reasonable because it produces a strong discontinuity in the value function at the border of $\mathcal{X}^-$: in $\bar{\mathcal{X}} = \mathcal{X} \setminus (\mathcal{X}^+ \cup \mathcal{X}^-)$ the value function Q only takes on finite values. The multi-layer perceptron is not able to approximate such strong discontinuities appropriately. Thus, the local costs in $\mathcal{X}^-$ are set to a comparatively high finite value. The choice of the local costs in the rest of the state space $\bar{\mathcal{X}}$ has not been restricted in any way by the determinations made above. Hence, this provides a degree of freedom for the controller design which is not available in other approaches. It can be used to specify an *optimality criterion*, e.g. time-optimal control, for the control trajectories. This is done by establishing a cost measure that 'counts' the control interactions outside the target region. Thus uniform costs are assigned to the rest of the state space, i.e. $r(x, u) = r(x) = const$. Because of the optimization approach described in more detail in Section 4.4.2 this creates an incentive to reduce the time spent outside the target region.

Other optimality criteria are conceivable. In some applications energy-optimal trajectories, for example, are of major interest. This is realized by defining a local cost measure $r(x, u)$ that is only dependent on u. In the case of the cart pole balancer, the action taken by the controller is the force F used to accelerate the cart. High absolute force values would be assigned high local costs in order to indicate high energy consumption. Thus, the concept of the local cost function is very flexible and allows to specify individually suited optimality criteria. In other approaches, e.g. CLARION, there always exists an incentive to quickly reach the target. This is due to the discount factor and the chosen local cost structure. Therefore, it is not possible to specify, for example, energy-optimality as the only optimization goal.

4.5.2 Parameterization of the Controller's Capabilities

In order to fulfil the specifications given above, the controller has to be provided with appropriate capabilities. These capabilities are determined by the action set. It has to be taken into account that the regulating unit is restricted to $|F| \leq 10N$. In contrast to the continuous state space, the action set has to be discrete due to the control concept. If the number of available actions increases, the action space is resolved finer; thus, the control accuracy generally rises but so does the complexity of the learning problem. This is due to the fact that the number of possible policies increases polynomially with $|\mathcal{U}|^N$ where $\mathcal{U}$ is the chosen action set and N is the length of the control trajectory which takes on values of about 100. For most of the plants, a set of quite few actions is sufficient. The cart pole balancer, for example, can be successfully controlled with only two or three actions. The action set chosen here is $\mathcal{U} = \{0N, \pm 10N\}$. This explicit specification of the action set automatically considers the restriction $|F| \leq 10N$ for the manipulated variable. Hence, it is not necessary to artificially bound the control action. This is often a problem when designing analytical linear controllers since the closed-loop system becomes nonlinear.

If using a small action set, it may happen that oscillations of the controlled variables occur when the system is in the target region. This is due to the fact that the controller is not provided with the whole spectrum of actions to exactly reach the control goal. Thus, it dynamically 'generates' the missing actions by using oscillating action sequences. This, however, leads to oscillations of the controlled variables which are especially conspicuous when the difference of subsequent actions is big. In order to reduce this difference, the idea is to extend the action set available in the target region $\mathcal{X}^+$ after training by adding the actions $\{\pm 1N\}$. The action set outside the target region is not altered. Due to the generalization property of the neural network used as function approximator, this extension of the action set preserves the general control behaviour as well as damping the oscillations significantly.

4.5.3 Parameterization of the Learning System

The neural network for representing the value function Q is a multi-layer perceptron with three layers. The input layer contains five neurons for the four-dimensional state vector and the action that is to be evaluated. In the hidden layer there are twenty neurons to provide appropriate generalization capabilities. The output layer consists of one neuron to compute the approximated costs of the state-action pair.

The training of the neural network is carried out corresponding to Section 4.4.3 along control trajectories starting with initial conditions chosen randomly from the training set $(s, \dot{s}, \theta, \dot{\theta}) \in [-0.25m, 0.25m] \times \{0\frac{m}{s}\} \times [-20°, 20°] \times \{0\frac{°}{s}\}$. The test set consists of four representative initial conditions $(s, \dot{s}, \theta, \dot{\theta}) \in \{-0.2m, 0.2m\} \times \{0\frac{m}{s}\} \times \{-10°, 10°\} \times \{0\frac{°}{s}\}$.

4.5.4 Integration of a priori Knowledge

In many cases at least partial knowledge about an appropriate control policy exists. It is necessary to use that a priori knowledge in order to enhance the learning process, because when learning a policy from scratch, the learning process often is unstable and the controller temporarily 'forgets' to avoid the forbidden region. As the controller should adapt itself to the possibly changing behaviour of the system, the learning process is not finished after a fixed amount of time. Thus, for an adaptive controller the performance should not decline drastically during learning. The used a priori knowledge can be incomplete or lead to still unsatisfying control behaviour. In the following, we present two different ways of integrating a priori control knowledge about the control policy.

First, a priori knowledge is integrated by modifying the action set. The idea is to provide the neural critic with the action u_{a_priori} from the a priori control knowledge. This a priori control knowledge can be any control characteristic $x \mapsto u$, as, for example, fuzzy or linear control laws. In the new action set $\mathcal{U}_{a\_priori}(x) = \{u_{a\_priori}(x), \pm 10N\}$, the action $0N$ is substituted in order to keep the complexity of the learning problem comparable. This modified action set leads to a hybrid controller that depending on the learned value function either mimics the a priori controller or chooses one of the extremal actions.

For the a priori controllers we use two fuzzy controllers that represent the knowledge of a human expert and a linear state feedback controller. The difference between the two fuzzy controllers consists in control quality and design time. The objective was, on the one hand, to quickly get a simple but functioning fuzzy controller, and, on the other hand, a well tuned one. The learned hybrid controllers should replace the a priori action by the actions $\pm 10N$ if necessary in order to obtain a better control behaviour.

4.6 Results

In the following, the course of learning and the control strategies of different controllers are compared. The simple fuzzy controller designed in about two hours is used as a priori control knowledge and considerably improved with the FYNESSE approach. We also demonstrate that the learning process becomes much more stable when using a priori knowledge than it is when learning a control law from scratch. Concerning the control behaviour, a graphical comparison of the hybrid controller with the controller learned from scratch is presented. Moreover, we analyze how the hybrid controller switches between the action of the a priori controller and the other actions provided. This gives a better understanding of what was actually learned. Afterwards, the results for the elaborate fuzzy controller are presented. Finally, we also investigate a linear controller as alternative source of a priori knowledge. The main results are summarized in tabular form.

4.6.1 The Simple Fuzzy Controller

Figure 4.6 shows the time histories for the four representative test initial conditions that have been created using the simple fuzzy controller. A great deal of improvement in control behaviour is still possible. Mainly the response time is too long and the controlled variables keep oscillating so much that the target region is left repeatedly. Nevertheless, the system is approximately controlled into the target region, and the pole does not fall down any more. Thus, the initial fuzzy controller fulfils basic control requirements, and it can be used as starting point for further controller design. The goal is to eliminate the disadvantageous characteristics of the simple fuzzy controller by using an autonomously learning component.

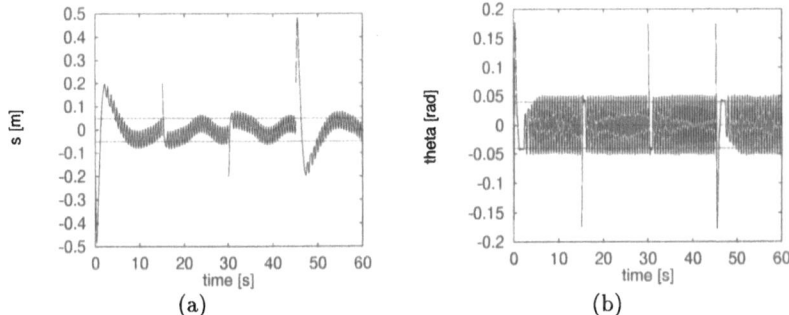

Fig. 4.6. Time histories for the controlled variables cart position (a) and pole angle (b) using the simple fuzzy controller. Starting from the four initial conditions control sequences of 15s each are depicted. The corresponding target region is dotted.

For the learning process, the action according to a priori knowledge is additionally presented to the neural critic in each control step. Based on the current knowledge represented by the learned value function an action is chosen. Thus, learning is performed along real trajectories. After 44000 such training sequences a very good hybrid controller has developed. This corresponds to a real time training of about 46h. In computer simulation on an Ultrasparc workstation half an hour was needed. For comparison an other controller was learned from scratch, i.e. without any a priori knowledge about control policies. The learning process is depicted in Figure 4.7. It shows the average costs of the control trajectories in the course of training where each control step outside the target region incurs local costs of 0.002. As our results clearly show, the costs for the best hybrid controller (training sequence 44000) are less than those of the best controller learned from scratch (training sequence 41000). Moreover, the learning process of the hybrid controller is much more stable than for the controller without a priori knowledge which keeps forgetting successful control strategies. A stable learning process is indispensable for an adaptive autonomously learning controller, because every instability would cause a substantial decline in control performance while adapting to the system behaviour.

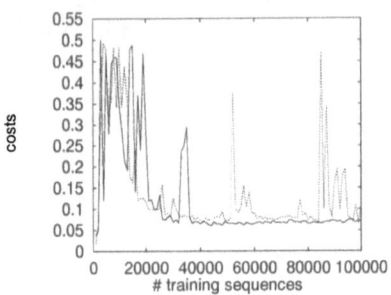

Fig. 4.7. Learning process in case of using a priori control knowledge in form of a simple fuzzy control law (solid line) and in case of using no a priori knowledge (dashed line).

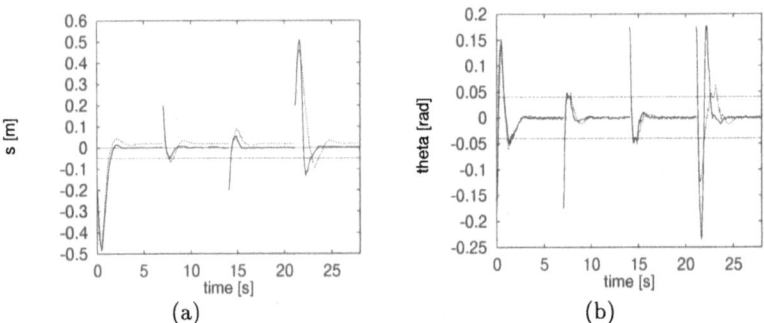

Fig. 4.8. Time histories for (a) cart position and (b) pole angle when using the hybrid controller (solid line) and the controller learned from scratch (dashed line). Starting from the four initial conditions control sequences of $7s$ each are depicted. The corresponding target region is dotted.

In Figure 4.8, the performance of the best controllers is shown by plotting the time histories for the controlled variables starting from the four representative initial conditions. As described in Section 4.5.2, the action set has been extended by $\{\pm 1N\}$ within the target region to damp the oscillations.

In comparison to the original fuzzy controller, the transient response of the hybrid controller is much faster. Moreover, the wave-like oscillations of the cart position could be eliminated during learning. Now the target region is reached quickly and permanently. The oscillations that would have occurred when not extending the action set would not have caused the system to leave the target region. Thus, extending the action set has not, in principle, altered the control behaviour but only damped the oscillations.

The controller without a priori knowledge as well, solves the control task but the transient response is slower which causes higher costs. Since the control task is fulfilled when the system reaches the target region, slight stationary inaccuracies may occur as can be seen in the case of the controller without a priori knowledge. As the initial fuzzy controller represented a symmetric control law, the hybrid controller could more easily develop an implicit symmetric switching line between the actions $-1N$ and $1N$. This leads to considerably higher stationary accuracy.

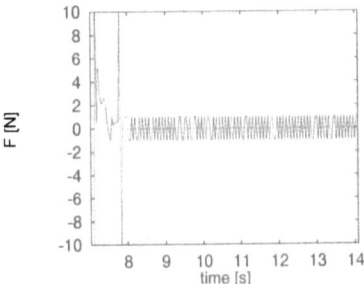

Fig. 4.9. Time history of the control action of the hybrid controller starting from the initial condition $(s, \dot{s}, \theta, \dot{\theta}) = (0.2m, 0, -0.175rad, 0)$. The corresponding time histories for the controlled variables are shown in the solid curves of the second trajectory in Figure 4.8 (a) and (b) respectively.

The learned hybrid controller can be seen as a switch between a priori action and the actions supplied by the user. In order to get an insight what was actually learned it is useful to have a look at the actions that are selected during control. Figure 4.9 shows which control actions are applied in the second control trajectory of the hybrid controller from Figure 4.8. One easily notices that the actions $\pm 10N$ are mainly chosen in the beginning of the trajectory. After reaching the target region the actions $\pm 1N$ are selected. These stages of control exactly represent the parts of the control task the simple fuzzy controller did not perform well. During the transient the a priori action is chosen quite frequently. This is because the task of controlling the system close to the target region was solved quite well by the fuzzy controller. Thus the hybrid controller takes advantage of the strength of the fuzzy controller and eliminates its weakness.

4.6.2 The Elaborate Fuzzy Controller

We have discussed using a simple fuzzy controller as source of a priori knowledge. Now we will investigate a more elaborate fuzzy controller that was designed in about 20 hours. Figure 4.10 depicts the time histories of the controlled variables for the initial fuzzy controller and the autonomously learned hybrid controller. The initial fuzzy controller already shows quite good control behaviour. The target region is reached permanently, and the pole does not fall down any more. However, the response time can still be improved. The slight oscillations only occur within the target region and are negligible. The hybrid controller reduces the time spent outside the target region by 37%. It quickly and permanently fulfils the control requirements. As the oscillations are only small the action set $\mathcal{U} = \{u_{a\_priori}, \pm 10N\}$ is unaltered, i.e. not extended by additional actions $\{\pm 1N\}$.

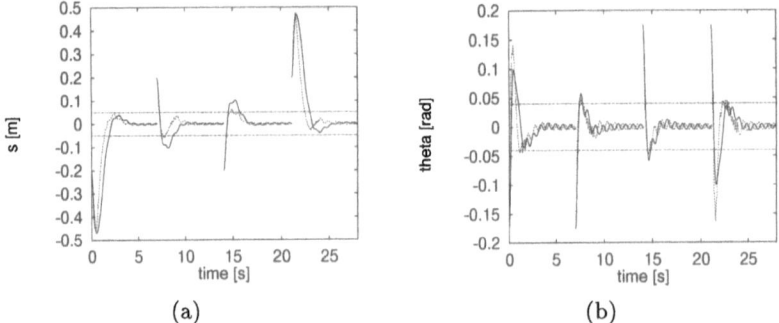

(a)   (b)

Fig. 4.10. Time histories for the controlled variables cart position (a) and pole angle (b) using (solid) the elaborate fuzzy controller and (dashed) the hybrid controller derived from it. Starting from the four initial conditions control sequences of 7s each are depicted. The corresponding target region is dotted.

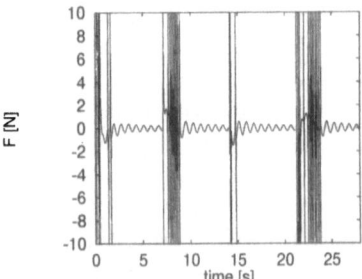

Fig. 4.11. Time history of the control action of the hybrid controller starting from the four initial conditions. The corresponding time histories for the controlled variables are shown in the dashed curves of Figure 4.10 (a) and (b) respectively.

Again the hybrid controller can be thought of as a switch between a priori action and the actions supplied by the user. Figure 4.11 shows the actions that are selected during the control trials of Figure 4.10. As can be seen, the a priori knowledge is used mainly in the target region. Thus, the hybrid controller has learned to exploit the strength of the elaborate fuzzy controller, namely to keep the system close to the goal state. During transition from the initial conditions to the control goal, the extremal actions $\{\pm10N\}$ are selected in order to quickly reach the target region.

4.6.3 The Linear Controller

The described approach of adding a priori actions to the action set evaluated by the neural critic can be applied for any control knowledge formulated in terms of a control characteristic. Hence, instead of a fuzzy controller, a linear state feedback controller can also be used. The following investigations are based on a linear controller that was developed using *linear quadratic regulator (LQR) design*. Thus, we obtained a very fast controller that fulfils the design requirements stated in Sections 4.5.1 and 4.5.2. Mainly, the restriction $|F| \leq 10N$ imposes constraints on the speed of the controller. Figure 4.12 depicts the time histories of the controlled variables for the initial linear controller and the autonomously learned hybrid controller. As can be seen, the initial linear controller already shows good control behaviour. The target region is permanently reached and the stationary accuracy is excellent. Only the response time could be further improved. This is done by the hybrid controller which reduces the time spent outside the target region by 35%. Since no oscillations occur the action set $\mathcal{U} = \{u_{a\_priori}, \pm10N\}$ is unaltered.

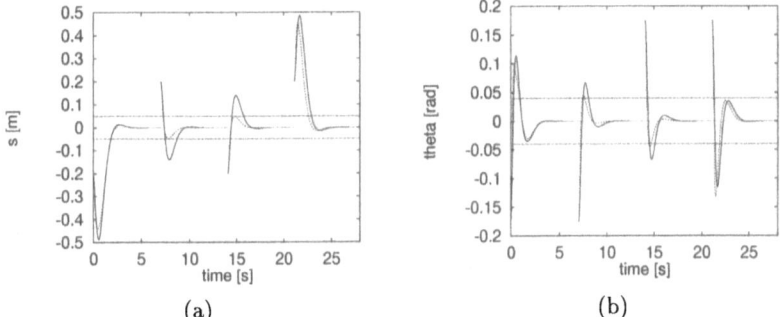

(a)   (b)

Fig. 4.12. Time histories for the controlled variables cart position (a) and pole angle (b) using (solid) the linear controller and (dashed) the hybrid controller derived from it. Starting from the four initial conditions control sequences of 7s each are depicted. The corresponding target region is dotted.

The time history for the actions selected during control is shown in Figure 4.13. The extremal actions $\{\pm10N\}$ are only applied in the very beginning of each control trajectory in order to obtain a quick transition from the initial conditions to the target region. For the rest of the trajectories the linear a priori action is selected. Thus, the hybrid controller again exploits the strength of the a priori control law and eliminates its weakness.

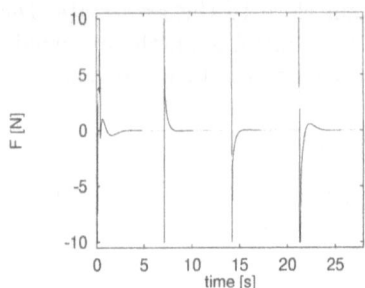

Fig. 4.13. Time history of the control action of the hybrid controller starting from the four initial conditions. The corresponding time histories for the controlled variables are shown in the dashed curves of Figure 4.12 (a) and (b) respectively.

4.6.4 Summary

The main characteristics of the controllers are summarized in Table 4.1. It depicts the results for the controllers that have been the subject of investigation in the previous paragraphs, namely the controller learned from scratch, the simple and elaborate fuzzy controller, as well as the linear controller that represent different sources of a priori control knowledge. The quality of the controllers is measured in terms of the number of steps outside the target region. Of course, there are many other measures to compare the quality of controllers like response time or degree of overshooting. However, as our approach is concerned with time-optimal control the number of steps outside the target region is the appropriate measure. Further qualitative information can be derived from the depicted time histories for the different controllers.

The performance of the hybrid controller based on the elaborate fuzzy controller shows a slight improvement in comparison to the hybrid controller designed using the a priori knowledge of the simple fuzzy controller. Although the design of the linear controller is much more time consuming because an analytic system model has to be developed, the performance of the derived hybrid controller is actually the same as for the elaborate hybrid controller. The expense for designing the a priori controller can therefore be kept to a reasonable minimum without losing performance concerning the hybrid controller.

The stability of the learned controllers is checked with the approach described in [14]. The training set is made discrete in the variables s and θ with $\Delta s = 0.01m$ and $\Delta \theta = 0.01rad$. The resulting grid points represent possible

a priori knowledge	#training seq.	#steps				Ø#steps
—	41000	37	16	26	59	34.5
fuzzy (simple)	initial controller	149	101	101	149	125
fuzzy (simple)	44000	45	16	17	42	30
fuzzy (elaborate)	initial controller	48	38	38	48	43
fuzzy (elaborate)	54000	37	17	17	38	27.25
linear	initial controller	46	37	37	46	41.5
linear	58000	46	12	12	38	27

Table 4.1. Comparison of controllers with different a priori knowledge. The table shows the number of training sequences until the controller is learned, the number of steps (control interactions with control interval $\Delta t = 0.04s$) outside the target region for all four initial conditions and the corresponding average value.

initial conditions for control trajectories. Starting from these initial conditions each learned controller reaches the target region and does not leave it any more. Thus, the closed-loop control systems are numerically stable for the chosen initial conditions. For the intermediate positions in the grid, stability of the controller can be assumed too because of the fine resolution of the grid and the continuity of the learned value function. Thus, a stability check is carried out for the region of the state space from which the initial conditions are taken.

4.7 Alternative Approach

In the previous sections, a priori knowledge about the control strategy is used to modify the set of possible actions $\mathcal{U}$. The global set of control actions $\mathcal{U} = \{0N, \pm 10N\}$ is changed to $\mathcal{U}_{a\_priori}(x) = \{u_{a\_priori}(x), \pm 10N\}$ which is dependent on the state x. In the case of an a priori fuzzy controller, the vagueness or uncertainty of the controller is lost with this approach. The fuzzy controller is defuzzified and simply used as a control characteristic. Therefore, the action set $\mathcal{U}_{a\_priori}(x)$ consists of non-specific extremal actions $\pm 10N$ and the a priori action $u_{a\_priori}(x)$, which is more or less good. FYNESSE learns to select the best action in a state. Consequently, the more specific the set of actions is, the better the resulting controller will be.

Since the a priori knowledge may be imprecise the corresponding a priori action may not be the correct action, but it is a clue about what action could be approximately correct. This suggests an alternative approach that extracts more information from the fuzzy control law than just the best action in a certain state x. Alternatively to formulating fuzzy control rules as *positive* knowledge about the process, it is also conceivable to formulate *negative* fuzzy control knowledge in terms of possibility distributions. In this way, it can be expressed, which actions are unlikely to be taken. These *impossible* actions are excluded from being selected in a certain system state by assigning them zero possibility. All other actions are said to be *possible without any restriction* [28, 9, 10, 22]. More about the relation of positive and negative information in the context of fuzzy systems can be found in [7, 23, 13].

When dealing with a continuous state space it is not practicable to use a specific action set for every system state. Therefore, the state space is partitioned in initial regions according to the a priori knowledge. After this initial partitioning the value function Q is learned and then used to split the regions and adapt the action sets in the different regions. That in turn corresponds to deriving more particular action sets for the state space by excluding actions that, in control experience, have proven not to be useful. This can be interpreted as an adaptation of the different possibility distributions. Below we will present a first experiment which demonstrates what promising results can already be achieved with an initial partitioning of the state space and quite simple action sets. The adaptation is still subject of future research.

The symbolic part of CLARION [24] looks similar to our approach at first glance, if we abstract from the representation of knowledge. The difference is that a symbolic rule in CLARION maps conditions onto a single action rather than a set of possible actions as in FYNESSE. The neural critic (as subsymbolic component) in FYNESSE selects the best action from this set of possible actions. As explained above this set depends on the state of the system. In this way, the search space can be reduced considerably. CLARION's subsymbolic component on the other hand evaluates *all* actions in a global unspecific action set (which is independent from the state) and combines these with the action that is proposed by the symbolic component. That means that the search space in CLARION cannot be reduced by symbolic knowledge; it only influences the action selection and in this way the exploration.

In the previous sections, the action set for the controller without a priori knowledge was defined to be $\mathcal{U} = \{0N, \pm 10N\}$. This ignores the knowledge that strongly accelerating the cart to the right with action $10N$ is not useful when the pole is already falling to the left, i.e. $\theta < 0$. This does not mean that any positive action is useless in that region of the state space. When approaching $\theta = 0$ or in case of $\dot{\theta} \gg 0$ it might be necessary to apply a positive force to the cart. Since the hyper-plane $\theta = 0$ obviously separates regions with fundamentally different behaviour, it is reasonable to initially partition the state space at that hyper-plane in two regions $\theta < 0$ and $\theta > 0$. For the reasons stated above the action $10N$ is shifted to $2N$ in the 'left' region $\theta < 0$ which means excluding $10N$ from the corresponding action set. In the 'right' region $\theta > 0$ the action $-10N$ is shifted to $-2N$ which likewise means excluding $-10N$ from the corresponding action set. Altogether this yields two region dependent action sets $\mathcal{U} = \{+2N, -10N\}$ if $\theta \leq 0$ and $\mathcal{U} = \{+10N, -2N\}$ if $\theta > 0$ where the action $0N$ is omitted for reasons of simplicity.

Though the a priori knowledge used for this initial partitioning and determination of the action sets is quite simple and not very specific, the learning behaviour of the system is very good. In Figure 4.14, the learning process for the prepartitioned controller is depicted in comparison with the controller using no a priori knowledge. As can be seen, the learning process is much more stable for the prepartitioned controller and the costs are a bit lower. When continuing the training beyond sequence 100000 which is not depicted in Figure 4.14, it turns out that from training sequence 140000 on there is still a significant improvement in the costs incurred during control. The number of steps outside the target region drops to an average value of 26.25, cf 34.5 from Table 4.1 when not using a priori knowledge.

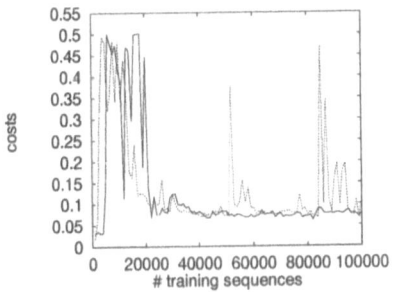

Fig. 4.14. Learning process in case of using a priori control knowledge in form of a prepartitioning of the state space (solid line) and in case of using no a priori knowledge (dashed line).

The resulting control behaviour of the two controllers is depicted in Figure 4.15. It shows that the prepartitioned controller reaches the target region much faster than the controller with no a priori knowledge. Eventually, the system is permanently kept in the target region.

These results show that the approach of formulating negative a priori knowledge is very promising. Future research will be directed towards adapting the action sets and increasing the use of fuzzy information for their determination.

4.8 Interpretation

Autonomous learning always involves the danger that the system does not learn what we expect it to. Two main reasons are:

1. the system does not learn long enough;
2. the formalization of the optimization goal is inconsistent with the learning task.

We observe the value function Q while learning and use it as a measure for the current quality of the controller. Nevertheless, local misbehaviour may

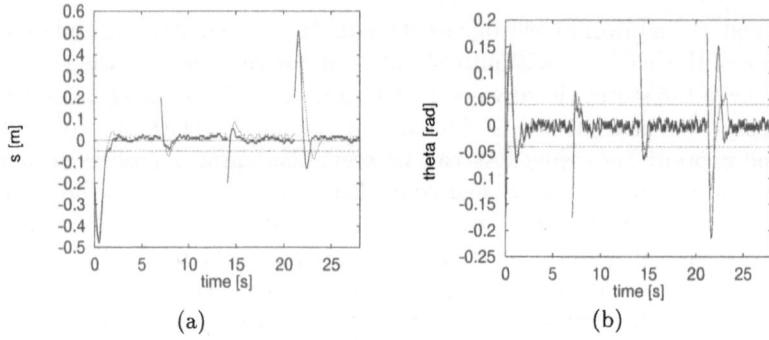

Fig. 4.15. Time histories for (a) cart position and (b) pole angle when using the prepartitioned controller (solid line) and the controller learned from scratch (dashed line). Starting from the four initial conditions control sequences of $7s$ each are depicted. The corresponding target region is dotted.

occur that must be detected. The second point may be a much more serious problem. A funny (real) example is the following: Someone wanted to train a little robot with two wheels (left and right). Its task was to drive around for a fixed time where start and finish were at the same point. The length of the path should be maximized. The result: At the end of the optimization procedure, the robot was just spinning on the starting point. The developer forgot to require that both wheels have to rotate in the same direction.

We are not able to criticize a control strategy in detail, for example, if in a certain state of the balancer a force $F = 3N$ is better than $F = 4N$. But that is not necessary. A rough qualitative interpretation of the strategy is sufficient for the detection of fundamental faults.

4.8.1 Techniques

From our point of view, the best ways for the interpretation are

1. fuzzy control rules;
2. control characteristics.

Obviously visualizations of control characteristics are restricted to three dimensions, e.g. two input variables and one output variable. On the other hand, they offer a fast overview over the global behaviour of the controller. In the case of more than two input variables we decide on the two variables we want to visualize and fix the others.

Fuzzy control rules on the other hand represent local information about the control strategy. As pointed out in Section 4.3, a vague description in terms of fuzzy rules is closely related to human understanding of functional dependencies. This becomes quite obvious when we look at a visualized control characteristic. We automatically start to interpret it as a set of fuzzy rules: "if the angle is *negative* and the angular velocity is *positive* then ...".

In FYNESSE, an initial fuzzy controller is used as a priori knowledge that improves the optimization procedure, since it leads to a more specific action set. The important point is that the selection of the control action is based on the value function $Q(x, u)$, and not on the fuzzy controller. That is, at the end of learning, the value function contains the relevant knowledge about the optimal control strategy.[4] Interpreting the control strategy is then somehow equivalent to an interpretation of the value function. This becomes even more obvious, when one realizes that $Q(x, u)$ is some kind of fuzzy relation between states x and control actions u, as well as fuzzy control rules.

The first step towards an interpretation in terms of fuzzy rules is a transformation of the learned value function Q into a fuzzy relation $\tilde{C}$ [19]: in each state x

- the best control action u_{best}^x is mapped to 1: $\mu_C(x, u_{best}^x) := 1$;
- the worst control action u_{worst}^x is mapped to 0: $\mu_C(x, u_{worst}^x) := 0$;
- all other control action are evaluated proportional to the best and worst action.

These points define the semantics of the fuzzy control relation which are not exactly the same as those of the fuzzy controller synthesized from expert knowledge. In the latter case, the initial control relation $\mu_R(x, u)$ expresses more a belief that u is a good control action in state x, i.e. uncertain or vague information about the control strategy. $\mu_C(x, u)$ on the other hand is clearly founded on learned costs. These are not uncertain at all if we neglect statistic effects in the optimization procedure, e.g. exploration techniques. Nevertheless $\tilde{C}$ is conform with $\tilde{R}$ in the sense that belief can be based on costs.

The fuzzy relation $\tilde{C}$ represents the meta-rule in equation (4.1). We generalize the formula in the following way:

$$\mu_C(x, u) := \sum_{i,j} \alpha_{ij}\mu_{x_i}(x) \cdot \mu_{u_j}(u) . \tag{4.14}$$

In this form we obtain rules that map an antecedent μ_{x_i} onto the linear combination $\sum_j \alpha_{ij}\mu_{u_j}$ of basic consequents μ_{u_j}. In the case of $\alpha_{ii} = 1$ and $\alpha_{ij} = 0$ for $i \neq j$ $\tilde{R} = \tilde{C}$ holds.

Based on a fixed set of antecedents and basic consequents, rule extraction is equivalent to the determination of the rule weights α_{ij}. We use standard least mean square algorithms for the calculation. The comparison between the initial and the learned controller becomes very easy: we use the same antecedents and basic consequents and compare the control strategies by the change in rule weights.

---

[4] We currently work on adaptive schemes for the fuzzy controller, as described in Section 4.7. The control knowledge is then transferred repeatedly from Q to the fuzzy controller during the learning procedure.

4.8.2 Results

For reasons of simplicity, we concentrate on two input dimensions, angle θ and angular velocity $\dot{\theta}$ and set $s = \dot{s} = 0$.

Figure 4.16 shows the control characteristics of the initial fuzzy controller and the resulting hybrid controller after learning. The plateaus in the edges of the initial control characteristic are due to the restriction of the inputs x of the fuzzy controller. The sensitive intervals are $\theta \in [-0.08rad, +0.08rad]$ and $\dot{\theta} \in [-0.9rad/s, +0.9rad/s]$. The learning process produces a hybrid controller where the transition area between $-10N$ and $+10N$ is smaller and rotated. Additionally, the plateaus have disappeared.

For the interpretation in terms of fuzzy rules the value function Q is transformed into a discrete fuzzy relation $\tilde{C}$. Afterwards, the rule weights are computed where the antecedents and consequents are the same as for the original fuzzy controller. The result is shown in Figure 4.17. The size of the letters corresponds to the respective rule weights. Again, we discover the rotation of the transition area between positive and negative force.

All in all, the strategy of the learned controller is plausible. Its qualitative behaviour is similar to that of the initial controller, which expresses our intuitive control knowledge. We do not discover any fundamental faults or local defects. The symmetry of the control problem can be detected in the control characteristic, as well.[5]

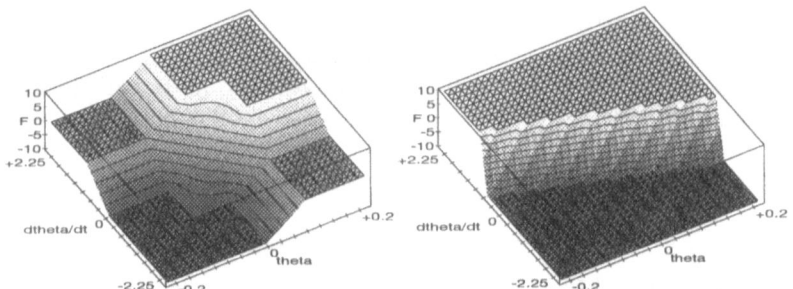

Fig. 4.16. Initial fuzzy (left) and learned control characteristic (right) for $s = \dot{s} = 0$.

4.9 Conclusions

Classical design concepts for controllers are, in general, highly problem dependent since they are mainly based on special model assumptions. FYNESSE avoids this problem by learning a control law in direct interaction with the

---

[5] It would have been sufficient to design the controller for "one side" of the state space. We did it for the complete state space because we wanted to investigate the learning behaviour of the algorithm.

$\dot\theta \setminus \theta$	N	0	P
P	0	P	P
0	N	0	P
N	N	N	0

$\dot\theta \setminus \theta$	N	0	P
P	0P	0P	0P
0	N0	N0P	0P
N	N0	N0	N0

Fig. 4.17. Original (left) and learned rule base (right) for $s = \dot s = 0$. The size of the consequents is proportional to their weights.

process. A model of the process is not necessary. Abstract optimization goals like time-optimal or energy-optimal control are defined independently of the process. The flexibility in defining these optimality criteria is a considerable advance in comparison with other approaches like CLARION or GARIC. However, this is an inevitable requirement for a serious controller design method. Moreover, constraints on controlled variables in terms of forbidden system states as well as constraints on manipulated variables can be formulated. During the learning process the experience of former control interactions is accumulated to obtain better policies.

The complexity of the learning task may lead to an instable learning process where learned policies are forgotten again. Concerning the adaptation to changing environmental conditions such instable behaviour is not tolerable. Therefore, in the FYNESSE framework the learning process is stabilized by using a priori control knowledge. The experiments show that even a simple controller is sufficient for that purpose. The fuzzy controller designed in two hours is only of inferior quality. However, the combination of the optimization approach with the fuzzy controller

1. optimizes the fuzzy controller and
2. stabilizes the learning process.

The neural network in FYNESSE approximates the optimal value function. Due to the interpolation property the network can adequately react in new situations that are similar to the ones already learned. The autonomously learned controllers are of high quality.

An alternative approach for the integration of a priori knowledge is introduced that takes into account the fuzziness of information. Furthermore, it allows an adaptation of the initial fuzzy controller in order to further improve the learning procedure. A first experiment demonstrates the quality of this approach.

The plausibility of the learned control strategy can be checked at the end of the learning procedure. The value function provided by the optimization algorithm is transformed into a fuzzy control relation which will be approximated by a set of fuzzy control rules. Together with the crisp control characteristic, the fuzzy control rules enable us to easily detect misbehaviour of the learned controller.

Altogether FYNESSE provides a design concept that is independent of the controlled process. It only needs little a priori knowledge which, moreover, may be imprecise. FYNESSE obviously unites the advantages of different fields of research: the learning properties of neural networks, the intuitive representation of fuzzy control knowledge in fuzzy controllers as well as the optimization approaches from the field of dynamic programming. In this way, symbolic and subsymbolic knowledge profit from one another in a single system.

Acknowledgement. The research project FYNESSE is supported by the Deutsche Forschungsgemeinschaft (DFG).

References

1. A. G. Barto, S. J. Bradtke, and S. P. Singh. Learning to act using real-time dynamic programming. *Artificial Intelligence*, (72):81–138, 1995.
2. A. G. Barto, R. S. Sutton, and C. W. Anderson. Neuron-like adaptive elements that can solve difficult learning control problems. *IEEE Transactions on Systems, Man, and Cybernetics*, 13:834–846, 1983.
3. R. E. Bellman. *Dynamic Programming*. Princeton University Press, Princeton, NJ, 1957.
4. H.R. Berenji and P. Khedkar. Learning and tuning fuzzy logic controllers through reinforcements. In *IEEE Trans. Neural Networks*, volume 3, pages 724–740, 1992.
5. D. P. Bertsekas. *Dynamic Programming*. Prentice-Hall, Englewood Cliffs, New Jersey, 1987.
6. M. Brown and C.J. Harris. A perspective and critique of adaptive neurofuzzy systems used in modelling and control applications. *Int. J. Neural Systems*, 6(2):197–220, 1995.
7. D. Cayrac, D. Dubois, and H. Prade. Handling uncertainty with possibility theory and fuzzy sets in a satellite fault diagnosis application. *IEEE Transactions on Fuzzy Systems*, 4(3):251–269, 1996.
8. C. de Boor. On calculating with B-splines. *Journal of Approximation Theory*, 6:50–62, 1972.
9. D. Dubois and H. Prade. *Possibility theory: an approach to computerized processing of uncertainty*. Plenum Press, New York, 1988.
10. D. Dubois and H. Prade. Fuzzy sets in approximate reasoning, part 1: Inference with possibility distributions. *Fuzzy Sets and Systems*, 40:143–201, 1991.
11. G. E. Farin. *Curves and surfaces for computer aided geometric design: a practical guide*. Academic Press, Boston, 3rd edition, 1993.
12. M.I. Jordan and R.A. Jacobs. Learning to control an unstable system with forward modeling. In D. S. Touretzky, editor, *Advances in Neural Information Processing Systems*, volume 2, pages 84–97. Morgan Kaufmann, San Mateo, California, 1989.
13. H. Kiendl. *Fuzzy control methodenorientiert*. Oldenbourg Verlag, 1997.
14. K. Michels and R. Kruse. Numerical stability analysis for fuzzy control. *Journal of Approximate Reasoning*, pages 3–24, 1997.
15. R. Munos and A. Moore. Variable Resolution Discretization in Optimal Control. *Machine Learning*, 1999. submitted.

16. M. Riedmiller. *Selbständig lernende neuronale Steuerungen.* PhD thesis, Universität Karlsruhe, 1996.

17. M. Riedmiller. High quality thermostat control by reinforcement learning - a case study. In *Proceedings of the Conald Workshop 1998*, Carnegie-Mellon-University, 1998.

18. M. Riedmiller. Reinforcement learning without an explicit terminal state. In *Proc. of the International Joint Conference on Neural Networks, IJCNN '98*, Anchorage, Alaska, 1998.

19. M. Riedmiller, M. Spott, and J. Weisbrod. First results on the application of the Fynesse control architecture. In *IEEE 1997 International Aerospace Conference*, volume 2, pages 421–434, Aspen, USA, 1997.

20. R.Schoknecht and M. Riedmiller. Using reinforcement learning for engine control. In *Ninth International Conference on Artificial Neural Networks (ICANN '99)*, Edinburgh, 1999. preliminary accepted.

21. M. Spott. Using classic approximation techniques for approximate reasoning. In *FUZZ-IEEE '98*, pages 909–914, Anchorage, USA, 1998.

22. M. Spott. A theory of possibility distributions. *Fuzzy Sets and Systems*, 102(2):135–155, 1999.

23. M. Spott and J. Weisbrod. A new approach to the adaptation of fuzzy relations. In *Proc. of EUFIT'96*, volume 2, pages 782–786, Aachen, Deutschland, 1996.

24. R. Sun and T. Peterson. A subsymbolic+symbolic model for learning sequential navigation. In *Fifth International Conference of the Society for Adaptive Behavior (SAB'98)*, Zurich, Switzerland, 1998. MIT Press.

25. R. S. Sutton. Learning to predict by the methods of temporal differences. *Machine Learning*, (3):9–44, 1988.

26. C. J. Watkins. *Learning from Delayed Rewards.* Phd thesis, Cambridge University, 1989.

27. J. Weisbrod. Fuzzy control revisited — why is it working? In P. P. Wang, editor, *Advances in Fuzzy Theory and Technology, Vol. III*, pages 219-244. Bookwrights, Durham (NC), 1995.

28. Lotfi A. Zadeh. Fuzzy sets as a basis for a theory of possibility. *Fuzzy Sets and Systems*, 1:3–28, 1978.

29. J. Zhang and A. Knoll. Constructing fuzzy controllers with b-spline models. In *FUZZ-IEEE '96*, New Orleans, USA, 1996.

Modeling for Dynamic Systems with Fuzzy Sequential Knowledge

[1] I. Takeuchi and[2] T. Furuhashi

[1] Nagoya Univesity & The Institute of Physical and Chemical Research
[2] Nagoya University

Abstract: This paper presents a fuzzy modeling method for dynamic systems, focusing on the knowledge representation framework. The basic idea lies in the use of "fuzzy" sequential knowledge for the description of dynamic characteristics of a system. Symbolic Dynamic System(SDS), a model for symbolic sequences, is extended to deal with "fuzzy" symbolic sequences. This approach introduces topological nature into the symbolic sequences, which allows an interpretation of the knowledge in numerical forms. The model consists of a mixture of sub-models and represents dynamic characteristics by fuzzy transitions among those sub-models. The parameter estimation algorithm, which performs steepest gradient descent in cost functions defined with fuzzy constraints, is presented. Numerical experiments demonstrate the feasibility of the proposed method.

5.1 Introduction

One of the important subjects for modeling is dealing with knowledge, such as introduction of *a priori* knowledge into the model, or extraction of knowledge from the identified model. For dynamic systems, we must pay attention to the use of a knowledge representation scheme which can easily describe their dynamic characteristics. Generally, dynamic characteristics have been described by differential equations. However in the modeling with differential equations, designers have to define state variables and the class of equations with their heuristics. These heuristic techniques require advanced mathematical skills. Moreover, the identified differential equations are inappropriate for knowledge extraction.

This paper presents a new modeling scheme for dynamic systems which is rich in the knowledge representation of dynamic characteristics. The proposed method is derived by introduction of "fuzziness" into Symbolic Dynamic System(SDS)[1]. SDS is a symbolic model for discrete dynamic systems, which processes symbolic sequences. Symbolic sequences are appropriate for approximate description of dynamic characteristics. The extended SDS is able to model dynamic characteristics and appropriate for knowledge representation.

This paper starts in section 5.2 with a discussion what kind of knowledge representation is appropriate for dynamic characteristics by taking some examples. In the next section, SDS is extended to deal with "fuzzy" symbolic sequences. Section 5.4 explains the identification algorithm for the extended SDS. Section5.5 demonstrates numerical experiments to verify the proposed method. The last section discusses our proposed method and concludes the paper.

5.2 Knowledge Representation for Dynamic Characteristics

This section discusses what kind of knowledge representation is appropriate for dynamic characteristics by taking two examples. Those examples demonstrate that the knowledge representation in symbolic sequential forms can be the candidate. Then, Symbolic Dynamic System(SDS), a symbolic model for discrete dynamic systems, is introduced as a model of the mechanism for symbolic sequential knowledge.

5.2.1 Symbolic Sequential Knowledge

Dynamic characteristics are generally interpreted as the state transitions of dynamic systems. What is desired for the knowledge representation scheme for dynamic characteristics is an ability to describe the state transitions. In this study we propose to use a knowledge representation given by symbolic sequential forms for a rough description of the state transitions. The following two examples demonstrate its effectiveness:

(Example 1) Physical System -A Simple Pendulum-
    At first, consider an example of physical system: the behavior of a simple pendulum. As shown in Fig.5.1(a), let the displacement and the velocity are denoted by x and v, respectively. By granularizing x and v into **P**ositive and **N**egative as

$$(x, v) = (\{\mathbf{P},\mathbf{N}\}, \{\mathbf{P},\mathbf{N}\}),$$

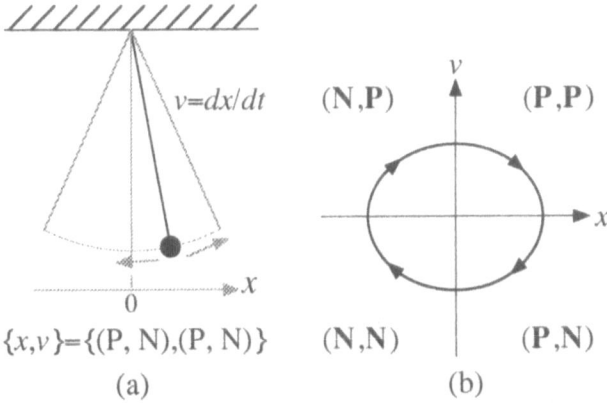

Fig. 5.1. Behavior of a pendulum(a) and state-space of the pendlum(b)

the behavior of the pendulum can be roughly described by a symbolic sequence such as

$$\cdots \to (\mathbf{P},\mathbf{P}) \to (\mathbf{P},\mathbf{N}) \to (\mathbf{N},\mathbf{N}) \to (\mathbf{N},\mathbf{P}) \to \cdots.$$

The behavior of the pendulum draws a locus in the 2-dimensional state-space as shown in Fig.5.1(b). Regarding the four quadrants of the state-space as subspaces labeled by $(\mathbf{P},\mathbf{P}),(\mathbf{N},\mathbf{P}),(\mathbf{N},\mathbf{N}),(\mathbf{P},\mathbf{N})$, respectively, the behavior of the pendulum is given by transitions among those subspaces.

(Example 2) Social System -Seasonal Adjustment Model-

Next, take an example of econometric models for social system: Seasonal Adjustment Model. This model accounts for time-series data by the mixture of trend component t_n for long-term variation, seasonal component s_n for periodic variation and observed noise w_n as

$$y_n = t_n + s_n + w_n. \tag{5.1}$$

Fig.5.2 shows an example of time-series data decomposed into those components.

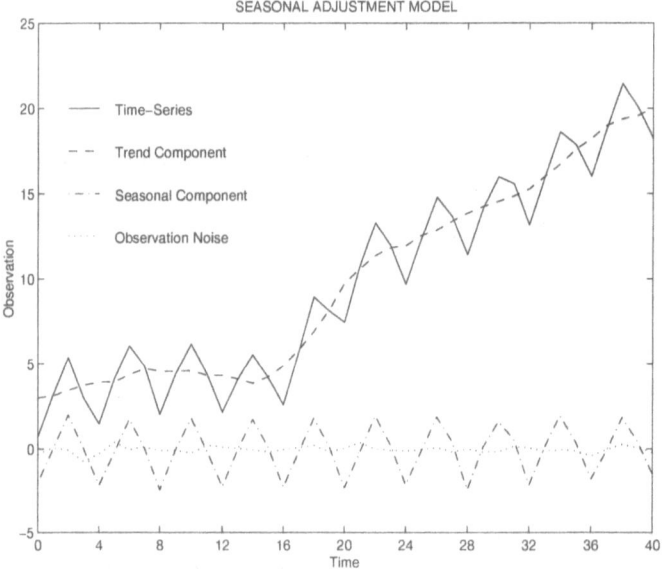

Fig. 5.2. An example of seasonal-adjustment-model

This example indicates significance of knowledge introduction. *A priori* knowledge is effective for the analysis of the identified model. In the example of Seasonal Adjustment Model, *a priori* knowledge such as long-term or periodic deviations, make it possible to analyze the trend and the seasonal components individually. By labeling four seasons as **Spring, Summer, Autumun, Winter**, respectively, a sequential knowledge $\cdots \to (\mathbf{Sp}) \to (\mathbf{Su}) \to (\mathbf{A}) \to (\mathbf{W}) \to \cdots$ is able to analyze the seasonal structure of the social systems.

These two examples demonstrate that the knowledge representation in the symbolic sequential forms can roughly describe dynamic characteristics.

5.2.2 Symbolic Dynamic System

In this subsection we introduce Symbolic Dynamic System(SDS) as a model of the mechanism for symbolic sequential knowledge.

SDS is defined by finite set of discrete states and transition rules among the states. Let the input vector, the output vector and the state at λ-th step are denoted by $v(\lambda)$, $\psi(\lambda)$ and $\xi(\lambda)$, respectively.

The behavior of SDS which has N discrete states $(\xi(\lambda) \in 1, 2, \cdots, N)$ is shown as

$$\xi(\lambda + 1) = \phi_{\xi(\lambda)}\{v(\lambda)\} \tag{5.2}$$

$$\psi(\lambda) = \gamma_{\xi(\lambda)}\{v(\lambda)\}, \tag{5.3}$$

where $\phi_{\xi(\lambda)}$ is a function which characterizes state transition rule at state $\xi(\lambda)$, $\gamma_{\xi(\lambda)}$ is a function which characterizes the output at state $\xi(\lambda)$. Fig. 5.3 shows an example of SDS. Given some kinds of sequential knowledge which describe the behavior of a dynamic system, a set $\boldsymbol{\Xi}$, whose members are combinations of the given symbols, would constitute an SDS that can represent all those symbolic sequential knowledge by its state transitions. SDS is a model of the mechanism for symbolic sequential knowledge of dynamic systems.

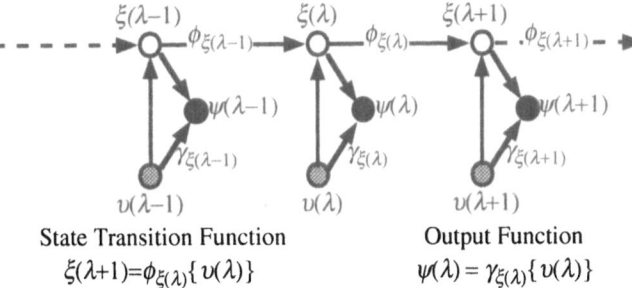

State Transition Function
$$\xi(\lambda+1) = \phi_{\xi(\lambda)}\{v(\lambda)\}$$

Output Function
$$\psi(\lambda) = \gamma_{\xi(\lambda)}\{v(\lambda)\}$$

Fig. 5.3. An example of sequential processing by symbolic dynamic system

5.3 Model for Fuzzy Symbolic Sequence

The guiding principle of fuzzy logic is in the idea that "knowledge is fuzzy". In this section, SDS is extended to deal with "fuzzy" sequential knowledge, which gives the characterization of a class of mathematical models.

5.3.1 SDS with Fuzzy States

To model "fuzzy" sequential knowledge, we consider fuzzy states [3] in SDS. It follows that the state of the system at time t is expressed by the grades of memberships $x_1(t)$, $x_2(t)$, $\cdots$, $x_N(t)$, each corresponds to the discrete state $\xi(1)$, $\xi(2)$, $\cdots$, $\xi(N)$, respectively. The extended SDS behaves as follows:

$$\Delta_t x(t) = \sum_{i=1}^{N} x_i(t) \, f_i\{u(t)\} \tag{5.4}$$

$$y(t) = \sum_{i=1}^{N} x_i(t) \, g_i\{u(t)\} \tag{5.5}$$

where $u(t)$, $y(t)$ denote the input and output vectors at time t respectively, and f_1, f_2, $\cdots$, f_N are functions which characterize the state transitions, g_1, g_2, $\cdots$, g_N are functions which characterize the outputs. Fig.5.4 illustrates the transformation from crisp to fuzzy granules in SDS. In the figure the discrete transitions such as $\xi(1) \to \xi(2) \to \xi(3)$ change into the fuzzy transitions such as $\tilde{\xi}(1) \to \tilde{\xi}(2) \to \tilde{\xi}(3)$. The architecture of SDS with fuzzy

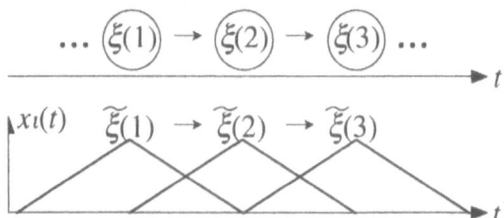

Fig. 5.4. Concept of fuzzification of discrete states of SDS

states are given as a mixture of each state transition function f_i and output function g_i weighted by the corresponding grade of membership $x_i(t)$ [4][5]. Fig.5.5 shows the block diagram of the model in the case of $N = 2$.

This fuzzification introduces a topological nature among discrete states. The membership vector $x(t) = \{\ x_1(t),\ x_2(t),\ \cdots,\ x_N(t)\ \}$ moves on the surface of convex polyhedron P, which is given by a set of extremal points $\{\ (1,0,\cdots,0),\ (0,1,\cdots,0),\ \cdots,\ (0,0,\cdots,1)\ \}$ in $[0,1]^N$ [1]. Then functions f_1,

---

[1] $x_1(t) + x_2(t) + \cdots + x_N(t) = 1$

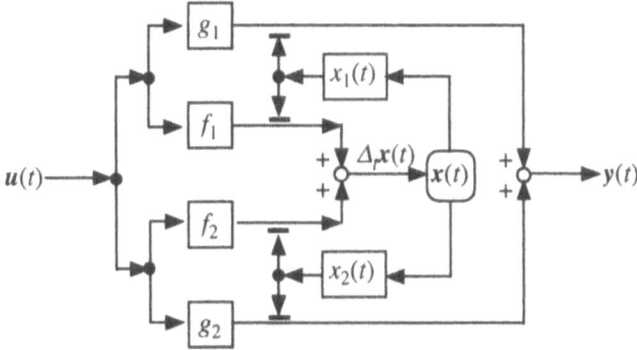

Fig. 5.5. Block diagram of SDS(N=2) with fuzzy states

$f_2, \cdots, f_N$ defines a vector field $\boldsymbol{P} \to \boldsymbol{P}$. Fig.5.6 illustrates an example of the dynamic characteristics of $x(t)$ on the convex polyhedron $\boldsymbol{P}$.

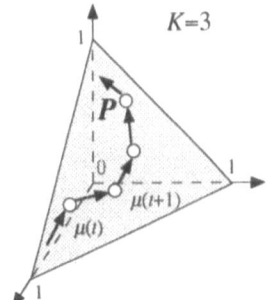

Fig. 5.6. An example of behavior of $x(t)$ on polyhedron P

5.3.2 Fuzzy Symbolic Sequence

SDS with fuzzy states brings symbolic sequential knowledge to an argument in the topological space: convex polyhedron $\boldsymbol{P}$. We consider a case where the symbolic sequential knowledge is given as $\boldsymbol{S} : \xi(1) \to \xi(2)$. It seems reasonable to suppose that if the sequential knowledge $\boldsymbol{S} : \xi(1) \to \xi(2)$ is unbiased, $\boldsymbol{S} : \xi(1) \to \xi(2)$ is expressed by the uniform linear motion on the line segment $\overline{\xi_1\xi_2}$ on the convex polyhedron $\boldsymbol{P}$ as shown in Fig.5.7(a). It is also reasonable to assume that "fuzzy" sequential knowledge $\boldsymbol{S}$ is given as the movement "like" that in Fig.5.7(b). $\boldsymbol{S}$ indicates the move "around" the line segment $\overline{\xi_1\xi_2}$ at "about" uniform speed.

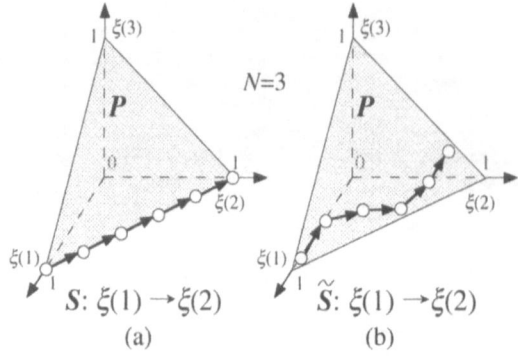

Fig. 5.7. Unbiased sequential knowledge(a) and fuzzy sequential knowledge(b)

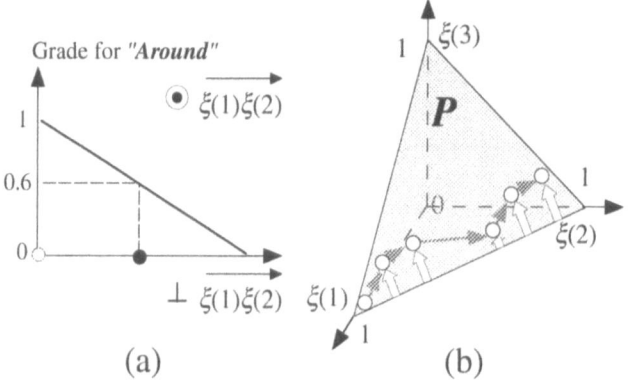

Fig. 5.8. Membership function for "around"

Next, let us define the fuzziness: "Around" and "About". Membership function μ_{Around} in Fig.5.8(a) quantifies the fuzziness: "Around" the line segment $\overline{\xi_1\xi_2}$ by its membership grade. μ_{Around} evaluates the perpendicular deviation from the line segment $\overline{\xi_1\xi_2}$ as shown by the white arrow in Fig.5.8(b). Membership function μ_{About} in Fig.5.9(a) quantifies the fuzziness: "About" uniform speed by its membership grade. μ_{About} evaluates the parallel deviation to the line segment $\overline{\xi_1\xi_2}$ as shown by the white arrow in Fig.5.8(b).

The above definition of membership functions μ_{Around} and μ_{About} make it possible to evaluate quantitatively and explicitly how much the sequential knowledge S is incorporated into the model. For example, if we want to introduce the unbiased sequential knowledge, the grades of these membership functions should be high. On the other hand, if we need a loose introduction of these knowledge, we can do it without taking care of these membership grades. In the parameter estimation process in the modeling, fuzzy constraints

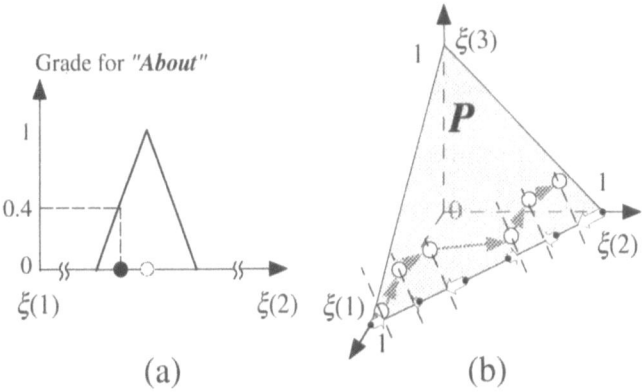

Fig. 5.9. Membership function for "about"

defined by these membership functions enable the quantitative handling of sequential knowledge. The fuzzification of SDS and fuzzy constraints give a characterization of a class of mathematical models.

5.4 Model Identification

This section starts with a formulation of modeling task. Then gives the parameter estimation algorithm which performs steepest gradient descent in appropriate cost functions.

5.4.1 Formulation of Modeling

The information given for the modeling are L sampled sequential data Z^{*1}, $Z^{*2}, \cdots, Z^{*L}$ and corresponding sequential knowledge $S^1, S^2, \cdots, S^L$. Z^{*l} consists of an input series $U^l = \{ u^l(1), u^l(2), \cdots, u^l(T(l)) \}$ and an output series $Y^{*l} = \{ y^{*l}(1), y^{*l}(2), \cdots, y^{*l}(T(l)) \}$. S^l is a sequential knowledge $\{ \xi^l(1), \xi^l(2), \cdots, \xi^l(\Lambda(l)) \}$.

Let us consider a set Ξ whose members are combinations of symbols in L sequential knowledge. An SDS whose discrete state is corresponding to each member of Ξ is able to represent all L kinds of sequential knowledge by its state transitions. To keep the following discussion simple, we will consider only one kind of sequences and omit the notation of l.

As mentioned in the previous section, the fuzzification of SDS and identification of the sets of functions $F = \{ f_1, f_2, \cdots, f_N \}$ and $G = \{ g_1, g_2, \cdots, g_N \}$ characterize a class of mathematical models: Fuzzy-SDS. Given the input series $U = \{ u_1, u_2, \cdots, u_T \}$, the sets of functions F and G calculate the state transition series $X = \{ x(1), x(2), \cdots, x(T) \}$ and the output series $Y = \{ y(1), y(2), \cdots, y(T) \}$. In this context, the modeling is formulated as the task to estimate parameters in F and G so that Y would approximate Y^* as good as possible on the condition that X follows the fuzzy constraints S [2]. In this algorithm, the sets of functions F, G must be differentiable with respect to every parameter of their own.

5.4.2 Parameter Estimation

To carry out the parameter estimation of the model formulated in the previous subsection, the following two cost functions

$$E_f(X,F) = \frac{1}{2} \sum_{t=1}^{T-1} \left| \Delta_t x(t) - \sum_{i=1}^{N} x_i(t) f_i(u_t) \right|^2 \tag{5.6}$$

$$+ \quad \alpha_{f1} \cdot \mu_{Around}(X)^{-1} + \alpha_{f2} \cdot \mu_{About}(X)^{-1}$$

$$E_g(X,G) = \frac{1}{2} \sum_{t=1}^{T} \left| y_t - \sum_{i=1}^{N} x_i(t) g_i(u_t) \right|^2 \tag{5.7}$$

$$+ \quad \alpha_{g1} \cdot \mu_{Around}(X)^{-1} + \alpha_{g2} \cdot \mu_{About}(X)^{-1}$$

must be minimized.

The first term in eqn. (5.6) evaluates that how the movement X should be on the convex polyhedron P and how F should be to realize the movement X. The second and third term in this equation denote the fuzzy constraints by the form of the reciprocal of membership functions $\mu_{Around}(X)$ and $\mu_{About}(X)$ given by

$$\mu_{Around}(X) = \sum_{t=1}^{T} |x(t) - x^{\perp}(t)|^{-2} \tag{5.8}$$

$$\mu_{About}(X) = \sum_{t=2}^{T-1} |x^{\perp}(t) - \frac{x^{\perp}(t-1) + x^{\perp}(t+1)}{2}|^{-2}, \tag{5.9}$$

respectively, where [3] $x^{\perp}(t)$ denotes the projection of $x(t)$ to the line segment $\xi(1)\xi(2)$ (in the case of $S : \xi(1) \rightarrow \xi(2)$) as shown by the next equation

$$x^{\perp}(t) = \frac{(e_2 - e_1)^T (x(t) - e_1)}{(e_2 - e_1)^T (e_2 - e_1)} (e_2 - e_1) + e_1 \tag{5.10}$$

---

[2] Note that the following parameter estimation algorithm presumes Markov process. It means that the error to be minimized in the algorithm is not given by $\sum_{t=1}^{T} |y(t) - y^*(t)|^2$. Given $x(t-1)$: the state of the system at time $t-1$, F calculates $\hat{x}(t)$: the estimate of the state at t. And G calculates $\hat{x}(t)$: the estimate of the output at t. The cost functions to be minimized in the algorithm is given by $\sum_{t=1}^{T} |\hat{y}(t) - y^*(t)|^2$

[3] Note that the ranges of these membership grades are not $[0,1]$. These are the reciprocal of the squared deviations defined in 5.3.2.

where e_1 and e_2 denote the extremal points of convex polyhedron P, each of which corresponds to $\xi(1)$ and $\xi(2)$, respectively. T indicates the transpose of vectors in eqn.(5.10).

The first term in eqn.(5.7) evaluates that how the movement X should be on the convex polyhedron P and how G should be to output the appropriate Y. The second and third terms are identical with those of eqn.(5.6).

$E_f(X, F)$ and $E_g(X, G)$ are functions of X and F, X and G, respectively. It requires that we should optimize X and the parameters of F and G simultaneously. Suppose that the optimal state transition $X^* = \{\ x^*(1),$ $x^*(2), \cdots, x^*(T)\ \}$ is already-known. Then the parameter estimation for F and G would be simplified. For the set of functions F, the error $E_f(X^*, F)$ given by eqn.(5.6) would be differentiable with respect to all the parameters in F, they could be updated with the steepest gradient decent method. Also for the set of functions G, the error $E_g(X^*, G)$ given by eqn. (5.7) would be differentiable with respect to all the parameters in G, they could also be updated.

However in reality, X^* is unknown. It must also be estimated. The next is to suppose that the sets of functions F and G are already optimized as F^* and G^*, respectively. In this case, the error given by eqn.(5.6) and (5.7) $E_f(X, F^*) + E_g(X, G^*)$ are differentiable with respect to $x(t)$ $(t = 1, 2, \cdots, T)$, we could update X by the steepest gradient descent method.

The above two assumptions imply that the iteration of update for the state transition X and the sets of functions F and G leads their parameters to one of the optima. This idea is derived from Expectation - Maximization (EM) algorithm [6][7]. Fig. 5.10 illustrates the basic concept of parameter estimation where state transition X and sets of functions F and G are updated alternately with fuzzy constraints S.

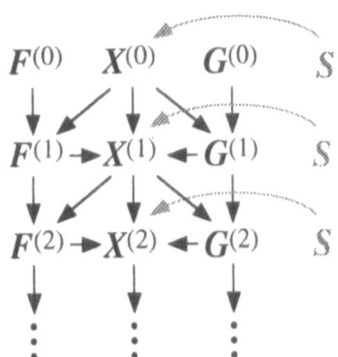

Fig. 5.10. Concept of parameter estimation

5.5 Numerical Experiment

This section describes the numerical experiment to verify the proposed method. 5.5.1 gives the information about the target system. 5.5.2 explains the analysis of the identified model. 5.5.3 describes the prediction experiment with the identified model.

5.5.1 Target System

We have assumed a function with two inputs and one output as the target system for this numerical experiment. Let the inputs and output at time t were denoted by $\{u_1(t), u_2(t)\} \in [0,1]^2$ and $y(t) \in [0,1]$, respectively. The target system was given by the equation:

$$y(t) = \Psi\{a_1(t)u_1(t) + a_2(t)u_2(t) - \frac{1}{2}(a_1(t) + a_2(t))\} \qquad (5.11)$$

where internal variables $\{a_1(t), a_2(t)\} \in [-1,1]^2$ were governed by the next differential equations:

$$\frac{da_1(t)}{dt} = \frac{2\pi}{T}(u_1(t) - \frac{1}{2})$$
$$\frac{da_2(t)}{dt} = \frac{2\pi}{T}(u_2(t) - \frac{1}{2}), \qquad (5.12)$$

which made the system be one of the dynamic systems. Ψ was the sigmoid function given by

$$\Psi(z) = \frac{1}{1 + \exp(-z)}, \qquad (5.13)$$

which made the target system nonlinear.

In the numerical experiment, four kinds of input series $U^1 \sim U^4$ ($L = 4$), corresponding output series $Y^{*1} \sim Y^{*4}$, and sequential knowledge $S^1 \sim S^4$: the outline of dynamic characteristics of the internal variables $\{a_1(t), a_2(t)\}$, were given in advance. $U^1 \sim U^4$ were expressed as

$$U^1 : \{u_1(t), u_2(t)\} = \{h(t) + \epsilon, h(t) + \epsilon\}$$
$$U^2 : \{u_1(t), u_2(t)\} = \{h(t) + \epsilon, -h(t) + \epsilon\}$$
$$U^3 : \{u_1(t), u_2(t)\} = \{-h(t) + \epsilon, h(t) + \epsilon\}$$
$$U^4 : \{u_1(t), u_2(t)\} = \{-h(t) + \epsilon, -h(t) + \epsilon\}.$$

with normalized cosine function $h(t)$ given by

$$h(t) = 0.5 \cos(\frac{2\pi}{T}t) + 0.5 \qquad (5.14)$$

and $\epsilon \sim N(0, 0.1)$. For example, Fig. 5.11 and 5.12 show an instance of the input series U^1. The output series Y^{*1} and the internal variables

$\{a_1(t), a_2(t)\}$ behaved as shown in Fig.5.13 and Fig.5.14, 5.15, respectively. In this experiment we assumed that the outline of dynamic characteristics of $\{a_1(t), a_2(t)\} \in [-1,1]^2$ were given by the sequential form with labels: **Positive**, **Zero** and **Negative**. The dynamic characteristics of both $a_1(t)$ and $a_2(t)$ were given as illustrated in Fig. 5.16, that was:

$$\boldsymbol{S^1} : \{\mathbf{Z,Z}\} \rightarrow \{\mathbf{P,P}\} \rightarrow \{\mathbf{Z,Z}\} \rightarrow \{\mathbf{N,N}\} \rightarrow \{\mathbf{Z,Z}\}$$

In the same way, $\boldsymbol{S^2} \sim \boldsymbol{S^4}$ were given by

$$\boldsymbol{S^2} : \{\mathbf{Z,Z}\} \rightarrow \{\mathbf{P,N}\} \rightarrow \{\mathbf{Z,Z}\} \rightarrow \{\mathbf{N,P}\} \rightarrow \{\mathbf{Z,Z}\}$$

$$\boldsymbol{S^3} : \{\mathbf{Z,Z}\} \rightarrow \{\mathbf{N,P}\} \rightarrow \{\mathbf{Z,Z}\} \rightarrow \{\mathbf{P,N}\} \rightarrow \{\mathbf{Z,Z}\}$$

$$\boldsymbol{S^4} : \{\mathbf{Z,Z}\} \rightarrow \{\mathbf{N,N}\} \rightarrow \{\mathbf{Z,Z}\} \rightarrow \{\mathbf{P,P}\} \rightarrow \{\mathbf{Z,Z}\}.$$

The number of symbols in $\boldsymbol{S^1} \sim \boldsymbol{S^4}$ was five($K = 5$), $\{\mathbf{Z,Z}\}$, $\{\mathbf{P,P}\}$, $\{\mathbf{P,N}\}$, $\{\mathbf{N,P}\}$ and $\{\mathbf{N,N}\}$. It defined the model architecture composed of 5 sub-models corresponding to these symbols. We have trained the model with $\boldsymbol{U^1} \sim \boldsymbol{U^4}$, $\boldsymbol{Y^{*1}} \sim \boldsymbol{Y^{*4}}$ and $\boldsymbol{S^1} \sim \boldsymbol{S^4}$ as explained in the previous section. In this experiment, we used 3 layered hierarchical neural networks for functions $\boldsymbol{f}_i$ and $\boldsymbol{g}_i$ $(i = 1, 2, \cdots, 5)$.

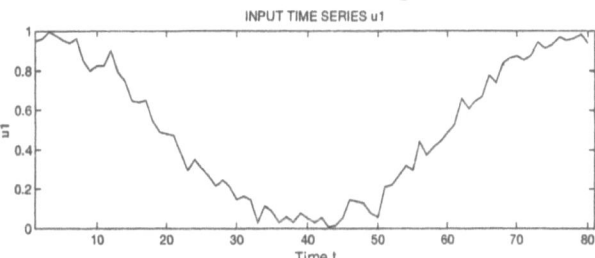

Fig. 5.11. Input series u_1

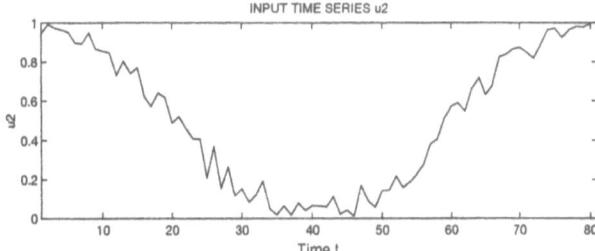

Fig. 5.12. Input series u_2

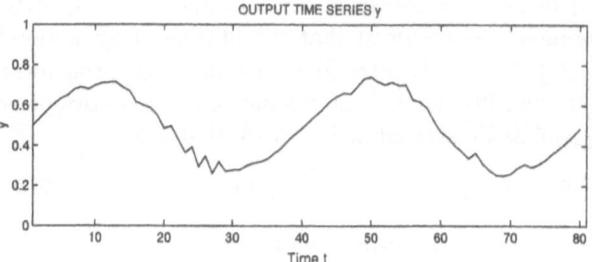

Fig. 5.13. Output series y

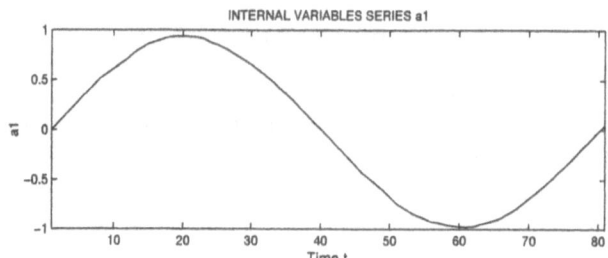

Fig. 5.14. Internal variable $a_1(t)$

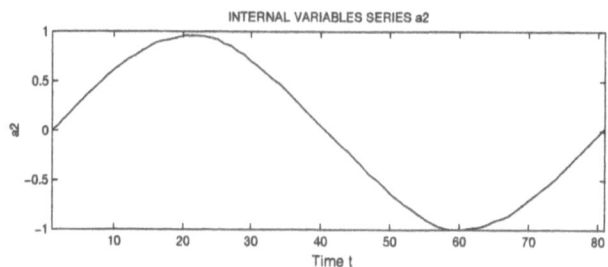

Fig. 5.15. Internal variable $a_2(t)$

5.5.2 Analysis of the Identified Model

This subsection explains the analysis of the identified model. Fig.5.17(a) represents the 2-dimensional state-space of the target system. The model is composed of five sub-models, each of which describes the corresponding fizzily divided subspace: {Z,Z}, {P,P}, {P,N}, {N,P} and {N,N}. Fig.5.18 shows the input-output characteristics obtained by output functions $g_{\{Z,Z\}} \sim g_{\{N,N\}}$. For example, in the case where the model followed the sequential knowledge S^1, the model performed by switching these output functions as

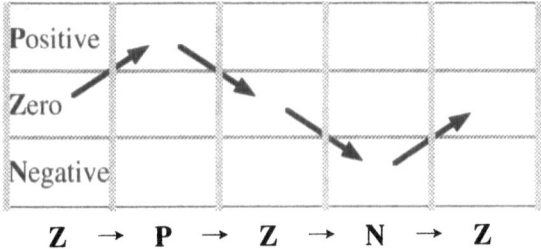

Fig. 5.16. Outline of dynamic characteristics

$$g_{\{Z,Z\}} \rightarrow g_{\{P,P\}} \rightarrow g_{\{Z,Z\}} \rightarrow g_{\{N,N\}} \rightarrow g_{\{Z,Z\}}.$$

Fig.5.19 shows the input-output characteristics obtained by the target system when $\{a_1(t), a_2(t)\}$ was fixed at the representative point of each subspace: $\{0,0\}$, $\{1,1\}$, $\{1,-1\}$, $\{-1,1\}$ $\{-1,-1\}$ as illustrated in Fig.5.17(b). With the comparison between Fig.5.18 and Fig.5.19, we can find the qualitative similarity in corresponding input-output characteristics. It demonstrates that each sub-model is identified to describe the corresponding subspace well.

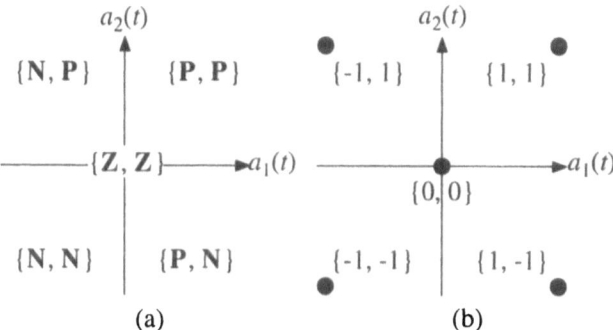

Fig. 5.17. State-space of object(a) and representative points in the state-space(b)

5.5.3 Prediction

This subsection reports the result of the prediction experiment with the identified model. In the class of dynamic systems which receive the input series [4], s-step ahead prediction is identical with spatial-temporal pattern transformation from $u(t+1)$, $u(t+2)$, $\cdots$, $u(t+s)$ to $y(t+1)$, $y(t+2)$,

---

[4] These systems were classified as non-autonomous dynamic systems

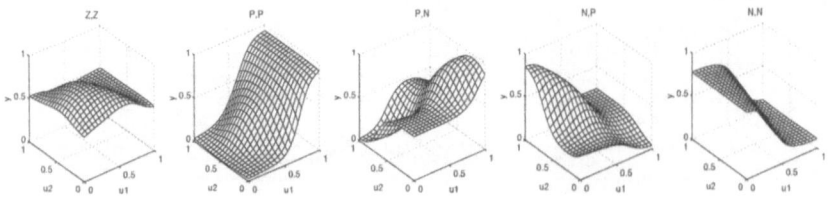

Fig. 5.18. I/O characteristics of output function in submodels

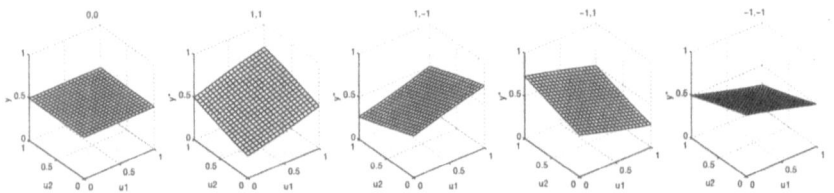

Fig. 5.19. I/O characteristics of object system at representative points

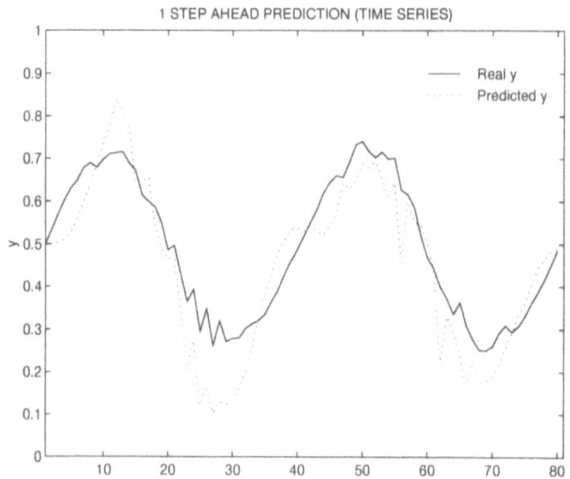

Fig. 5.20. Result of 1-step ahead prediction (time series)

$\cdots, y(t + s)$. Fig.5.20 indicates the real series Y^* and the predicted series Y given as an instance of the results in the case of $s = 1$, that is 1-step ahead prediction. Fig.5.21 specifies the correlation between Y^* and Y in the above instance, where the horizontal and vertical axes denote the distribution of Y^* and Y, respectively, which evaluates the prediction results with how close the distribution is to the straight line in the figure.

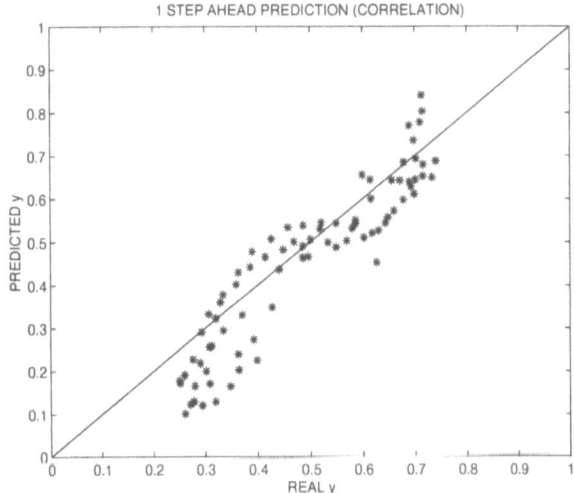

Fig. 5.21. Result of 1-step ahead prediction (correlation)

In the assumption that $x(t)$: the state of the target system at time t is already known, we tried the cases where $s = 1, 2, 3, 4, 5, 10, 15$ and 20. The results are presented in Table.5.1, the value in the table denotes the improved rate of prediction performance: (RMSE [5] before parameter estimations)/(RMSE after parameter estimations). As you find in Tab.5.1, we could get the better improved rates in the case of the smaller s in comparison with those in the case of the larger s. The reason for that would be in the assumption of Markov process in the parameter estimation algorithm.

Table 5.1. Improved rate: (RMSE befor learning)/(RMSE after learning)

s	Improved Rate	s	Improved Rate
1	4.90	2	3.20
3	2.59	4	2.30
5	2.13	10	1.56
15	1.29	20	1.19

5.6 Conclusion

This paper presented a fuzzy modeling method for dynamic systems. We confined our attention to the knowledge representation for dynamic systems that

---

[5] RMSE is the abbreviation of Root Mean Squared Error.

requires the description for dynamic characteristics of the system. In our proposed method we used sequential knowledge as the knowledge representation form and introduced Symbolic Dynamic System(SDS) as the mechanism to generate the sequential knowledge. SDS was extended to deal with the "fuzziness" included in the sequential knowledge, which characterized the class of mathematical models. Parameter estimation which performs steepest gradient descent in the defined class was also presented. The proposed model consisted of sub-models each of which described the dynamic characteristics and the input/output characteristics for corresponding fuzzily divided subspace in the state-space. Knowledge introduction into the model and extraction from the model were easy for its architecture derived by the fuzzification of symbolic model.

References

1. Metropolis, N. and Stein, M. and Stein, P, "On finite limit sets for transformations on the unit interval", *Journal of Combinatorial Theory*, vol.15, pp.25-44,1973
2. T.Takagi and M.Sugeno, "Fuzzy Identification of Systems and Its Applications to Modeling and Control", *IEEE Trans. on SMC*, vol.15, num.1, pp.116-132,1985
3. R. Kruse and R. Buck-Emden and R. Cordes, "Processor Power Considerations -An Application of Fuzzy Markov Chains ", *Fuzzy Sets and Systems*, vol.21, num.3, pp.289-299,1987
4. T.W.Cacciatore and S.J.Nowlan, "Mixtures of controllers for jump linear and nonlinear plants", *Advances in Neural Information Processing Systems*, vol.6, pp.719-726,1994
5. Y. Bengio and P. Frasconi, "Input-Output HMM's for Sequence Processing", *IEEE Trans. on Neural Networks*, vol.7, num.5, pp.1231-1249,1996
6. A. P. Dempster and N. M. Laird and D. B. Rubin, "Maximum likelihood from incomplete data via the EM algorithm", *Journal of the Royal Statistical Society series B* vol.39, pp.1-38,1977
7. G. E. Hinton and T. J. Sejnowski, "Learning and relearning in Boltzmann machines", in D. E. Rumelhart and J. L. Mclelland, editors, *Parallel Distributed Processing, MIT Press, Cambridge, MA*, 1986

Hybrid Machine Learning Tools: INSS - A Neuro-Symbolic System for Constructive Machine Learning

Fernando Osório[1], Bernard Amy[2], and Adelmo Cechin[1]

[1] UNISINOS - Computer Science Dept.
Av. Unisinos, 950 - CP 275 - CEP 93022-000
São Leopoldo - RS - BRAZIL
Web : http://www.inf.unisinos.tche.br/
E-mail: {osorio,cechin}@exatas.unisinos.tche.br

[2] Laboratoire LEIBNIZ - IMAG - INPG
46, avenue Felix Viallet 38031
Grenoble Cedex 1 - FRANCE
Web : http://www-leibniz.imag.fr/RESEAUX/
E-mail : amy@imag.fr

Abstract: In this paper we present the INSS system, a new hybrid approach based upon the principles of KBANN networks. It represents an important improvement in comparison with its predecessor because the learning and the knowledge extraction process are faster and are accomplished in an incremental way . INSS offers a new approach applicable to constructive machine learning with high-performance tools, even in the presence of incomplete or erroneous data. *Keywords:* Constructive machine learning, hybrid neuro-symbolic systems, Cascade-Correlation, Neural Networks, rule insertion, rule extraction.

6.1 Introduction

Various Artificial Intelligence methods have been developed to reproduce intelligent human behavior. These methods allow to reproduce some human reasoning process using the available knowledge. Each method has its advantages, but also some drawbacks. Hybrid systems combine different approaches in order to take advantage of their respective strengths. These hybrid intelligent systems also present the ability to acquire new knowledge form different sources and so to improve their application performance.

The main argument, and the most used one, to justify the study and the application of hybrid symboli-connectionist systems is the complementarity of symbolic AI methods and sub-symbolic connectionist methods (Artificial Neural Networks - ANN).

Such a justification is a very general one. And it remains to be more precise about the real contribution of the hybrid approach. What exactly provides the combination of neural networks and knowledge based systems? Researchers claim that hybrid systems take advantage of their respective component strengths. Is it a real property of the existing hybrid neuro-symbolic systems? And what are these advantages?

To validate an hybrid system, one have to answer these questions, and to describe what really can be done with this system which was hardly done with just one of its components. Particularly the system has to be given proof of the following properties:

- Possibility to use and to take into account several kinds of knowledge representation, like empirical data and expert knowledge (examples, production rules and fuzzy rules).
- Best efficiency of the global system when compared to each of its components.
- Strong coupling between the components, leading to an exchange of knowledge between all of these components. This knowledge has to be proved consistent and useful. The best way for implementing such a coupling is to choose the integration mode called co-processing [17, 23], in which the different components of the hybrid system work on the same level and exchange information between both themselves and their environment.
- Possibility of global learning. The whole system is able to adapt its various sets of knowledge to the variations of the data domain. This tuning can be done following two ways : either learning (or forgetting) new examples, or modifying the architecture of the neural component.

In this paper we describe a system, called INSS (Incremental Neuro-Symbolic System [24, 25]), endowed with these properties. In section 2 we explain the origin of our system and the reasons of our choices. Section 3 describes INNS system. Then, in section 4, to validate the system, we present some practical results allowing to show that INSS has the sought properties. Section 5 presents the application of INSS in a medical domain.

6.2 The Co-processing Integration Mode

In the classification task domain, the hybrid neuro-symbolic systems, such as SYNHESYS [15] and KBANN [35], exploit their capacity to use at the same time theoretical knowledge (set of symbolic rules) and empirical knowledge (set of observed examples). These two systems are significant examples of the coprocessing integration mode in hybrid systems, allowing a bi-directional knowledge transfer between the symbolic and connectionist modules. Figure 6.1 shows the general architecture of this kind of systems.

We chose to base our study on the KBANN model, a well-known hybrid neuro-symbolic system that represents, among others, the state-of-the-art in this domain. This system is able to compile a knowledge base into the form of an ANN. Then, it learns from an example data set, and after that it extracts new rules. This approach allows a refinement of initial knowledge, as we can see in Figure 6.2. Such a system constructs robust networks: the insertion of a priori theoretical knowledge leads to quicker learning; we can use small data sets during the learning phase; all available knowledge about

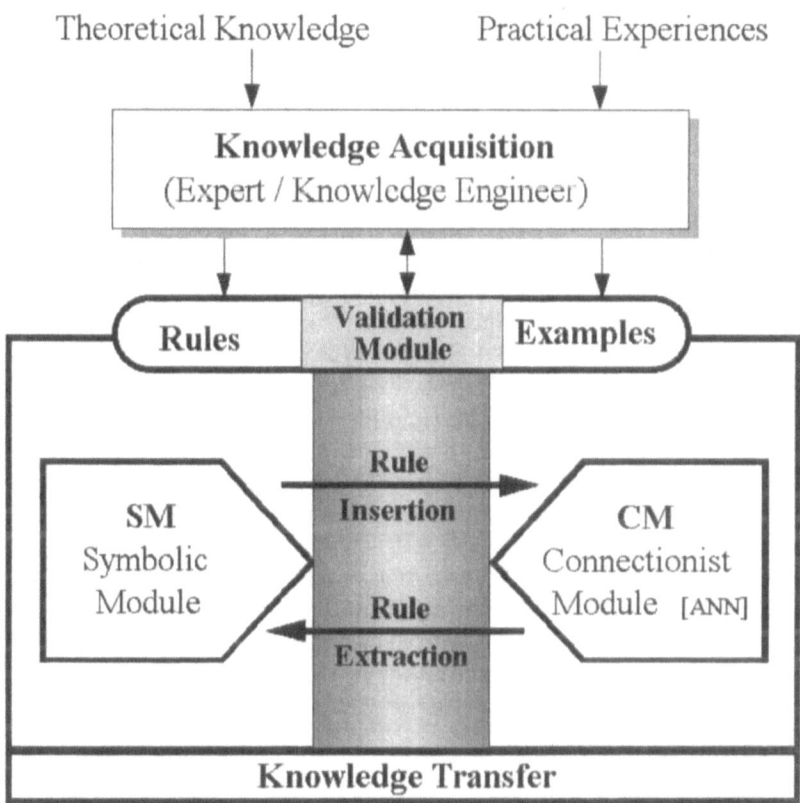

Fig. 6.1. Hybrid neuro-symbolic systems and knowledge transfer

124

the problem (whether theoretical or empirical) is used; and thus the system is more adapted to process incomplete and/or erroneous data.

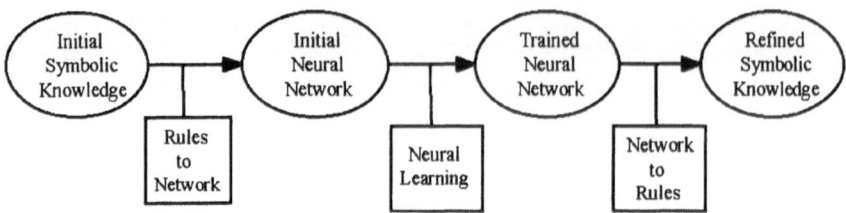

Fig. 6.2. Knowledge refinement using KBANN

However, the KBANN system has some important limitations due to the choice of its ANN model and learning method, the Back-Propagation algorithm [28]:

1. KBANN networks are based on static networks, so it is difficult to change or to add new knowledge. A simple change in old knowledge requires a retraining of the whole network. Furthermore, if new knowledge is dicovered that turns invalid the old knowledge, it is difficult to correct it;

2. due to the use of the Back-Propagation algorithm, the learning is slow. Back-Propagation as a first order (first derivative) successive approximation algorithm brings with him performance problems (for example, the "flat spot" problem) that can be solved by better training algorithms and strategies like QuickProp, Cascor, RProp, Scaled Conjugate Gradient ALgorithm, etc. [29];

3. in the KBANN since the rule extraction process must consider the whole network after the rule insertion and training, all the rules must be extracted. That is, a fully new knowledge base is created, which may include the old rules or not. The interpretation of this new knowledge base by a human becomes then a time consuming task, since he has to throw away all the previous analysis.

It is the reason why we developed the new system called INSS to improve KBANN networks and to overcome its main limitations. This new system also authorises insertion, refinement and rule extraction, but, unlike the KBANN system, each process performs incrementally. Moreover, instead of using the Back-Propagation algorithm, based on static networks, INSS uses the Cascade-Correlation learning method [14] which proceeds by adding new units (neurons) during learning. Our approach allows to obtain a constructive network that is able to develop its structure and its knowledge, while keeping unchanged the principal properties of a hybrid neuro-symbolic system. The main feature, that constitutes the originality of our system, is that we are able to perform an incremental rule extraction [11]. The rule extraction process may analyze only the new added units and occurs as new knowledge is acquired. This way, the old knowledge remains intact and is progressively incremented by the new one. Furthermore, the user is able to determine the degree of exactness or of generality of the extracted rules. Less rules give him a overview of the data being modelled but with little exactness. As more rules are extracted from a more refined network, more details can be added to the old ones. We do not know any other neuro-symbolic system able to extract rules in a such incremental way.

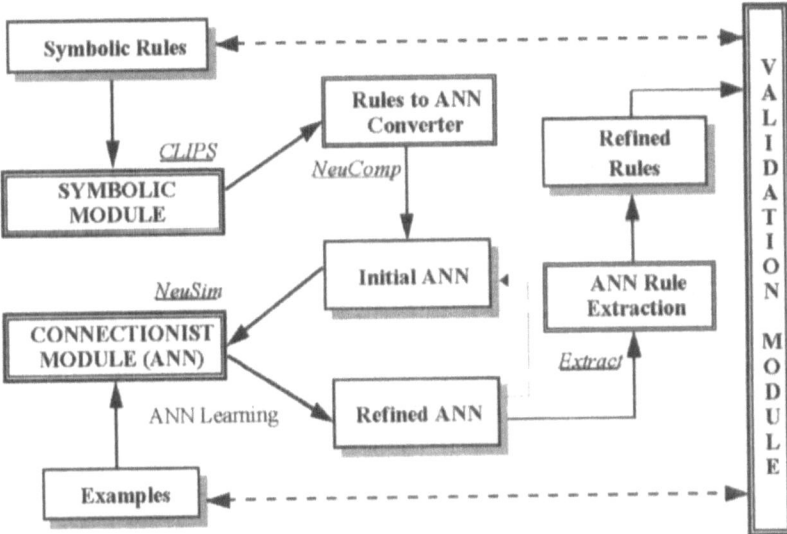

Fig. 6.3. INSS System: Constructive knowledge refinement

6.3 The INSS System

The *INSS system* is composed of five modules: *Symbolic-Module* (Symbolic Inference Engine), *NeuComp* (Construction of a network from rules), *NeuSim* (ANN learning and recall), *Extract* (Rule extraction), and *Valid* (Validation of acquired knowledge, by means of study of relations between rules and examples). The INSS system components are represented in Figure 6.3.

Our system uses the CLIPS language (*C Language Integrated Production System*) [16], developed by the STB-NASA, as its symbolic module. Our system also provides facilities to transfer rules and examples to/from the specific syntax used in this language and the syntax used in our tools (Neu-Comp/NeuSim/Extract). The NeuSim module can be also used as a forward-chaining inference engine once the symbolic rules have been transferred to the connectionist module.

126

6.3.1 Rule Insertion

The NeuComp module can process elementary production rules (simple propositions) which we called "rules of order 0". These rules are equivalent to IF/THEN forms such as:

```
IF <Condition>(TRUE/FALSE) AND/OR
   <Condition> (TRUE/FALSE)...
THEN <Conclusion>
```

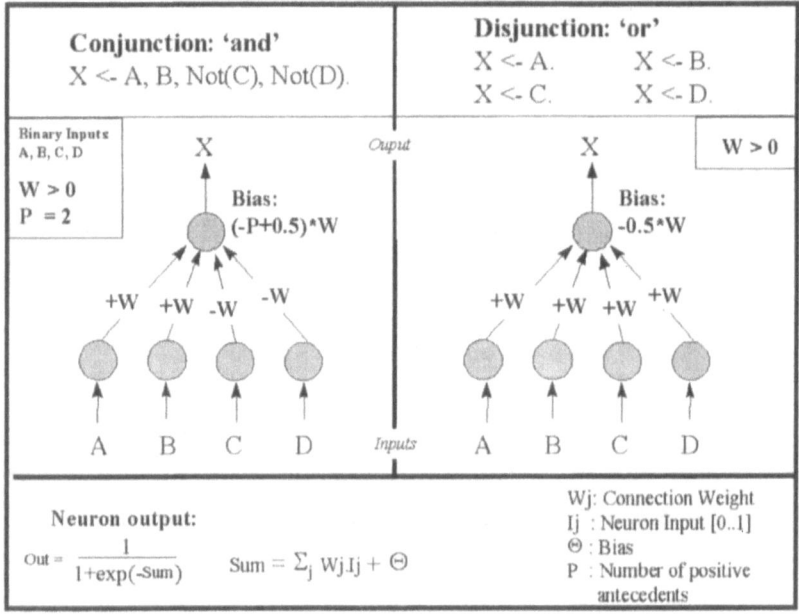

Fig. 6.4. Rules to network translation ("rule insertion")

The rule compilation follows the method described by Towell [35, 37]. The result of the translation is a network composed of a set of units linked by weighted connections (see Figure 6.4). The activation of this network, before learning, leads exactly to the same results (outputs) as those obtained with the set of rules.

We also extended the rules used by KBANN to "high level rules" [26, 27]: production rules of order 0+, which are rules including value intervals. As application problems, where this type of rules were used, we cite:

– Robotic applications. Ex.: an autonomous robot using left and right sensors can be controlled by rules of the form: "if the left sensor signal is higher than the right one, then it is closer to the left wall". Using only boolean operators or boolean logic rules does not allow such a conclusion.

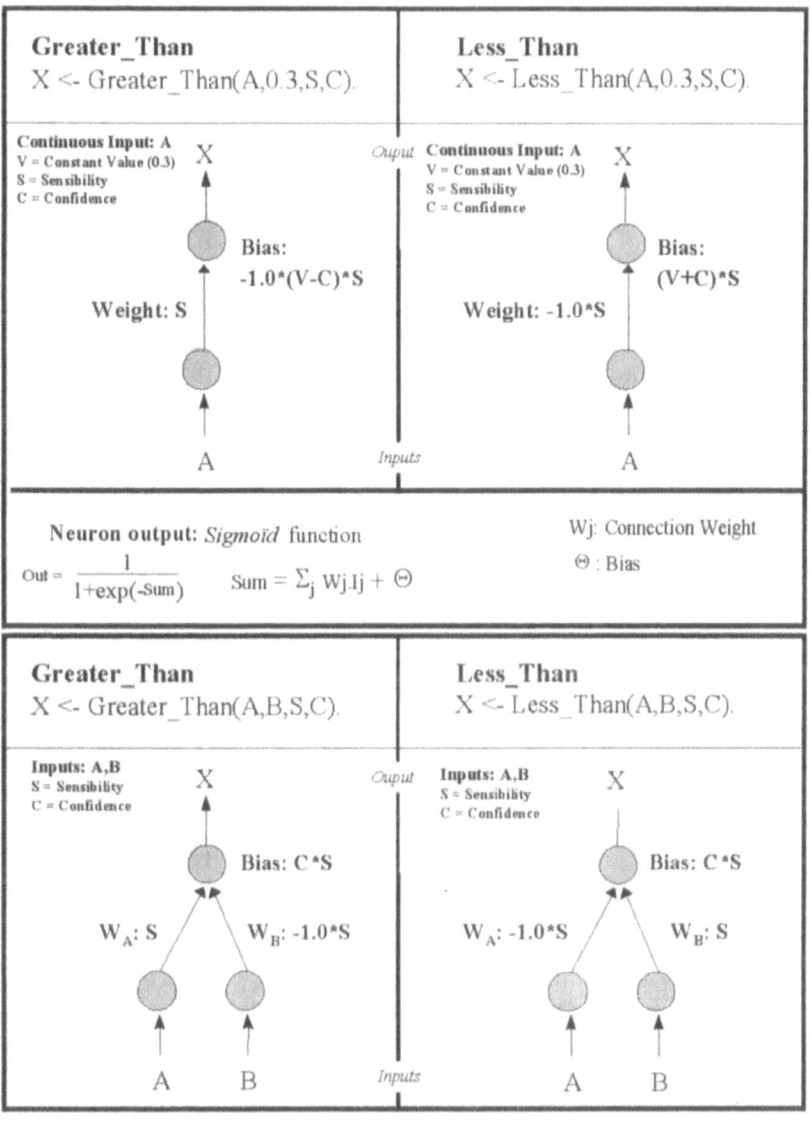

Fig. 6.5. Compiling rules of 0+ order

– Medicine. Ex.: an alarm equipment in a hospital can indicate the state of a patient through rules of the form: "if the temperature is higher than 37 degrees or lower than 35 degrees, then please call the nurse".

The introduction of this kind of rules was necessary to express and to introduce the existent knowledge (expert knowledge) to NeuComp in projects conducted by the authors of the paper.

We implemented the usage of comparison functions of the following type:

```
<Operator>(<Feature>, <Value>)      or
<Operator>(<Feature>, <Feature>),
where <Operator> is GreaterThan, LessThan or Equal.
```

Resulting in rules of this kind:

```
IF GreaterThan(Sensor_S1, 1.0) AND
   LessThan(Sensor_S1, Sensor_S2)
THEN Conclusion_C1
```

These rules can be compiled into an ANN composed by simple Perceptron like units (we create feed-forward multi-layer networks with sigmoïd based units). A detailed description of all compilation processes, used within INSS, can be found in [25], and we show a brief description of the compilation process in Figure 6.5. We added two new parameters to our symbolic rules that allow us to specify the "sensibility" (slope of the output curve) and the "confidence" (displacement of the output curve related to the specified activation threshold). So, with these two parameters we are able to compile rules like: less than or equal to X, greater than or equal to X, less than and not equal to X, in range (including or excluding limit values), etc. The "sensibility" parameter acts like the "W" value used with KBANN nets [35].

We show in Figure 6.6 examples of the neurons output. These neurons were obtained using our compilation process of 0+ order rules. We can observe rules that compare one input value with one constant value (Greater_than [Feature, ConstValue]), and rules that compare one input value with another input value (Greater_than [Feature, Feature]).

As the symbolic rules allow to establish some initial knowledge and then give an initial structure to the network, this approach solves two important problems related to Artificial Neural Networks: on one hand this simplifies the choice of the number and distribution of units, on the other hand we obtain a good assignment of initial values to the connection weights.

6.3.2 Learning

The use of the Cascade-Correlation learning algorithm instead of Back-Propagation, in the NeuSim module, allows a quicker learning [14, 29], with higher performance results [29, 34]. Figure 6.7 shows an example of the network

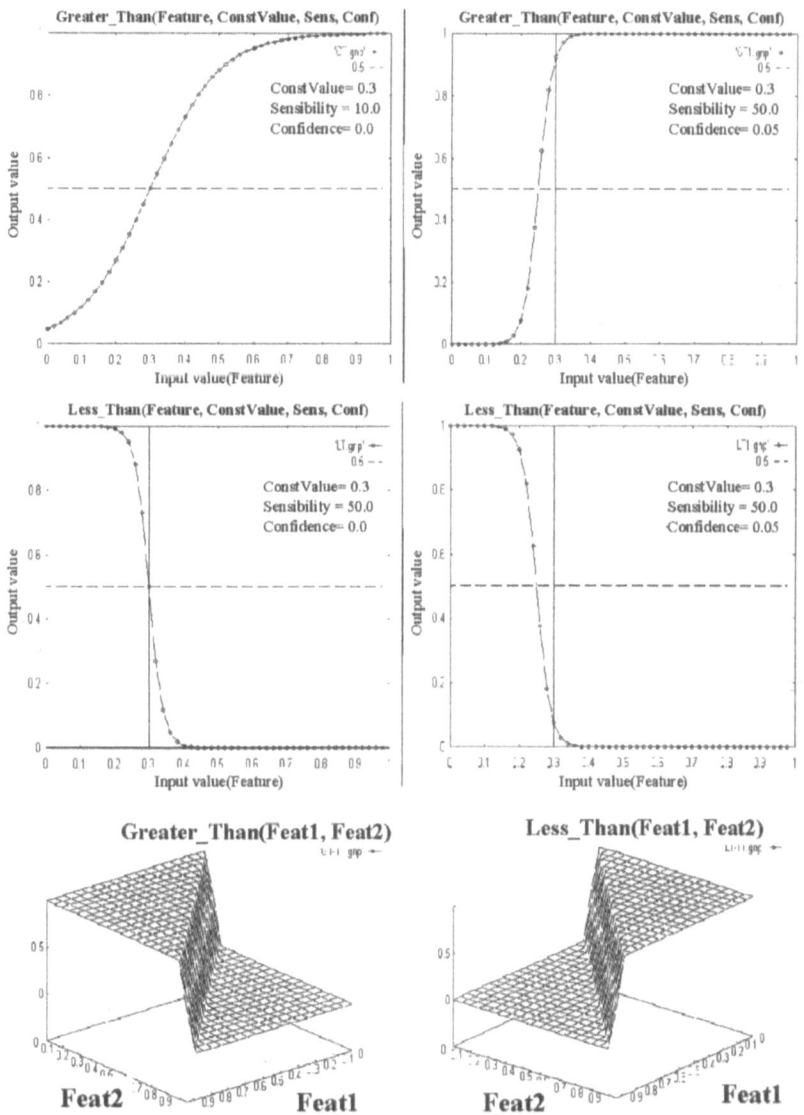

Fig. 6.6. Compiled neurons output - GreaterThan, LessThan

130

structure evolution when we apply the Cascade-Correlation learning algorithm. It allows especially constructive learning where the initial knowledge is not mixed with the new acquired knowledge. New units are added to the initial network structure in order to correct or complete the initial knowledge.

The importance of such a choice of the learning method is reinforced by studies [30, 31] showing that Cascade-Correlation networks can be used to model some aspects of human cognitive development.

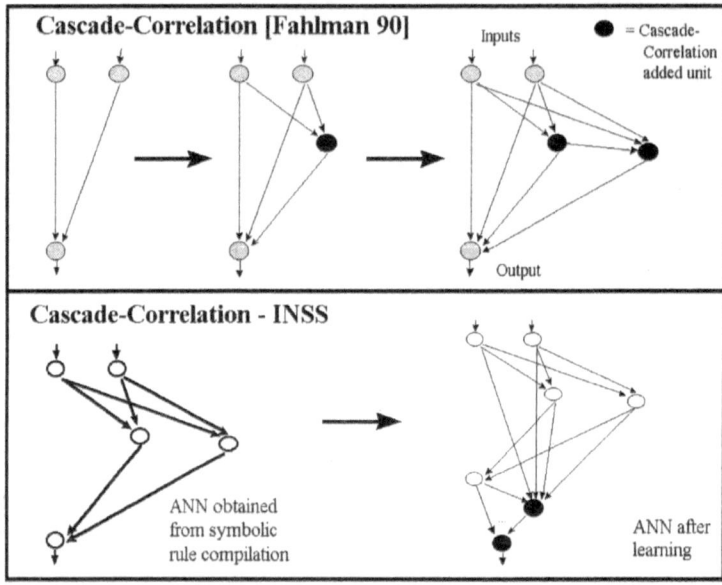

Fig. 6.7. ANN structure evolution using Cascade-Correlation

The Cascade-Correlation algorithm developed by Fahlman and Lebiere [14], in contrast to static neural learning algorithms such as Back-Propagation [28], is a generative technique to network construction and learning. Instead of merely adjusting weights in a network of fixed topology, Cascade-Correlation starts with a minimal network of input and output units. During learning, it may add hidden units one at a time, installing each on a separate layer. This is done in the following way: if the net is not reducing error fast enough with its current topology, it will select and install a new hidden unit whose output activations correlate best over all training cases with the existing network error. Once one new unit is installed in the network its weights are frozen, and this unit keeps unchanged its learned weights. So, Cascade-Correlation will reduce step-by-step the network output error by a cyclic process of output units learning and hidden unit addition/learning. In essence, Cascade-Correlation searches not only in weight space but also in the space of network topologies.

Learning in a network by adding new units allows to complete, to change, or to refine the initial knowledge. In INSS, using the Extract module, one can be able to analyse only the new added units and the modified output units. The old units always keep their function and their meaning in comparison with the initial rules introduced into the network. As we can preserve unchanged the initial knowledge acquired, this technique makes the main difference of our system in comparison with the KBANN system [11, 12, 25].

6.3.3 Rule Extraction

The Extract module [11, 12] implements an improved version of the SUBSET algorithm [2, 35, 36] of rule extraction from neural networks. This algorithm was improved in two ways. First, the extraction process is a lot simpler and quicker since we look only at a small part of the network. We do not need to extract all network knowledge, but just the new acquired knowledge. Second, we developed heuristic methods for network simplification (remove less significant units and links), used before extraction. The use of a simplified network helps us to reduce the complexity of the extraction procedure.

We included in our system the use of expert and fuzzy rules, since a) the inputs of a neural network can be interpreted as the state of the system; b) the mapping performed by the network of the system state to an output can be interpreted as the inference mechanism performed by production systems; c) the output of the network can be interpreted as the action to be taken on the system.

The use of fuzzy rules in this context is mainly due to:

- for some kinds of neural networks (RBF networks), there is a proof of equivalence between the neural network and fuzzy inference systems ([19];
- the smooth continuous mapping implemented by some feedforward neural networks (like MLP) can be easily represented by fuzzy rules;
- *counterpropagation networks* use proximity concepts, which are very similar to membership functions of the fuzzy techniques.

The main disadvantage in the use of fuzzy rules is that one rule interferes with the others making the rules less modular. This disadvantage is partly suppressed by the use of mutually exclusive rules.

Unfortunately most of the extraction algorithms work only with a dedicated structure, where the network has special neurons with special activation functions connected in a special way. The result is a mirroring of the fuzzy algorithm in form of a network. There are fuzzyfication neurons, inference neurons and defuzzyfication neurons. A simple look at the network reveals the fuzzyfication, inference and defuzzyfication methods of the corresponding fuzzy inference system. So we should limit ourselves to work only with MLP networks.

Two problems arise when studying the diverse architectures and working with transparent networks (networks offering the possibility to extract knowledge in the form of rules):

1. How to obtain an initial input space partition to be expressed in form of fuzzy sets (see figure 6.8): there are 4 methods to partition the input space: grid partition, tree partition, scatter partition [18] and linear partition. These fuzzy sets are used then to form the rules. The grid partition is commonly used: divide each input variable range in 3 fuzzy sets with linguistic values *low*, *medium* and *high* and then combine them with the intersection (see figure 6.8(a)). The disadvantage of the grid partition is that the number of fuzzy sets increases exponentially with the number of input variables. The number of fuzzy sets is important because this number corresponds to the number of rules, which is the most important index about the comprehensibility of a fuzzy inference system. The tree and scatter partitions increase the comprehensibility of rules, but have the disadvantage that, depending on the application and on the distribution of the data, many of them may be required to cover the training set. For example, when the data is distributed diagonally to the input variables, or when there are dependencies among the input variables. The scatter partition has the disadvantage that the partitions are not mutually exclusive. The linear partition has the advantage that it produces the smallest number of rules but the membership functions are more difficult to comprehend.

2. How to tune or to train the fuzzy inference system: the rules alone are not enough to implement a good mapping from the inputs to the outputs. A training with data is necessary to adapt the parameters of the rules.

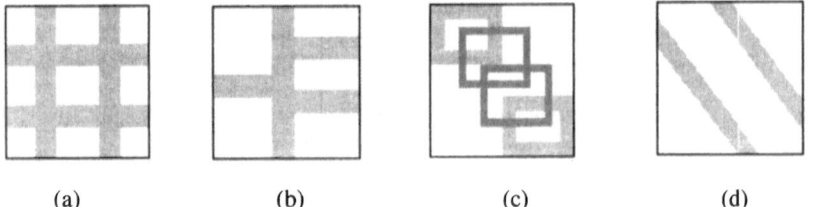

(a)   (b)   (c)   (d)

Fig. 6.8. Various methods for partitioning the input space: grid partition (a); tree partition (b); scatter partition (c); linear partition (d).

These two problems are very similar to the problems of determining the number of hidden units in a sigmoid neural network and determining the structure of the network.

Therefore, the most common strategies to solve the problems above were identified and listed below.

1. The use of special structures representing the structure of the fuzzy inference system: this facilitates the introduction of fuzzy rules in the network and the solution of the problem of the input partition. At the same time, this facilitates the extraction of the rules.
2. The use of special units representing the elementary operations of a fuzzy inference systems: min, max, multiplication, division.
3. The use of gradient descent algorithms to solve the problem of parameter tuning: most algorithms are a modification of Backpropagation adapted to the new units and architectures. The problem with such a generalization in the use of gradient descent algorithms is that some care must be taken with units whose nonlinear function has a zero derivative somewhere or units, whose effect on the learning is to adapt the wrong parameters of the network.
4. The use of a partition aligned to the input variable axis and mutually exclusive (see figure 6.8(a) and (b)).
5. The use of a partition defined by the user: this is considered by many authors as an advantage, since knowledge about the problem can be introduced into the network.
6. The computation of all combinations of the linguistic values of the input variables in the premises: this simplifies the algorithm but increases the number of rules generated.
7. The use of reinforcement learning or stochastic search to solve the control problem. Both methods require the possibility to experiment with the process or with some model of the process. The stochastic search requires also an objective function to be minimized.

Furthermore the different rule extraction systems generate two types of fuzzy rules: Mamdani or Sugeno fuzzy rules.

A **Mamdani Fuzzy Inference System** with two inputs x_1 and x_2 and one output y contains a set of Mamdani Rules with the form [20]:

$$\text{IF } x_1 \in F_1 \text{ AND } x_2 \in F_2 \text{ THEN } y = F \qquad (6.1)$$

where F_1, F_2 and F are fuzzy sets. Their membership functions μ_{F_1}, μ_{F_2} and μ_F have normally the form of triangles ($\mu_{F_1}(x_1) = 1 - \min(k_1|x_1 - k_2|, 1)$), where k_1 defines the steepness and k_2 is the center of the triangle. The membership functions of a fuzzy inference system constructed with Mamdani rules should cover the input space, at least the points which can occur in practice. The fuzzy logic operation AND is implemented with the min operator, the rule of inference is computed using the min operator and the composition is computed with the max operator.

The final result is a fuzzy set. A real value must still be computed from the membership function using some defuzzyfication method.

A **Sugeno Fuzzy Inference System** with input variables $x_1, \cdots, x_n$ and output variable y contains a system of Sugeno rules with the form [33]:

$$\text{IF } f(x_1 \text{ is } F_1, \cdots, x_i \text{ is } F_i, \cdots, x_n \text{ is } F_n) \text{ THEN } y = g(x_1, ..., x_n) \qquad (6.2)$$

where $F_1, \cdots, F_n$ are fuzzy sets representing the region of the input space where the rule is valid, f is the fuzzy logic operation (AND, OR) that connects the propositions $(x_i \text{ is } F_i)$ in the premise and g is the function which computes the value of y when $x_1, \cdots, x_n$ satisfies the premise.

The two main advantages of the Sugeno rules in relation to the Mamdani ones are: first to solve the problem of the need of too many implications to cover the whole input space and second to simplify the computation effort of the defuzzyfication process. If the input has many components, then the space is too large to be covered by the rules. The functional relations in the consequence part between inputs and outputs make an additional dependence between the two spaces. This turns the premises valid in a larger set and then the number of implications needed is reduced. Second, the defuzzyfication includes normally the computation of some integrals. This is a laborious computation which takes a lot of time and can be a problem in real-time applications.

Although the function g was generically defined, Takagi and Sugeno report only the use of a linear function $g(x_1, ..., x_n) = k_0 + k_1 x_1 + \cdots + k_i x_i + \cdots + k_n x_n$ where k_i are constants.

Based on the last analysis of different fuzzy inference systems, we present now the idea for the extraction of fuzzy rules from a neural network of the type MLP. Consider the network with the structure as in figure 6.9 (left). This figure shows that the threshold unit separates the input space into two mutually exclusive regions. Each region is described by two pieces of information: where it is located (its region) and the corresponding mapping equation performed by the network. Its region can be expressed in form of an inequality: $a_3 > 0$ for the grey region and $a_3 \leq 0$ for the white region, where a_3 is the activation of the unit 3.

Consider now the network in figure 6.9 (right) with shortcut connections, *sigmoid* units instead of *threshold* units and *add* unit at the network output. Since the sigmoid function is continuous there is no sharp limit separating the white from the grey region as in figure 6.9 (left). In this case, the relations $a_3 > 0$ and $a_3 \leq 0$ must be generalized to a fuzzy relation with defining membership functions μ_1 and μ_2.

Now, associated with each region there is a membership function (for example, $\mu_1(x_1, x_2)$) and a linear equation (for example, $y = x_1 w_{51} + x_2 w_{52} + (w_{50} + w_{54})$) expressing a dependance of the network output on the network inputs in this region. The computation of the output of the network can be performed multiplying (implementation of a fuzzy inference) the membership function by the corresponding linear expression and afterwards added up (implementation of a fuzzy composition):

$$y = \mu_1(x_1, x_2)(x_1 w_{51} + x_2 w_{52} + w_{50} + w_{54})$$
$$+ \mu_2(x_1, x_2)(x_1 w_{51} + x_2 w_{52} + w_{50} - w_{54})$$

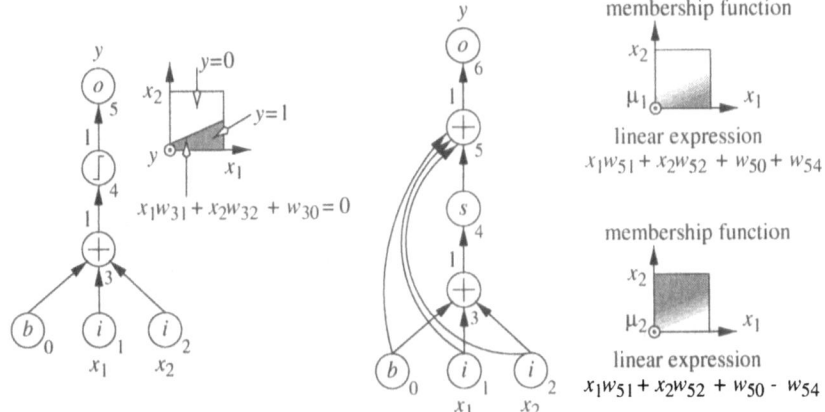

Fig. 6.9. Neural network with one *threshold* unit (marked with an *s*) (left). Neural network with one *sigmoid* unit (right). w_{ij} is the weight of the connection from the j-th to the i-th unit. The symbol $\odot$ is to be understood as an arrow pointing to the reader.

or expressed in form of Sugeno fuzzy rules:

$$\text{IF } (x_1, x_2) \text{ is } G_1 \text{ THEN } y = x_1 w_{51} + x_2 w_{52} + w_{50} + w_{54}$$
$$\text{IF } (x_1, x_2) \text{ is } G_2 \text{ THEN } y = x_1 w_{51} + x_2 w_{52} + w_{50} - w_{54}$$

where G_1 and G_2 are the fuzzy sets with membership functions μ_1 and μ_2, respectively.

This idea can be expanded for MLPwith short-cut connections and any number of hidden layers. This was developed in the FAGNIS (Fuzzy Atomatically Generated Neural Inferred System) system ([5] [6]). In [5] a proof of the equivalence between the neural network and the generated fuzzy inference system was performed, in dependence only of the choice for the membership functions. In that work an exact definition of the extraction problem is shown with theorems, which define the limits and conditions for the rule extraction.

To maintain an easy interpretability of the membership functions associated with the fuzzy rules generated some constraints were imposed on them:

1. The fuzzy set $F_i(x)$ is a convex fuzzy set, whose membership function is the highest at only one point with value 1. This way, it is guaranteed that the degree of membership decreases as the input values get farther from this point.

2. **Mutual exclusiveness of the fuzzy sets.** Mathematically, this constraint is expressed by $\sum_{i=1}^{n} F_i(x) \leq 1$. The system of fuzzy rules shall not have more than one rule completely active at a certain state.

3. **Region of influence constraint.** The region of influence (where the membership function has a value different of 0) should be occupied by as

few membership functions as possible. For the one-dimensional case this number should not be greater than two.

The FAGNIS system of rule extraction was already tested on some applications. First in the control area [8]. These ideas were applied to the control of the angle and position of the inverted pendulum with a specialized network. There, FAGNIS was compared with a Deadbeat controller (linear state controller). These ideas were adapted later to treat a second problem, the control of an interferometer in the MIPAS (Michelson Interferometer for Passive Atmospheric Sounding [22]) experiment at the Nuclear Research Center Karlsruhe, which was investigated and published in [7] [13].

A second application of FAGNIS was in the chemistry area where it was used to interpret neural networks trained to predict separation factors in the gas chromatography ([6][9][10]).

6.3.4 System Improvements

Since we can not be totally sure if all symbolic knowledge (rules) are really perfect with no inconsistencies, and also we can not be totally sure if all examples in learning database are really perfect, so we need to check the validity of our old rules against the new symbolic rules (obtained by rule extraction) and the available learning examples. The Valid module [3] finds out the probably incorrect rules and examples. Thus, we will need to submit these inconsistencies to an expert analysis, or to increase our learning and rule databases with more informations. This module is very important and complex and it is under development.

In summary, the INSS system presents some important advantages over its predecessor, KBANN. Our system improvements allow us to eliminates some drawbacks of KBANN nets:

- The INSS constructive neural architecture allows to work with incomplete symbolic rule sets and also with incorrect symbolic rule sets. Our system can easily add new rules (neurons) or even make broader changes in the existing ones. The KBANN networks, as they use static networks, restrict learning to less important changes to the rule set. If we need to 'learn' a new rule from examples in KBANN we should add manually specific units for this purpose.
- The KBANN network algorithm tries not to change unit meaning, and tries to keep the symbolic label significance associated to them. We can not be sure that, during the KBANN learning process, its units will not suffer a meaning shift. The Cascade-Correlation, used within INSS, keeps unchanged the initial acquired knowledge (compiled rules) by freezing the network connection weights, and does not have any problem of meaning shift.
- The learning algorithm used in INSS is faster than KBANN's Back-Propagation based algorithm. Besides, this algorithm allows an incremental net-

work construction, by improving the connection weights as well as the network topology.

- Our rule extraction algorithm does not need to analyse all the ANN structure, but instead we just consider the new acquired network knowledge by analysing the new added units. This leads to an important reduction of the rule extraction process complexity.
- We are not restricted to using binary inputs (rules of order 0), nor obligated to pre-process continuous inputs in order to discretizate them. Our system allows symbolic rule compilation of proposition rules of order 0+.
- The integration of efficient fuzzy rule extraction algorithms into the INSS system due to its modular construction expands its capabilities. This represents an improvement in the knowledge representation power of the generated rules and so in the range of applications of the system.

6.4 Validation of INSS : Practical Results

The possibility to use and to take into account several kinds of knowledge representation appears clearly in the description of the functionning of INSS. It is the same for the possibility of global learning. INSS can not only adapt its various sets of knowledge to the variation of the data domain, but also to learn by modifications of its architecture.

It remains to show that the hybridisation increases the efficiency of the system, and that the knowledge extracted by INSS is a "good" knowledge. With this aim in view we have applied INSS on a relatively simple application, the *Monk's Problem* [34]. This problem is a set of tests developed for performance comparison of different learning algorithms. There are three Monk's problem data sets. Here we will discuss only the results we obtained within the first one, the Monk1 problem, although our tests cover all three problem data sets.

Table 6.1. Monk1: Description of the symbolic rule set

Input Features:
HEAD_SHAPE = { ROUND, SQUARE, OCTAGON }
BODY_SHAPE = { ROUND, SQUARE, OCTAGON }
IS_SMILING = { YES, NO }
HOLDING = { SWORD, BALLOON, FLAG }
JACKET_COLOUR = { RED, YELLOW, GREEN, BLUE }
HAS_TIE = { YES, NO }
Symbolic Rules:
(1) Monk1 ← HEAD_SHAPE = ROUND, BODY_SHAPE = ROUND
(2) Monk1 ← HEAD_SHAPE = SQUARE, BODY_SHAPE = SQUARE
(3) Monk1 ← HEAD_SHAPE = OCTAGON, BODY_SHAPE = OCTAGON
(4) Monk1 ← JACKET_COLOUR = RED

The Monk1 problem data set is composed by one set of four symbolic rules (see table 6.1 for the complete domain theory), by one generalization test set of 432 examples (covering all the input space), and by one learning set of 124 examples. The examples are exactly those available in the original data [38]. In our experiments we used portions of the rule set and the examples set in order to study the generalization capacity of our system. Just the learning set and the rule set were partitioned, for its part, the generalization test set was preserved unchanged in all experiments.

6.4.1 First Experiment : Validity of the Extracted Knowledge

This experiment aims at verifying if the system is able to find again the complete rule set from a partial set of knowledge. This is accomplished by means of learning an example base built up with the complete set.

In a first test, we created a network by compiling 75% of the rules (3 among the 4 available rules). Then we applied the rule extraction method. The extraction process has been applied only on two units, the output and one hidden unit, because one unit only has been added to the network during the learning period. We repeated such a test for all the configurations of the incomplete rule set : one rule eleminated among four available rules. In any case, the extraction method allowed to retrieve the rule removed from the initial set.

In a second test, we used another incomplete rule set constructed by suppressing 50% of the rules contained into the complete set. As in the first test, we refined this initial knowledge by using the original learning data set. The result we obtained is the same one: *we rediscovered all the rules eliminated from the original rule set.*

This set of experiments leads to two remarks :

- In any case, the retrieved rules were found by rule extraction from the ANN added units. That shows the process of modification of the network architecture is consistent.
- The fact we rediscover the eliminated rule means the removed rule was implicitly present in the examples learned by the neural network. The extracted knowledge is sound and not in contradiction to the example set.

6.4.2 Second Experiment : Efficiency of the Hybridisation

The results obtained (see table 6.2) show that INSS is able to treat this problem using all available learning examples, or using a combination of the theoretical knowledge (rules) and empirical knowledge (examples). We showed that we always obtain a superior generalization rate when we use at the same time rules and examples. Lower generalization rates are obtained when we used just one information source at the same time.

Table 6.2. Monk1 problem: Using rules and examples to improve generalization

Portion of Rule Set	Portion of Examples Set	Generalization using INSS	Generalization Just rules	ANN Generaliz. Just examples
-	100%	100%	-	100%
-	75%	89.21%	-	89.21%
-	50%	70.92%	-	70.92%
100%	-	100%	100%	-
75%	-	83.33%	83.33%	-
50%	-	72.22%	72.22%	-
75%	100%	100%	83.33%	100%
50%	100%	100%	72.22%	100%
75%	75%	100%	83.33%	89.21%
75%	50%	100%	83.33%	70.92%
50%	75%	100%	72.22%	89.21%
50%	50%	89.86%	72.22%	70.92%

* Generalization scores represents the average obtained from 5 different runs
+ Our system and the data used in these tests are available for comparisons

6.5 Medical Diagnosis and Other Applications

In order to study the behavior of INSS on a real application, the system has been also tested on a medical diagnosis application : diagnosis of toxic coma. When a comatose patient is admitted in an emergency care unit, the clinician makes an early tentative diagnosis by collecting clinical and biological parameters. The diagnosis may be later confirmed or rejected by toxicological analysis. So, for the initial therapeutic action to be as adequate as possible, there is a need for an accurate prediction of the toxic cause, without waiting for the toxicological analysis. The use of an intelligent automated system to help in this diagnosis task seems to be very useful. Until now, there is no complete model for describing this knowledge by means of rules.

Our goal was to use INSS to aid to identify the causes of a psychotrope induced coma. We have available a case base of 505 pre-analysed examples of patients. Each example is described with 13 parameters or symptoms obtained directly when the patient is admitted, without waiting for the toxicological analysis. The diagnosis should aid to identify the presence or absence of each one of the 7 individual toxic causes (Alcohol, ADT, Benzodiazepines, Barbiturates, Carbamates, Morphine or Phenothiazines). A more detailed description of this problem can be found in the technical report of the Esprit MIX Project [1].

Table 6.3 reproduces the results we obtained comparing INSS to other machine learning systems applied to this medical diagnosis problem. All the systems were tested with exactly the same learning and testing data sets, and the results expressed in this table are the average of 10 different runs. The systems we compared with INSS are described in the MIX report [1].

The scores showed in Table 6.3, related to the other methods (K-PPV, C4.5, and ProBis), were reproduced from the results obtained by other researchers [21]. As we were constrained to use the same experiment protocol in order to be able to compare these different methods, we show here just a brief performance comparison. Although we published in [1] a more detailed list of the results obtained with INSS related to this problem.

Table 6.3. Comparison of the generalisation test rate after learning

Method → Class ↓	K-PPV	C4.5	ProBIS	INSS
Alcohol -E	66.56%	65.40%	68.94%	**74.50%**
ADT - a	55.39%	55.26%	57.63%	**60.79%**
Barbituriques - B	65.65%	63.32%	64.60%	**82.45%**
Benzodiazepines-b	62.37%	64.34%	63.95%	**83.37%**
Carbamates - c	81.58%	**87.64%**	84.87%	87.28%
Morphine - m	97.23%	97.50%	**97.97%**	97.88%
Phenothiazines - p	66.45%	71.26%	68.95%	**75.36%**

As we can observe from Table 6.3, the INSS system shows a remarkable performance in this task compared with the other techniques. In some classes the percentage differences between INSS and other methods are quite small, but INSS is always near to the best performance obtained. However we have to remark that in some classes we get relatively poor classification results for all methods. That is due to the intrinsic complexity of this problem and the strong overlapping of the different classes : this kind of complexity is a typical feature of the medical diagnosis.

We also tried to extract rules from the trained ANN. The extracted rules were presented to one expert of this domain, and he immediately recognised them as "valid rules". He also noted that a great part of the rules had captured important relations between certain input features and the presence of one specific toxic substance (e.g., intermediate pupil size, normal eye movement, low core temperature, and prolonged cardiological QT interval, are factors that indicate the possible presence of ADT).

This research resulted in the development of an experimental user interface to give access to our system through the WWW (World-Wide-Web). This program allows the consultation of the INSS system for toxic coma diagnosis. The user can fill-in a form with the patient's clinical and biological parameters and get back the ANN answer indicating the possible toxic substances absorbed. Presently, the system answer is based upon an ANN trained with the 505 cases database. However, this small number of available cases has proved to be insufficient for a good diagnosis of all toxic substances.

We are currently using the INSS system in two other domains: autonomous robot control and models of human cognitive development (e.g., balance scale problem [30, 31]). A description of our preliminary results obtained with these applications can be found in [25].

6.6 Conclusion

The INSS system presented here offers many advantages compared to the KBANN system by which it was inspired. This system has a better performance and allows incremental acquisition/extraction of network knowledge. Furthermore, it is based upon an incremental learning method already used to model human cognitive development. This learning method allowed us to develop a system perfectly adapted to the concepts proposed in the framework of constructive machine learning systems. The system was tested on different applications (classification tasks, medical diagnosis, autonomous robot control) obtaining satisfactory results. Actually our main goals are to develop a deeper study of the real-world applications of INSS, as well as to study the aspects related to the constructive acquisition of knowledge.

Our future work is the implementation of a complete hybrid machine learning tool based on ANN allowing diverse input and output forms of knowledge. Figure 6.10 shows the structure of such a system for introduction and extraction of different forms of knowledge. In the future with the addition of interface routines for format conversion, such a system could process other forms of knowledge transforming it into and from Neural Networks.

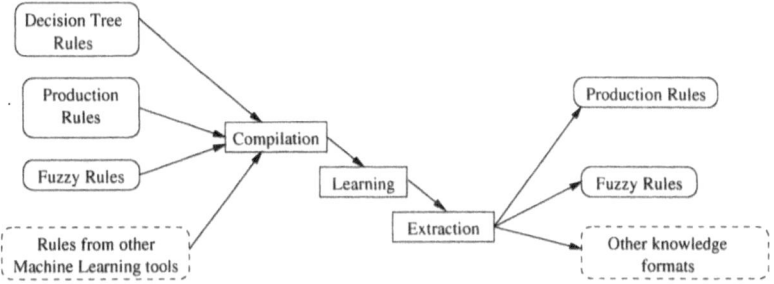

Fig. 6.10. Generic system for introduction and extraction of knowledge

Acknowledgements: Thanks to Scott Fahlman, Geoffrey Towell, Vicent Danel and Daniel Memmi for their contribution to our research and/or to the production of this article. We would like also to thank Prof. Wolfgang Rosenstiel and to the "Neuro-Group" at the Tübingen University for the enlightening discussions and support. This research was supported in part by a fellowship from CAPES-Brazil and Cofecub-France, by a fellowship from CNPq and by the german Government (DFG project).

142

References

1. Amy, B. et al. (1997) *MIX Medical Application (Final Report - Deliverable D16).* Technical Report, Project Esprit- BRA 'MIX' - European Community (May 1997). Web: http://www-leibniz.imag.fr/RESEAUX/public.html . Ftp: ftp://-ftp.imag.fr/pub/LEIBNIZ/RESEAUX-D-AUTOMATES/MIX-FMR.ps.gz
2. Andrews, R.; Diederich, J.; Tickle, A. B. (1995) *A Survey And Critique of Techniques For Extracting Rules From Trained ANN.* Technical Report - Neurocomputing Research Centre - QUT (Queensland University of Technology, Brisbane - Australia, January 1995). Also published in: Knowledge-Based Systems 8(6), p.378-38 (1995). Web: http://www.fit.qut.edu.au/NRC/ Ftp:ftp://-ftp.fit.qut.edu.au/pub/NRC/tr/ps/QUTNRC-95-01-02.ps.Z
3. Blond, P.-Y. (1996) *Validation de Connaissances dans un Système Hybride Neuro-Symbolique à Apprentissage Incrémental.* Rapport du D.E.A. en Sciences Cognitives (Lab. LEIBNIZ - IMAG, Grenoble - France, 1996).
4. Boz, Olcay (1995) *Knowledge Integration and Rule Extraction in Neural Networks.* Technical Report, EECS, Lehigh University. (October 1995). Web: http:// www.lehigh.edu/ ob00/ integrated.html
5. Cechin, A.: *The Extraction of Fuzzy Rules from Neural Networks.* Fakultät für Informatik der Eberhard-Karls-Universität zu Tübingen, Shaker Verlag, Aachen, ISBN 3-8265-3541-3, 1998.
6. Cechin, A., Epperlein, U., Koppenhoefer, B. and Rosenstiel, W.: *The Extraction of Sugeno Fuzzy Rules from Neural Networks.* in Michel Verleysen (editor): *Proceedings of the European Symposium on Artificial Neural Networks,* 49–54, Brussels, Belgium, 1996. D facto publications.
7. Cechin, A. and Eppler, W.: *Automatic Design of a Fuzzy Controller from a Neural Process Modell.* in H.-J. Zimmermann (editor): *Proceedings of the 2nd European Congress on Intelligent Techniques and Soft Computing,* Aachen, Germany, 1994.
8. Cechin, A. and Eppler, W.: *Automatischer Entwurf eines Fuzzy-Reglers aus einem neuronalen Prozeßmodell.* in B. Reusch (editor): *4. Dortmunder Fuzzy-Tage,* Dortmund, Germany, 1994. Poster.
9. Cechin, A., Epperlein, U., Koppenhoefer, B. and Rosenstiel, W.: *The Extraction of Sugeno Fuzzy Rules from Neural Networks.* in Robert Andrews and Joachim Diederich (editors): *Proceedings of the Rule Extraction from Trained Artificial Neural Networks Workshop,* 16–24, Brighton, United Kingdom, 1996.
10. Cechin, A., Epperlein, U., Koppenhoefer, B. and Rosenstiel, W.: *Fuzzy Rules Extraction from Neural Networks Applied to Molecular Recognition.* in A.B. Bulsari, S. Kallio and D.T. Tsaptsinos (editors): *Proceedings of the International Conference on Engineering Applications of Neural Networks,* 107–110, London, United Kingdom, 1996.
11. Decloedt, L., Osorio, F., Amy, B. (1996) RULE_OUT Method: A New Approach for Knowledge Explicitation from Trained Artificial Neural Networks. *Proceedings of the AISB'96 − Workshop on Rule Extraction from Trained Neural Nets, p.34-42.* (QUT - Andrews and Diederich Eds. 1996). Web: http:// www-leibniz.imag.fr/ RESEAUX/ public.html Ftp: ftp:// ftp.imag.fr/ pub/ LEIBNIZ/ RESEAUX-D-AUTOMATES/ osorio.aisb96.ps.gz
12. Decloedt, Loïc (1995) *Explicitation de Connaissances dans un Système Hybride d'Intelligence Artificielle.* Rapport du D.E.A. en Informatique, Laboratoire LIFIA − IMAG, INPG (Grenoble − France, Juin 1995). Web: http:// www-leibniz.imag.fr/ RESEAUX/ public. html Ftp: ftp:// ftp.imag.fr/ pub/ LEIBNIZ/ RESEAUX−D−AUTOMATES/ DEA/ decloedt.dea.ps.gz

13. Eppler, W., Gemmeke, H. and Cechin, A.: *Stabilization of a Stratospheric Balloon Experiment by a New Fuzzy Controller with a Neural Process Model.* in *IEEE Nuclear Science Symposium,* 422–426, Norfolk, USA, 1994.

14. Fahlman, S. E., Lebiere, C. (1990) *The Cascade-Correlation Learning Architecture.* Carnegie Mellon Un., Technical Report - CMU-CS-90-100. (1990) Web: http:// www.cs.cmu.edu/ Reports/ index.html . Ftp: ftp:// archive.cis.ohio-state.edu/ pub/ neuroprose/ fahlman.cascor-tr.ps.Z

15. Giacometti, A. (1992) *Modèles hybrides de l'expertise.* Thèse de Doctorat, LIFIA - IMAG (Grenoble − France, 1992). Web: http:// www-leibniz.imag.fr/ RESEAUX/ public.html . Ftp: ftp:// ftp.imag.fr/ pub/ LEIBNIZ/ RESEAUX-D-AUTOMATES/ giacometti. these. ps.tar.gz

16. Giarratano, Joseph C. (1993) *CLIPS User's Guide - Version 6.0.* Lyndon B. Johnson Space Center, Software Technology Branch, NASA (U.S.A., 1993). Web: http:// www.jsc.nasa.gov/ clips/ CLIPS.html or http:// home.haley.com/ clips.html Ftp: ftp:// ftp.cs.cmu.edu/ afs/cs/ project/ ai-repository/ ai/areas/ expert/ systems/ clips/ 0.html

17. Hilario, M. (1996) An Overview of Strategies for Neurosymbolic Integration. In: *Connectionist-Symbolic Integration: From Unified to Hybrid Approaches.* Ron Sun (Ed.) - Chapter 2. (Kluwer Academic Publishers, 1996). Ftp: ftp://-cui.unige.ch/AI/

18. Jang, J.-S.R. and Sun, C.T.: *Neuro-Fuzzy Modeling and Control.* Proceedings of the IEEE, 83:378–406, 1995.

19. Jang, J.-S.R. and Sun, C.T.: *Functional Equivalence Between Radial Basis Function Networks and Fuzzy Inference Systems.* IEEE Transactions on Neural Networks, 4:156–159, 1993.

20. Kruse, R., Gebhardt, J. and Klawonn, F.: *Fuzzy-Systeme.* B.G.Teubner, Stuttgart, 1993.

21. Malek, Maria. (1996) *Un modèle hybride de mémoire pour le raisonnement à partir de cas.* Thèse de Doctorat, UJF - LEIBNIZ (Grenoble - France, 1996). Web: http:// www-leibniz.imag.fr/ RESEAUX/ public.html . Ftp: ftp:// ftp.imag.fr/ pub/ LEIBNIZ/ RESEAUX-D-AUTOMATES/ malek.these.ps.gz

22. Oelhaf, H., Clarmann, T., Fergg, F., Fischer, H., Friedl-Vallon, F., Fritzsche, C., Piesch, C., Rabus, D., Seefeldner, M. and Völker, W.: *Remote Sensing of Trace Gases with a Ballon Borne Version of the Michelson Interferometer for Passive Atmospheric Sounding (MIPAS).* in *Proceedings of the 10th ESA-Symposium on European Rocket and Balloon Programmes,* 207–213, Mandelieu-Cannes, France, 1991.

23. Orsier, Bruno (1995) *Etude et application de systèmes hybrides neuro-symboliques.* Thèse de Doctorat, UJF - LIFIA (Grenoble - France, 1995). Web: http:// www-leibniz.imag.fr/ RESEAUX/ public.html . Ftp: ftp:// ftp.imag.fr/ pub/ LEIBNIZ/ RESEAUX-D-AUTOMATES/ orsier.these.ps.gz

24. Osorio, F. S. & Amy, B. (1995) *INSS: A Hybrid Symboli-Connectionist System that Learns from Rules and Examples (text in portuguese).* Panel'95 - XXI Latin-American Conference on Computer Science (Canela, Brazil, August 1995). Web: http:// www-leibniz.imag.fr/ RESEAUX/ osorio/ papers/ diret.html

25. Osorio, F. S. (1998) *INSS: Un Système Hybride Neuro-Symbolique pour l'Apprentissage Automatique Constructif.* Thèse de Doctorat, INPG - Laboratoire LEIBNIZ - IMAG (Grenoble, France, 1998). Web: http:// www-leibniz.imag.fr/ RESEAUX/ public.html . Ftp: ftp:// ftp.imag.fr/ pub/ LEIBNIZ/ RESEAUX-D-AUTOMATES/ osorio.these.ps.gz

26. Reyes, Gerardo (1997) *Etude des Connaissances dans les Réseaux de Neurones Artificiels : Représentation et Explicitation de Règles d'Haut Niveau.* Rapport du D.E.A. en Sciences Cognitives, LEIBNIZ - IMAG. (Grenoble - France, 1997).

27. Reyes, G.; Osorio, F.; Amy, B. (1997) Neural Learning of "High Level Rules": The Balance Scale Problem. In: *HELNET'97 International Workshop on Neural Networks.* (Montreux, Swiss, October 1997). Web: http:// www-leibniz.imag.fr/ RESEAUX/ public.html . Ftp: ftp:// ftp.imag.fr/ pub/ LEIB-NIZ/ RESEAUX-D-AUTOMATES/ osorio.helnet97.ps.gz

28. Rumelhart, D., Hinton, G., Willians, R. (1986) Learning Internal Representations by Error Propagation. In: *Parallel Distributed Processing - Explorations in the Microstructure of Cognition,* V1. (Cambridge - MIT Press, 1986).

29. Schiffmann, W.; Joost, M. & Werner, R. (1993) Comparison of Optimized Back-propagation Algorithms. In: *Proceedings of the European Symposium on Artificial Neural Networks, ESANN'93.* p.97-104. (Brussels, 1993) Web: http:// www.uni-koblenz.de/ schiff/ publications.html

30. Shultz, T. R., Schmidt, W. C. (1991) A Cascade-Correlation Model of Balance Scale Phenomena. In: *Proceedings of the Thirteenth Annual Conf. of the Cognitive Science Society.* p.635-640. (Hillsdale, NJ - Erlbaum, 1991). Web: http:// www.psych.mcgill.ca/ labs/ lnsc/ html/ Lab-Home.html (or Pub-cog-dev.html). Ftp: ftp:// ego.psych.mcgill.ca/ pub/ shultz/ balcog.ps.gz

31. Shultz, T. R., Mareschal, D., Schmidt, W. (1994) Modeling Cognitive Development on Balance Scale Phenomena. In: *Machine Learning.* No.16, p.57-86. (Kluwer Publishers, 1994). Web: http:// www.psych.mcgill.ca/ labs/ lnsc/ html/ Lab-Home.html (or Pub-cog-dev.html). Ftp: ftp:// ego.psych.mcgill.ca/ pub/ shultz/ balml.ps.gz

32. Sun, Ron & Alexandre, Frederic (1997) *Connectionist-Symbolic Integration: From Unified to Hybrid Approaches.* (Lawrence Erlbaum Associates, 1997).

33. Takagi T. and Sugeno, M.: *Fuzzy Identification of Systems and Its Application to Modeling and Control.* IEEE Transactions on Systems, Man, and Cybernetics, 15:116–132, 1985.

34. Thrun, S. B. et al. (1991) *The Monk's Problem - A Performance Comparison of Different Learning Algorithm.* Carnegie Mellon University, Technical Report CMU-CS-91-197. (1991). Web: http:// www.cs.cmu.edu/ thrun/ . Ftp: ftp:// archive.cis.ohio-state.edu/ pub/ neuroprose/

35. Towell, G. (1991) *Symbolic Knowledge and Neural Networks: Insertion, Refinement and Extraction.* Ph.D. Thesis, University of Wisconsin-Madison - Computer. Science Dept. (1991). Web: http:// www.cs.wisc.edu/ shavlik/ uwml.html Ftp: ftp:// ftp.cs.wisc.edu/ machine-learning/ shavlik-group/ (towell.thesis.*.ps)

36. Towell, G. & Shavlik, J. (1993) Extracting Refined Rules From Knowledge-Based Neural Nets. In: *Machine Learning.* pp.71-101, 13. (Kluwer Academic Publishers - Boston, 1993). Web: http:// www.cs.wisc.edu/ shavlik/ uwml.html . Ftp: ftp:// ftp.cs.wisc.edu/ machine-learning/ shavlik-group/ towell.mlj93.ps

37. Towell, G. & Shavlik, J. (1994) Knowledge-Based Neural Nets. In: *Artificial Intelligence.* pp.119-165, 70. (1994). Web: http:// www.cs.wisc.edu/ shavlik/ uwml.html . Ftp: ftp:// ftp.cs.wisc.edu/ machine-learning/ shavlik-group/ towell.aij94.ps

38. UCI-ML Repository (1997) *UCI - University of California, Irvine Machine Learning Databases and Domain Theories.* (1997). Web: http:// www.ics.uci.edu/ mlearn/ MLRepository.html . Ftp: ftp:// ftp.ics.uci.edu/ pub/ machine-learning-databases/ README

A Generic Architecture for Hybrid Intelligent Systems

Hans–Arno Jacobsen
Humboldt University, Berlin
Institute of Information Systems
D-10178 Berlin
jacobsen@wiwi.hu-berlin.de .

Abstract: The integration of complementary learning and adaptation techniques, to overcome limitations of individual approaches and achieve synergetic effects through hybridization or fusion, has in recent years contributed to a large number of new intelligent system designs. Many of these approaches, however, follow an ad hoc design methodology, further justified by success in certain application domains. Due to the lack of a common framework it remains often difficult to compare the various systems conceptually and evaluate their performance comparatively.

In this work we first aim at classifying state–of–the–art intelligent systems, which have evolved over the past decade in the soft computing community. We identify four categories, based on the systems' overall architecture: (1) single component systems, (2) fusion–based systems, (3) hierarchical systems, and (4) hybrid systems.

We then review a unifying paradigm, well known in the artificial intelligence community. This paradigm serves us as conceptual framework to better understand, modularize, compare, and evaluate the individual approaches. We think it is crucial for the design of intelligent systems to focus on the integration and interaction of different learning techniques in one model, rather then merging them to create ever new techniques.

Two original instantiations of this framework are presented and evaluated. A reinforcement–driven fuzzy adaptation architecture and an expert guided neural fuzzy system. For the former architecture we go into great detail demonstrating the interaction between the different system components and the adaptive techniques developed. The latter architecture is briefly described to show an alternative instantiation of the agent framework. We conclude by presenting several open research problems stimulating further explorations.

7.1 Introduction

Complex adaptive systems, also referred to as *intelligent systems*, have in recent years been developed for modeling expertise, for decision support, and for process control, among others. Many of these approaches go beyond simply applying one problem solving technique, but rather, combine different knowledge representation schemes, decision making models, and learning strategies in one system. This integration aims at overcoming limitations of individual techniques through hybridization or fusion of various techniques.

These ideas have lead to the emergence of many different kind of intelligent system architectures in the soft computing community in the past decade. We have identified four categories based on the systems' overall architectural design. We distinguish between single and multi–component approaches and between hybridization and fusion based approaches.

Most systems are designed in an ad hoc manner, further justified by demonstrations of successful applications. Such approaches make it often hard to adapt the design ideas to domains governed by different conditions. Moreover, this makes it difficult to compare the individual approaches and evaluate their relative performance, since no common basis for such comparison is available. It remains therefore difficult to precisely pinpoint merits and demerits of the different approaches. Especially, when new techniques, based on the integration of know algorithms are presented, the respective evaluation constitutes a major drawback.

In an attempt to alleviate these problems we review a paradigm, well known in the *artificial intelligence* community, as conceptual framework to better understand, modularize, evaluate, and compare the individual approaches. This framework defines an intelligent system in a modular manner which allows one to focus on the interaction of different system components and their overall utility for the problem solving task.

We think it is crucial for the design of intelligent systems to primarily focus on the integration and interaction of different techniques, rather than merge different methods to create ever new techniques. Techniques, already well understood, should be applied to solve specific domain problems within the system. Their weaknesses must be addressed by combining them with complementary methods. The focus must therefore lie on the component–wise integration of different methods and be geared towards studying their mutual dependencies, synergetic effects, and precise interactions.

In a first step to achieve this goal we present two instantiations of the conceptual agent framework. We show how different learning techniques may be combined in a hybrid manner to achieve complementary effects.

The rest of the paper is organized as follows. Section 7.2 surveys state–of–the–art intelligent systems and identifies four distinct categories. Section 7.3 reviews the *learning agent paradigm* as discussed by Russell and Norvig (Russell and Norwig 1995). In Section 7.4 and Section 7.5 we instantiate this framework with two original intelligent systems. A reinforcement–driven fuzzy relation adaptation architecture (Section 7.4) and an expert guided neural fuzzy system (Section 7.5). For the former architecture we go into greater detail demonstrating the interaction between the different system components. The latter architecture is briefly described to show an alternative instantiation of the agent framework. Section 7.6 presents several open research problems and issues for future work.

7.2 Intelligent Systems Based on Neural and Fuzzy Techniques

Neural networks are well suited for learning and adaptation tasks. In general, however, a neural network constitutes a black box. This means it is not possible to understand how a neural system works. Furthermore, it is very hard to incorporate human a priori knowledge into a neural network. This is mainly due to the fact that the connectionist paradigm gains most of its strength from a distributed knowledge representation.

Fuzzy knowledge based systems, on the other hand, exhibit complementary characteristics. The incorporation and interpretation of knowledge is straight forward, whereas learning and adaptation constitute major problems. Table 7.1 gives a more clear cut juxtaposition of these characteristics.

neural concepts	fuzzy concepts
learnable, adaptive devices	static devices. a priori non–adaptive
black–boxes, not interpretable	rule–based, interpretable
learns from scratch	domain knowledge expressed in rules

Table 7.1. Juxtaposition of complementary characteristics of pure neural and pure fuzzy systems.

Due to this complementarity it is not surprising that many approaches have evolved which combine neural network and fuzzy techniques in one system. A complete survey of all these approaches is out of the scope of this chapter. Rather, we try to focus on the different kind of architectures developed over the past few years. Figure 7.1 depicts the different approaches metaphorically, characterized below.

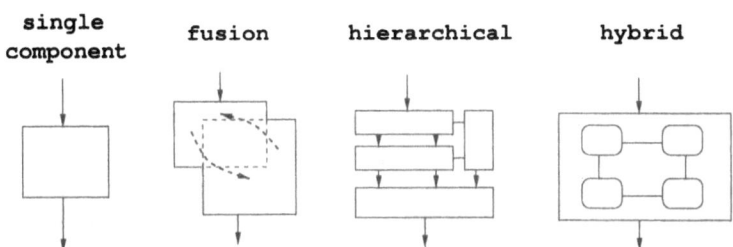

Fig. 7.1. Different categories of intelligent system designs based on neural and fuzzy techniques.

The four categories we have identified are: *single component system, fusion based systems, hierarchical systems,* and *hybrid systems.* The boundaries between the different categories are not strict. For many cases one could argue that a given system could belong to more than one class.

The **single component system** class contains systems based solely on one technique. It contains the "puristic" approaches, such as plain fuzzy control, TSK–control, or multi–layered perceptron based approaches. Many successful applications of such approaches have been demonstrated in the literature.

The **fusion based system** class includes systems which combine different techniques into one single computational model. Instances of this class are, for example, ANFIS (Jang 1992), NEFCON (Nauck and Kruse 1992), FUN (Sulzberger, Tschichold-Gürman, and Vestli 1993), Eppler's approach (Eppler 1993), FINEST (Tano, Oyama, and Arnould 1996), and FLINS (Okamoto and et al. 1995), among many others.

Common to these approaches is their network–like architecture which is often based, in one way or another, on the five staged fuzzy rule base evaluation scheme (fuzzification, premise evaluation, truth value propagation, conclusio aggregation, and defuzzification). Like the approaches in the previous class, these systems realize a mapping from an input space to an output space. The system does not contain other components which perform strategic planing or self–assessment.

The **hierarchical system** class comprises more architecturally complex systems. Its instances are build in a hierarchical fashion, associating a different functionality with each layer (e.g., preprocessing of sensor data, planing, and action selection). The correct operation of the system depends on the correct operation of all layers; a possible error in one layer is propagated up through the hierarchy directly effecting the system output. Example systems include (Arao, Tsutsumi, Fukuda, and Shimojima 1995), (Tano 1997), and (Tano, Namba, Sakao, Tomita, and Aoshima 1997), among others.

Finally, the **hybrid system** class contains approaches that put different techniques on a side by side basis and focus on their interaction in the problem solving task. It is this interaction which we deem important, since it allows to integrate alternative techniques and exploit their mutuality. Furthermore, the conceptual view of the agent allows one to abstract from the individual techniques and focus on the global system behavior, as well as study the individual contribution of each component. Examples include ARIC (Berenji 1992), GARIC (Berenji and Khedkar 1992), FYNESSE (Riedmiller, Spott, and Weisbrod 1997), SHADE (Jacobsen, Iordanova, and Giacometti 1994; Jacobsen and Iordanova 1994), and our work on the fuzzy relation adaptation architecture (Jacobsen 1995; Jacobsen and Weisbrod 1996; Jacobsen 1998).

We are proponents of this latter class of systems. As we believe, they exhibit greater potential for solving difficult tasks (learning, classification, and control), due to the inherent self–assessment capabilities of the approaches and their potential to gracefully degenerate with the loss or unavailability of one of their component functions.

7.3 Review of the Learning Agent Paradigm

We now review an abstract framework of a learning agent architecture to more easily capture the complexity of intelligent systems, to better understand and modularize such systems, and to obtain a terminological framework within which future intelligent system designs can be evaluated and compared. This form of conceptualizing a learning agent goes back to Russell and Norvig who also present many applications of the learning agent (cf. (Russell and Norwig 1995)). The agent architecture is depicted in Figure 7.3 (adapted from (Russell and Norwig 1995)).

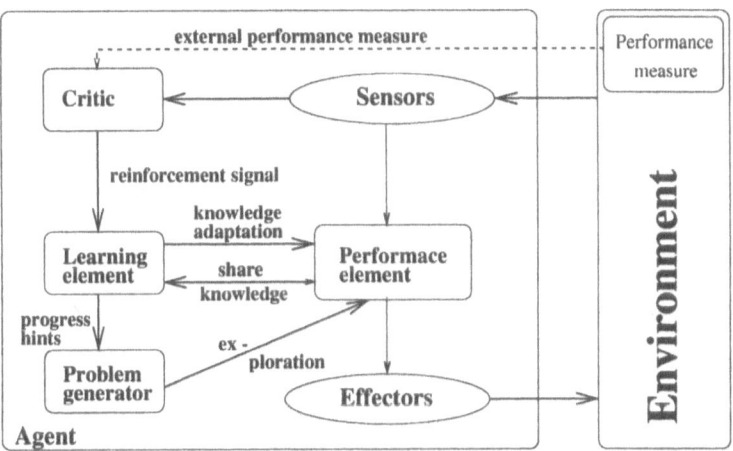

Fig. 7.2. Conceptual learning agent architecture according to Russell & Norvig (adapted from *"Artificial Intelligence a modern approach"*,1995, Prentice Hall, p. 526).

This framework should be seen as a tool to characterize and analyze complex intelligent systems. Its basic principles may be found with varying degrees in all systems presented earlier. The architecture consists of four components (Russell and Norwig 1995) and the *environment* upon which the agent acts:

The **environment** constitutes the problem task, e.g., the process to be controlled, the decision space to be analyzed, or the learning problem to be solved. Abstractly speaking, it is described by a state vector perceived by the agent through its **sensors** and influenced by it through its **effectors**.

The **performance element** (PE) is the actual "controller" mapping environment states to actions.

The **learning element** (LE) updates the knowledge represented in the PE in order to optimize the agent's performance with respect to an outside performance measure. It has access to the environment state, the agent's past actions, and an immediate reinforcement signal indicating the appropriateness of the action that last influenced the environment. Given this information it updates the PE so that in future situations more pertinent actions are chosen over less pertinent ones.

The **critic** faces the problem of transforming an external reinforcement signal into an internal one. The crux is that the external reinforcement signal may be very poor, an indication of failure, for example, and it may even be delayed, indicating failure after an entire sequence of actions has influenced the environment. The internal reinforcement signal, on the contrary, must be more informative and immediate. It indicates for each action taken whether it was beneficial or not. This problem is discussed in the AI literature as *credit assignment problem* (CAP): Depending on the overall situational outcome credit or blame have to be distributed among actions and decision steps involved in the agent's reaction behavior. Sutton (Sutton 1984) differentiates between *temporal credit assignment* and *structural credit assignment*. Temporal credit assignment is the distribution of credit for outcomes to actions. The question is *when* the action occurred that caused the outcome. Structural credit assignment is the distribution of credit for actions to internal decisions that caused the action. It effects the internal structure of a system. With this differentiation it is clear that the critic faces the temporal CAP and the LE the structural CAP.

The **problem generator**'s role in the agent architecture is to contribute to the exploration of the problem space. Abstractly speaking, it proposes different actions which might lead to the discovery of new and better solutions. In most existing systems it is realized by adding a small amount of random noise to the output action. The amount added depends on the system performance. If the system performs well the need for new and better solution is not as urgent as if it performs poorly.

Clearly, this framework does not require the use of a specific technique for realizing the individual components. These techniques may be chosen entirely according to their strength and according to the problem task at hand.

Russell and Norvig (Russell and Norwig 1995) present a rich set of instantiations of this framework with diverse machine learning techniques that implement different components of the agent. In the soft computing community, however, little attention is paid to conceptual learning agent frameworks. We are aiming at closing this gap. We now introduce two instantiations of this framework partially explored in previous work (Jacobsen 1992; Jacobsen and Iordanova 1994; Jacobsen 1995; Jacobsen and Weisbrod 1996; Jacobsen 1998).

7.4 Reinforcement–Driven Fuzzy Relation Adaptation

This section describes and experimentally evaluates the *reinforcement–driven fuzzy relation adaptation* algorithm and architecture. The algorithm has previously been introduced in (Jacobsen and Weisbrod 1996; Jacobsen 1995) and the architecture has been motivated in (Jacobsen 1998; Jacobsen 1995). This architecture is part of the hybrid category of systems described above. Each of its components is instantiated by a separate machine learning technique. Figure 7.3 shows how the system's architecture derives from the framework presented above.

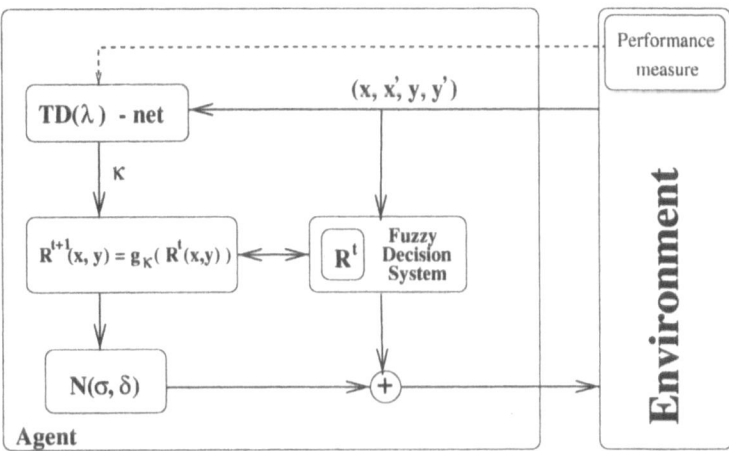

Fig. 7.3. Reinforcement–driven fuzzy relation adaptation architecture.

The *performance element* is instantiated by a rule–based fuzzy decision support system, i.e., a mapping from observed input states to an output decision (action). The mapping is defined by a fuzzy rule base. The *learning element* is instantiated with the reinforcement–driven fuzzy relation adaptation algorithm developed for the aggregated relation representation of the fuzzy rule base (cf. 7.4.4 for details). The *problem generator* is a module that adds a small amount of random noise to the output, depending on the performance of the system. It thus gives the system its explorative behavior. The *critic* is implemented by a feed–forward neural network trained with the TD(λ) rule (Sutton 1988).

This approach resembles the *adaptive critic* developed by Barto *et al.* (Barto, Sutton, and Anderson 1983), with the obvious differences in terms of component techniques applied here. Another closely related architecture is FYNESSE (Riedmiller, Spott, and Weisbrod 1997). FYNESSE successfully shows how the combination of a neural network and an, on fuzzy relations based, fuzzy controller may be applied to solve dynamic control problems.

We now discuss the methods applied in the performance element and the learning element in greater detail. At first, however, we review the theoretic foundation of our approach — the fuzzy relation calculus.

7.4.1 Fuzzy Relation Calculus

The following review of the fuzzy relation calculus draws from work in (Weisbrod 1995) and (Jacobsen and Weisbrod 1996; Jacobsen 1995). In the following, without loss of generality, we will consider only a *one input/one output* system. All results are easily extended to systems with many input and many output variables. We will therefore, consider here just two variables, the input variable x and the output variable y, with their respective universes of discourse $\mathcal{U}_x$ and $\mathcal{U}_y$. Additionally, we denote the generic elements of $\mathcal{U}_x$ and $\mathcal{U}_y$ by u and v, respectively. Furthermore, let $\tilde{A}_i$ and $\tilde{B}_i$ represent fuzzy sets on the universes of discourse $\mathcal{U}_x$ and $\mathcal{U}_y$, respectively ($i \in \{1,\ldots,n\}$). We will denote the fuzzy rule:

$$\text{"IF } x \text{ is } \tilde{A}_i \text{ THEN } y \text{ is } \tilde{B}_i\text{"}$$

by $[\tilde{A}_i \Rightarrow \tilde{B}_i]$.

The general framework for handling a fuzzy rule base

$$[\tilde{A}_i \Rightarrow \tilde{B}_i]$$

is to transform each rule into a fuzzy relation

$$\tilde{R}_i = transform(\tilde{A}_i, \tilde{B}_i)$$

on $\mathcal{U}_x \times \mathcal{U}_y$, to aggregate these implication relations to

$$\tilde{R} = aggregate(\tilde{R}_i),$$

and to apply the resulting so called meta rule $\tilde{R}$ by using max–min composition. That is, given the actual input $\tilde{A}'$ on $\mathcal{U}_x$, the result $\tilde{B}'$ on $\mathcal{U}_y$ of applying the fuzzy rule base $[\tilde{A}_i \Rightarrow \tilde{B}_i]$ is determined by computing:

$$\tilde{B}' = \tilde{A}' \circ \tilde{R}, \tag{7.1}$$

$$\mu_{B'}(v) = \max_{u \in \mathcal{U}_x} \min \{\mu_{A'}(u), \mu_R(u,v)\}. \tag{7.2}$$

The meta rule $\tilde{R}$ is given as follows:

$$\tilde{R}_i = transform(\tilde{A}_i, \tilde{B}_i) = \tilde{A}_i \cap \tilde{B}_i, \quad \text{and} \tag{7.3}$$

$$\tilde{R} = aggregate(\tilde{R}_i) = \bigcup \tilde{R}_i = \bigcup_i (\tilde{A}_i \cap \tilde{B}_i). \tag{7.4}$$

with the appropriate t/t-co-norms (*min* and *max* in our case).

The meta relation can thus be computed, given the fuzzy production rules governing the problem task. However, during the adaptation step there is no need to consider the way the meta rule is constructed. We may just take the fuzzy relation $\tilde{R}$ for granted and adapt it according to the critic's reinforcements. This is due to the fact, that *any* meta rule is processed using max–min composition according to eq. (7.1 and 7.4).

But in the second phase, i.e., the knowledge interpretation phase, this information will become essential because one has to look for the inverse operations of *transform* and *aggregate* in order to reduce the resulting fuzzy relation $\tilde{R}'$ into a set of simple fuzzy rules.

Graphic Interpretation of Fuzzy Relation Calculus

To better illustrate our approach we now motivate the above steps graphically. Given a rule base:

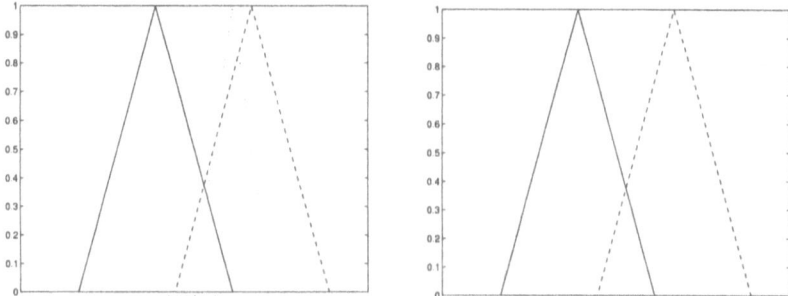

Fig. 7.4. Partitioning of input and output domains of discourse.

$$\mathcal{R}_1 : \quad \textbf{If } [x \text{ is } \tilde{A}_1] \textbf{ THEN } [y \text{ is } \tilde{B}_1]$$

$$\vdots$$

$$\mathcal{R}_n : \quad \textbf{If } [x \text{ is } \tilde{A}_n] \textbf{ THEN } [y \text{ is } \tilde{B}_n]$$

and an input $[x \text{ is } \tilde{A}']$. The rules are evaluated according to the inference scheme discussed above, i.e., the rule base is aggregated and the control input is applied to the aggregated relation.

Figure 7.4 depicts the partitioning of the input and output domains of discourse. The input domain of discourse also shows the fuzzy set of the input provided ($[x \text{ is } \tilde{A}']$).

Figure 7.5 shows the fuzzy relations of the individual fuzzy rules in the product space (i.e., $\tilde{R}_i = transform(\tilde{A}_i, \tilde{B}_i) = \tilde{A}_i \cap \tilde{B}_i$, for $i = 1, i = 2$). In this example the rule base consists of two fuzzy rules. The rules associate one of the input fuzzy sets from Figure 7.4 with one of the output fuzzy sets from the same figure (i.e., $[\tilde{A}_i \Rightarrow \tilde{B}_i]$).

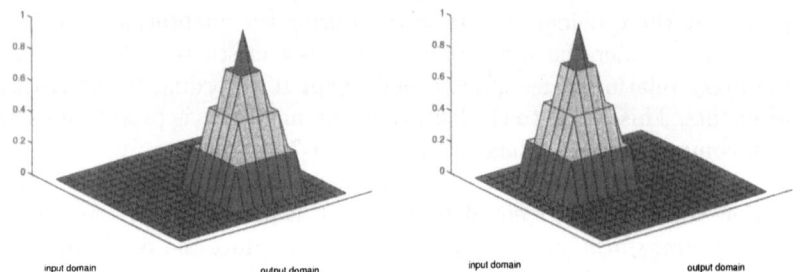

Fig. 7.5. Single rules in the product space. In this example the rule base consists of two fuzzy rules, relating the respective input and output fuzzy sets.

As before we want to infer $\tilde{B}'$ from $\tilde{A}'$ and $\tilde{R}$, as above with CRI [1] we obtain

$$\mu_{B'}(v) = \max_u(\min\{\mu_{A'}(u), \mu_R(u,v)\})$$
$$= \max_u(\mu_{R'}(u,v))$$

where

$$\mu_{R'}(u,v) = \min\{\mu_{A'}(u), \mu_R(u,v)\} .$$

Figure 7.6 depicts the cylindric extension of the fuzzy input set in the product space and the, over the individual fuzzy rule relations, aggregated fuzzy relation (above denoted as "meta rule" — $\tilde{R} = aggregate(\tilde{R}_i) = \bigcup \tilde{R}_i = \bigcup_i (\tilde{A}_i \cap \tilde{B}_i)$). The cylindric extension of the fuzzy set defined on $\mathcal{U}_x$ results in a fuzzy relation defined in the product space. For the max–min composition both operands must be defined on the same domain (product space). The *cylindric extension* of a fuzzy set $\widetilde{A'} \subseteq \mathcal{U}_x$ onto $\mathcal{U}_x \times \mathcal{U}_y$:

$$\tilde{S} = (\widetilde{A'} \uparrow (\mathcal{U}_x \times \mathcal{U}_y)) : \mathcal{U}_x \times \mathcal{U}_y \to [0,1]$$

is defined as

$$\mu_S(u,v) = \mu_{A'}(v) \quad \forall u \in \mathcal{U}_x, \ \forall v \in \mathcal{U}_y .$$

The application of the compositional rule of inference ($\tilde{B}' = \tilde{A}' \circ \tilde{R}$) results in the fuzzy set depicted in Figure 7.7 (second figure). The first figure shows the intermediate result — $\mu_{R'}(u,v) = \min\{\mu_{A'}(u), \mu_R(u,v)\}$. From the result fuzzy set a crisp control output is commonly determined by one of the common defuzzification operators (cf. (Lee 1990)).

---

[1] Compositional rule of inference (Zadeh 1973).

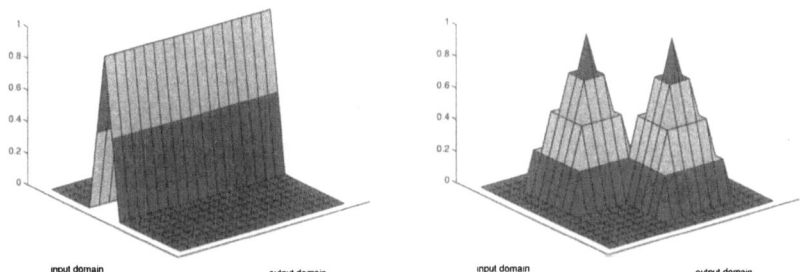

Fig. 7.6. Cylindric extension of the fuzzy input set and aggregated relation of the rule base in the product space.

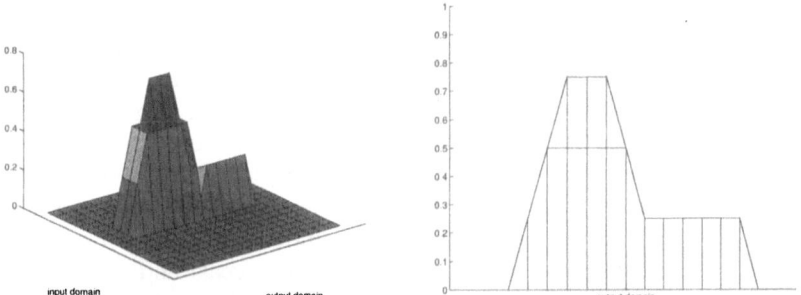

Fig. 7.7. Resulting relation after the application of the inference operations and the final output fuzzy set.

7.4.2 Adaptation of Fuzzy Relations

The fuzzy relation adaptation process can be divided into two stages which are repeated in a cyclic manner: an *action selection* stage and a *knowledge update* stage. The former selects a control action to be transmitted to the process, the latter adapts the fuzzy relation underlying the knowledge representation. Figure 7.8 depicts this learning cycle and also shows how the different components of the learning agent intervene in the learning process.

```
while  (learning has not converged)
       select an initial state x^t at random
       while  (not out of control)
              y^t ← Performance_Element (x^t)
              apply y^t to process
              observe new state x^{t+1}
              r^t ← Critic^H (x^t, x^{t+1}, y^t)
              Learning_Element (r^t)
       end
end
```

Fig. 7.8. Loop executed by the learning agent. The different functions correspond to the components shown in previous figures.

7.4.3 Choosing the Right Action — Action Selection Stage

After inferring the output fuzzy set $\mu_{B'}(v)$ from the meta rule $\tilde{R}$ (cf. Section 7.4.1) a crisp control action has to be derived and emitted to the process. This step is known as *defuzzification*. Several operators have been defined for this purpose (see (Lee 1990) for an overview). For example the *maximum defuzzification* operation selects the control action with the maximum membership value among all maxima from the output fuzzy set. Any deterministic defuzzification scheme, however, does not allow the control agent to *experiment* with the available control actions since the same action is selected over and over again for the same input situation. Hence, the agent cannot experience better or worse situations as a result of applying different actions in the same state and can therefore not adapt its knowledge. If the represented knowledge is sufficient for meeting the performance goals and there is no need for improvements a deterministic defuzzification is all that is needed. But if the available control knowledge is incomplete, inconsistent or even partly wrong the agent needs mechanisms to acquire, fine–tune, or reconfirm it. This is accomplished by the *trial and error* strategy undertaken in reinforcement learning.

The objective is that the agent learns to reliably judge the expected outcome of taking a specific action in a given state. This information will then be reflected in the output fuzzy set associated with the current input situation.

To stimulate this kind of explorative behavior we introduce a *randomized defuzzification* scheme. It is similar to the maximum defuzzification operation discussed above. Control actions are chosen randomly from the set of possible control actions according to their degrees of membership in the output fuzzy set. Control actions with higher degrees of membership have a greater chance of being selected as output as ones with lower degree of membership.

7.4.4 Updating the Control Rules — Knowledge Update Stage

Given the input x and the output y we know exactly *how* and *why* the selected output action was chosen from the set of possible actions. Observing the effect of the output on the process it becomes thus possible to reinforce the selection of the same control action or to suppress its selection in future situations. This is achieved by directly modifying the underlying knowledge relation. Figure 7.9 motivates this step.

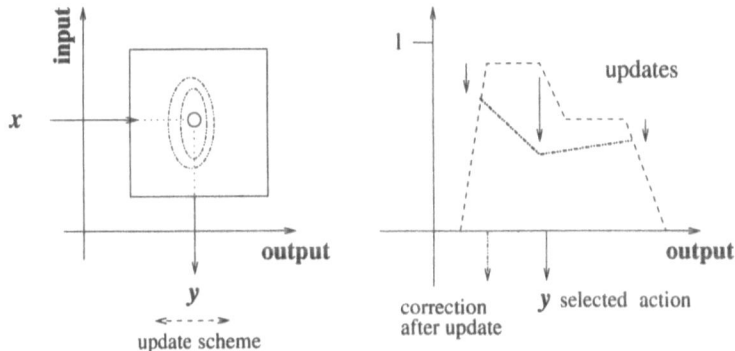

Fig. 7.9. Conceptual description of the fuzzy reinforcement scheme. Left figure shows the fuzzy relation (top view) with crisp input x and crisp output y and their relationship in the fuzzy relation. The right figure shows the output fuzzy set and demonstrates the effects of an update on the selected output action.

Clearly, the objective is to reinforce good actions and to suppress bad actions. Several different parameterizable families of *reinforcement schemes* for updating the knowledge relation have been developed:

1. point–wise updates,
2. neighborhood incorporating updates, and
3. fuzzy set oriented updates.

We now denote $\mu_R(u, v)$ by $\tilde{R}(u, v)$ to better emphasize the relational nature of the approach. Note, u, v denote the generic elements of $\mathcal{U}_x$ and $\mathcal{U}_y$, respectively, whereas x, y denote the specific system input and observed output values.

We assume that the critic element can provide for every action taken an immediate feedback. The feedback indicates whether the emitted action may be considered as *good* or as *bad* action, i.e., should be positively reinforced or rather suppressed in the future.

Point–Wise Update

The action selection stage determines the control action that is to be emitted to the process given a system state as input. If the control action is *favorable*, the simplest way to ensure its selection in future situations is to increase its membership value in the relation given by the input state and the control action (cf. 7.9). Alternatively, if the control action turns out to be *less favorable* a decrease in the relation will prevent it from being selected again. The following update scheme implements this concept. The *simple update* is defined as follows:

$$R(x, y) = \min\{1, \max\{0, R(x, y)\} + \alpha \kappa\},$$

with $0 \leq \alpha \leq 1$ a learning rate and κ the reinforcement signal ($\kappa > 0$ for rewards and $\kappa < 0$ for punishments). The $\min, \max$ operations serve to enforce the boundary conditions. The learning rate α determines the speed of growth of the relation, it has to be set depending on the task and depending on the reliability of the immediate internal reinforcement signal, the following section investigates the influence of this parameter in different learning situations.

Assuming a *perfect* internal reinforcement signal it is reasonable to update the relation by an amount relative to its current membership degree. For rewarding situations a total membership is desired, i.e., the membership value of the current situation should be maximized. Conversely, in negative situations the relation should be restraint as fast as possible. The *relative update* captures this idea. It weights the amount of change with a learning rate, to compensate for possible disturbances, which would otherwise update the relation in a very crisp manner. The *relative update* is defined as follows:

$$R(x, y) = \begin{cases} R(x, y) + \alpha\,(1 - R(x, y)) & \text{if } \kappa > 0 \quad \text{(reward)} \\ R(x, y) - \alpha\,R(x, y) & \text{if } \kappa < 0 \quad \text{(punishment)} \end{cases}$$

where $0 \leq \alpha \leq 1$ is the learning rate.

Neighborhood Incorporating Update

Both, of the above, update schemes operate on single points in the relation. The fuzzy relation, however, is a topological representation of the control knowledge with localized meaning. Along the output dimension, for example, the fuzzy output set for a given input state is represented in degrees of membership for the corresponding control actions. Updating a whole region centered around the point specified by the state–action pair has the effect of interpolation in the learning process. Not as many training runs have to be performed since an entire neighborhood benefits from a single update with the positive effect of speeding up the learning. The neighborhood incorporating updates capture this idea. The *more dimensional simple neighborhood update* is defined as follows:

$\forall u_i \in \mathcal{U}_x$ and $\forall v_j \in \mathcal{U}_y$

$$R^t(u_i, v_j) =$$

$$\min\{1, \max\{0, R^t(u_i, v_j) + \alpha\, \kappa\, R^t(u_i, v_j)\, e^{(-(d_{u_i,v_j}^{x_{i_0}, y_{j_0}})^2)/\sigma_t^2}\}\}$$

The *more dimensional relative neighborhood update* is defined as follows:

$\forall u_i \in \mathcal{U}_x$ and $\forall v_j \in \mathcal{U}_y$

$$R^t(u_i, v_j) = \begin{cases} R^t(u_i, v_j) + \alpha\,(1 - R^t(u_i, v_j))\, e^{(-(d_{u_i,v_j}^{x_{i_0}, y_{j_0}})^2)/\sigma_t^2} & (1) \\ R^t(u_i, v_j) - \alpha\, R^t(u_i, v_j)\, e^{(-(d_{u_i,v_j}^{x_{i_0}, y_{j_0}})^2)/\sigma_t^2} & (2) \end{cases}$$

(1) - reward, (2) - punishment,

with α and κ as above. σ_t an adaptive variance defined below and d the Euclidean distance from the center point (x_{i_0}, y_{j_0} — the state–action pair). Now, the update scheme is additionally a function of time. With increasing time (number of iterations) the updated neighborhood decreases, finally converging to the center point.

Clearly, these last two update schemes contain additional parameters which have to be set beforehand. By decreasing an initially *large* neighborhood we want to achieve that, at first, a large region is updated, which, as learning progresses, converges to a small very localized region. The function used to decrease the "radius" of the neighborhood defining function has been chosen according to a function used in self–organizing feature maps for similar effects (Hertz, Krogh, and Palmer 1991).

The adaptive variance is determined by an initial variance $\sigma_{initial}$ and a final variance σ_{final}. Initially, a large neighborhood should be considered decreasing with time, so that the final neighborhood contains just the state–action pair itself; t, t_{max} denote the current time and the maximum number of steps. For tasks where the maximum number of steps is not known an approximative value has to be taken. The adaptive variance is defined as follows:

$$\sigma^t = \sigma_{initial} \left(\frac{\sigma_{final}}{\sigma_{initial}} \right)^{t/t_{max}}$$

The exponent is initially zero and grows until it attains one so that σ_t is initially $\sigma_{initial}$ and decreases after t_{max} steps reaching σ_{final}.

This update scheme involves a *time-decaying* neighborhood. An alternative approach is the *fixed* neighborhood incorporating update scheme that operates on a fixed neighborhood. It follows from the above operator by setting $\sigma_i = \sigma_f$.

Fuzzy Set Oriented Update

Another update scheme, also incorporating a neighborhood, is the *fuzzy set oriented update*. It is determined by defining a fuzzy set around the state-action pair in consideration. We choose symmetric triangular fuzzy sets but any fuzzy set may be used. These fuzzy sets are combined into a fuzzy relation on the Cartesian product of the input and output domains. The *fuzzy set oriented update* is defined as follows:

$\forall u_i \in \mathcal{U}_x$ and $\forall v_j \in \mathcal{U}_y$

$$R(u_i, v_j) = \max\{\gamma\, R(u_i, v_j), \min\{\mu_{I_{w_2}}(u_i), \mu_{O_{w_1}}(v_j)\}\},$$

with $0 < \gamma \leq 1$ a discount factor and w_1, w_2 parameters specifying the fuzzy set $\tilde{I}$ on the input domain and the fuzzy set $\tilde{O}$ on the output domain centered around the crisp state-action pair (x, y). The *discount factor* γ was introduced to discount the relation update in situations where the process response patterns change.

7.4.5 Learning Visualized

This section provides a better understanding of the learning algorithm by illustrating its behavior graphically. The algorithm is applied to function approximation tasks. In these tasks a controller learns to approximate a given function. At this point we want to emphasize on the learning algorithm by closely monitoring its behavior and the resulting fuzzy relation. For function approximation tasks we assume that the critic knows the correct function and judges the from the performance element transmitted action as either *good*, if it falls within an ϵ-neighborhood of the true value, or as *bad*, otherwise. Figure 7.4.5 shows snapshots of the fuzzy relations learned by the controller and depicts the controller's approximation behavior after the indicated number of iterations. The controller is evaluated on the sample points only in these snapshots.

7.4.6 Experiments

In this section the adaptation schemes are applied to function approximation tasks. In these tasks a controller is adapted such that it approximates a given function. The static character of these tasks allows us to study the fuzzy relation adaptation process isolated from the adaptive critic since the internal

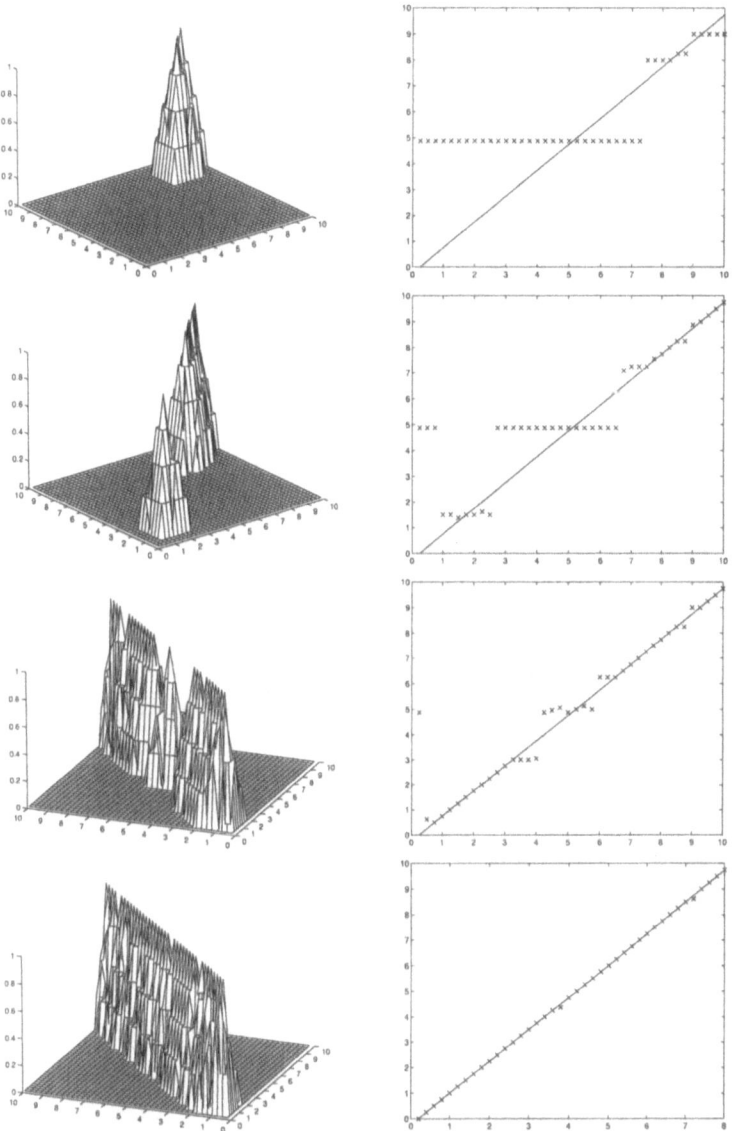

Fig. 7.10. Approximation of a linear function with the fuzzy set oriented update as reinforcement scheme. The left column above depicts the fuzzy relation learned in the product space of input and output domains of discourse. The right column depicts the learners approximation behavior based on the fuzzy relation learned. The true function is plotted as solid line, the approximation behavior is visualized as 'x'. The snapshots were taken after 50, 200, 500 and 1000 learning cycles.

reinforcement signal can be easily generated by comparing the real value of the function to be approximated with the through fuzzy inference computed value. If this difference is sufficiently small the controller performance is judged as *good* and otherwise as *bad*. We observe the adaptation process by means of the mean square error between the real function and the, through the fuzzy controller approximated function. The below presented, error curves show the development of the error over the number of iterations, averaged over the number of repetitions. One iteration involves an entire learning cycle (i.e., one execution of the inner loop of the control algorithm (cf. Figure 7.8). It should be noted that the error measure depends on the chosen discretization and the range of function values. The error must therefore be interpreted in a relative manner.

Adaptation with and without a Priori Knowledge

Figure 7.11 shows error curves for the approximation of $f(x) = x, x \in [0, 10]$. The meta relation was initialized with a set of rules describing f in straight forward manner (uniform partitioning of domain, 4 rules). The rules were randomly distorted. The positive effect of initializing the meta relation with prior knowledge (i.e., known rules) can be seen by comparing the error with the error in Figure 7.13. Both figures make reference to approximating the same function.

Figures 7.12 compares the behavior of the above developed update schemes. It follows that the fuzzy set oriented update performs best with regard to speed of learning and smoothness of adaptation. The neighborhood incorporating update lies between the fuzzy set oriented update and the point–wise update. These results are conform with other experiments completed in (Jacobsen 1995).

Figure 7.13 shows the influence of the parameter γ. Due to the static character of the task only slight effects are observable. The best performance is achieved with γ close to 1. The second graph in Figure 7.11 shows the influence of the parameter r. As the width of the fuzzy set, defining the update operator, increases, the speed and accuracy of learning augments. Intuitively, this can be interpreted as: if one updates more in a single step, less overall updates have to be effected.

Adaptation in Changing Environment

To investigate the *on-line adaptive* capabilities of the proposed algorithm we defined a learning task that simulates processes which exhibit sudden changes in their response patterns. This is achieved by altering the function underlying the approximation task in the above experiments. Figures 7.14 and 7.15 show the results for different parameters. (cf. (Moore and Harris 1994) for similar experiment in a supervised learning setting.)

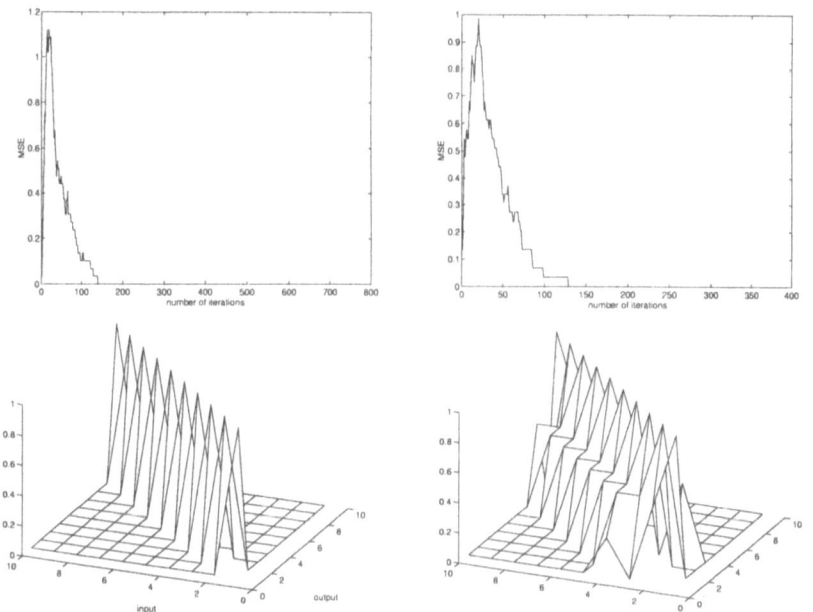

Fig. 7.11. Error for point-wise update ($\alpha = 1$ and fuzzy set oriented update ($r = 2, \gamma = 1$). Learning with a priori knowledge. Second row: Adapted fuzzy relations for the approximation of $f_1(x) = x, x \in [0, 10]$.

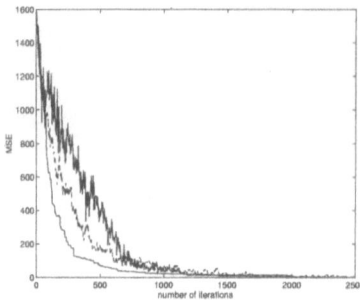
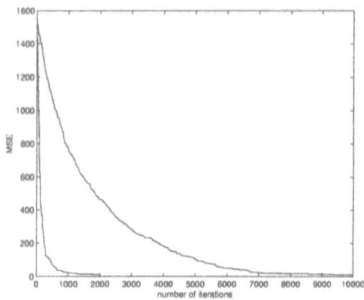

Fig. 7.12. Comparison of the error measures for the approximation of a complex partly linear function. Fuzzy set oriented update (both figures, solid line, $\gamma = 1$, $r = 5$), two dimensional update fixed variance (left figure, dashed line, $\sigma = 0.4$), two dimensional update time-decaying variance (left figure, solid line, $\sigma_i = 1.5, \sigma_f = 0.2$) and point-wise update (right figure, solid upper line, $\alpha = 0.7$).

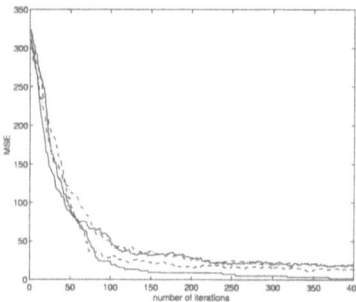
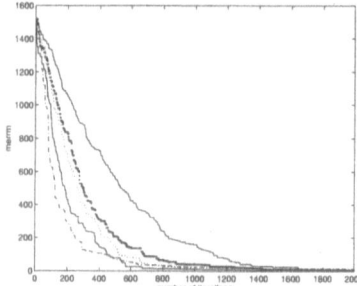

Fig. 7.13. First figure: Influence of the discount factor γ ($\gamma = 1$ (solid line), $\gamma = 0.8$ (dash dot line), $\gamma = 0.5$ (dashed line), $\gamma = 0.3$ (solid line)). Function f from above. Second figure: Study of parameter r (half-width of fuzzy set) ($r = 5, 1.25, 1.0, 0.75, 0.5$ from left to right in the figure; $\gamma = 1$). Complex partly linear function. Learning without a priori knowledge.

7.5 Expert–Guided Hybrid Neuro–Fuzzy System

The previous section discussed a fuzzy system architecture that is fully autonomous, with all system components being instantiated by different machine learning techniques. In this section we briefly present another instantiation of the learning agent framework that involves a human expert to guide the system in its learning stage. Figure 7.16 shows how the system's architectures derives from the agent framework presented above. This architecture has been discussed and evaluated in (Jacobsen and Iordanova 1994; Jacobsen, Iordanova, and Giacometti 1994) and is closely related to work by Giacometti (Giacometti 1992). Our approach differs in that it deploys fuzzy rules and appropriate reasoning schemes and different mechanisms to transfer knowledge between the system components.

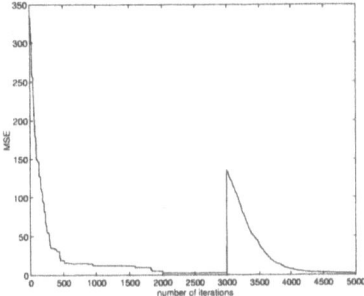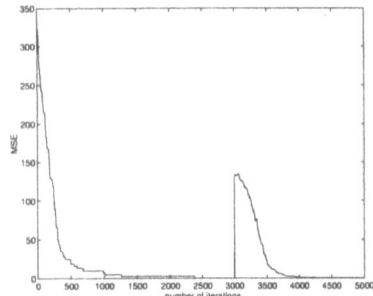

Fig. 7.14. Approximation of $g_1(x) = x$ changing after $T = 3000$ to $g_2(x) = x^2$ for $x \in [0, 1]$. (Fuzzy set oriented updates, $r = 2, r = 4$, respectively; $\gamma = 0.93$ in both runs).

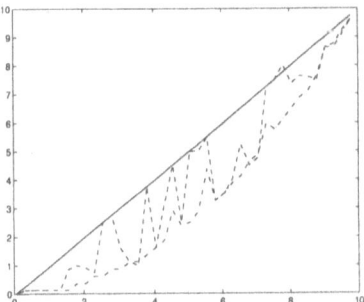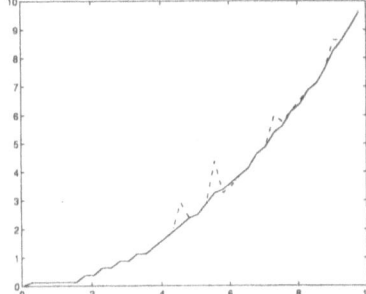

Fig. 7.15. Approximation behavior during the change in response characteristic in process occurred. Left figure : solid line at $T = 3000$; dashed line after $T = 3500$; dashed dotted line after $T = 4000$. Right figure : dash dotted line after $T = 4500$; solid line after $T = 5000$.

The performance element (PE) is instantiated by two entirely independent modules, a feed–forward neural network (NN) and a rule–based fuzzy decision support (FDS) system. Both map the system input state to an output decision (action). The neural network component is trained on a sample set (if available) by back propagation. The FDS is derived in concert with a human domain expert and an additional fine tuning stage. In our system we rely on a manual tuning stage, but any number of algorithms explored for this design stage could equally well be employed. The final PE output is determined by a conflict resolution scheme and depends on the operational mode of the system. We chose mechanisms as developed in previous work (Jacobsen and Iordanova 1994; Jacobsen, Iordanova, and Giacometti 1994) (emphasize on NN or on FDS depending on the domain knowledge available; action combination through a resolution operation.) To obtain exploratory behavior these resolution schemes must account for a slight degree of randomness according to system performance (the role of the problem generator in this architecture).

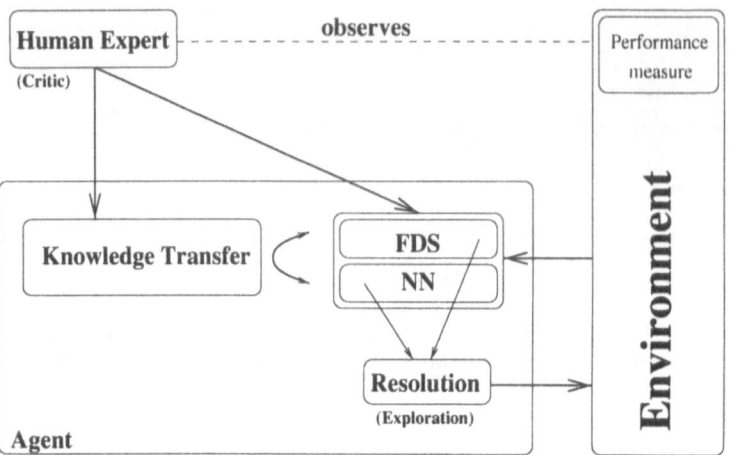

Fig. 7.16. Expert–guided hybrid neuro–fuzzy system

The learning element is a *knowledge transfer* component which allows knowledge to be explicitly transferred from either one of the modules, inherent to the PE, to the other. Several modes of operation are possible, see Table 7.2.

The system requires the assistance of a human critic which evaluates the decisions inferred and possibly intervenes to tune the system's parameters until it operates reliably. This approach is less appropriate for online learning due to the human interactions required. We plan to experiment with an automated critic in the future.

The overall architecture derives from the SHADE system fully explored in (Giacometti 1992) incorporating a symbolic, on classical logic based, expert system. In (Jacobsen 1992; Jacobsen, Iordanova, and Giacometti 1994; Jacobsen and Iordanova 1994) we extended the system to incorporate a fuzzy inference mechanism, generalizing the expert system component of the system, and extend the knowledge transfer operations available.

7.6 Discussion of Research Questions

In this section we discuss and raise some interesting further research questions. Many of these questions arise due to the introduction of fuzzy relations rather than fuzzy rules in the control system architecture. The relation based approach has the advantage of a sound theoretically foundation, but, practically, it is more complex to manage.

Due to the modular architecture of the discussed hybrid learning system and its well–defined interfaces, different techniques can easily be substituted for realizing the diverse functions in the system. The architecture provides

From NN to FDS
Rule extraction algorithm explored in (Jacobsen 1992) (Jacobsen and Iordanova 1994) that describes the neural network in terms of fuzzy production rules.
From FDS to NN
Bootsrapping of a neural network with the inverse of the extraction algorithm described in (Jacobsen 1992; Jacobsen and Iordanova 1994).
Generation of samples by applying randomly generated inputs to the FDS, inferring an output and training the NN with the random sample.

Table 7.2. Knowledge transfer modes.

therefore a framework for testing the complementarity of various learning techniques. It provides also a testbed for comparing different fuzzy inference schemes and learning algorithms within the same environment. We have aimed at demonstrating this through presenting two original system instantiations. Further work needs to quantitatively explore the complementarity of the machine learning techniques used within the individual system components.

Dynamic Data Structure for Fuzzy Relation Representation

The representation of the control knowledge by a fuzzy relation is more memory intensive than its representation by individual rules. Although, the relation is usually only sparsely populated, it has so far been stored as entire structure. As we have demonstrated above, the aggregated fuzzy relation could be computed for each decision step anew, thus trading off computing time for memory. An alternative would be the design of an optimized data structure for the fuzzy relation storage and manipulation.

Let the control knowledge be represented in an n-array fuzzy relation (n-1 inputs and one output, for SISO — single input, single output systems). Let n_i denote the number of sample points of the i-th domain of discourse. The entire relation thus holds $m = \prod_{i=1}^{n} n_i$ membership values. Since accuracy of membership values is not critical, one byte of storage to represent the membership value is sufficient. Still m bytes of storage are needed. So far we have neglected the questions of discretization of the domains of discourse involved, however, this is an important parameter that determines the accuracy of learning (Jacobsen 1995). For applications with more than one input dimension (and more than one output) the storage of the fuzzy relation as entire memory structure may become a problem. An efficient dynamic data structure for storing and manipulating fuzzy relations is needed to support these kind of systems.

Fuzzy Relation Interpretation

For the reinforcement–driven fuzzy relation adaptation algorithm we have exploited the immediate relationship between system input and output in the relation to adapt the underlying knowledge representation. The initial relation is computed by transforming the expert given fuzzy rules into the meta relation (cf. 7.4.1). However, this abandons the explicit representation of the linguistic values making up the fuzzy rules and the rules themselves, now implicitly represented in the relation. In the following we will refer to this transformation as *mapping* from rules to relation.

This mapping does not have one unique inverse which could be applied to the relation re–generating the underlying rules. Rather, several sets of rules exist which give rise to the same relation. Finding an exact solution by decomposing the relation is a rather hard problem. The following discussion will briefly illustrate the encountered difficulties in decomposing a fuzzy relation. To simplify the discussion let us assume that the number of rules to be constructed is fixed[2]. The decomposition problem thus reduces to finding an appropriate set of rules which generates the given relation.

To establish the result of non–uniqueness of this solution let us consider the following simple example. Given the fuzzy rule $[\tilde{A} \Rightarrow \tilde{B}]$ with premise fuzzy set $\tilde{A}$ and consequent fuzzy set $\tilde{B}$. The relation modeling the implication operator is given by:

$$\tilde{R} = \tilde{A} \circ_R \tilde{B} = (0.3, 1) \circ_R \begin{pmatrix} 0.5 \\ 0 \end{pmatrix} = \begin{pmatrix} 0.3 & 0.5 \\ 0.0 & 0.0 \end{pmatrix}$$

where $\circ_R$ is the minimum implication relation[3]. Now $\widetilde{A_1} = (0.3, 0.9)$ and $\tilde{B}$ as above are for example possible fuzzy sets generating the same relation:

$$\widetilde{A_1} \circ_R \tilde{B} = (0.3, 0.9) \circ_R \begin{pmatrix} 0.5 \\ 0 \end{pmatrix} = \begin{pmatrix} 0.3 & 0.5 \\ 0.0 & 0.0 \end{pmatrix} = \tilde{R} \quad .$$

This example proves the following property.

Property:
Given a fuzzy relation $\tilde{R} \subseteq \mathcal{U} \times \mathcal{V}$ then the decomposition of $\tilde{R}$ in a set of rules $[\tilde{A}_i \Rightarrow \tilde{B}_i]$ where $\tilde{A}_i \subseteq \mathcal{U}$ and $\tilde{B}_i \subseteq \mathcal{V}$ such that

$$\tilde{R}_i = \tilde{A}_i \circ_R \tilde{B}_i \quad \text{and} \quad \tilde{R} = \bigcup_{i=1}^{n} \tilde{R}_i$$

is in general not unique.

---

[2] This is not a trivial assumption but facilitates the formulation of the following results.

[3] We use a vectorial notation instead of the common *fractional* notation which is sufficient for this example. The underlying universe is an abstract body of objects which is of no further importance.

From this example it can be seen that the task of decomposing a fuzzy relation into a set of rules or finding all sets of rules generating the relation is non trivial. Important questions with regard to such a decomposition are to find minimal sets of rules, interpretable sets of rules with respect to an a posteriori interpretation, and algorithmic tractable solutions for decomposition. The *fuzzy relation decomposition problem* has gotten little attention in the fuzzy set theory literature. To the best of our knowledge (Efstathiou and Tong 1981; Jacobsen 1995; Riedmiller, Spott, and Weisbrod 1997) are the only ones looking at this problem in greater detail.

Adaptive Discretization

In this work we have assumed that a discretization of the domains of discourse of input and output variables were given. The discretization influences the achievable accuracy of the controller fundamentally. It therefore is a crucial parameter that has to be chosen by the system designers. A further extension would be an approach that tries to "learn" an appropriate discretization, possibly one with different resolutions at different intervals of the domains. Moreover, a continuous function approximation of a fuzzy relation would solve this problem as well, and constitute an interesting new concept.

Adaptive Critic

The development of a sophisticated adaptive critic element, capable of solving the *sequential decision problem* is a further important issue. The critic has to learn to judge the appropriateness of having taken a given action in a given state, relative to other actions available in the same state. It passively observes the sequence of process states and the associated control actions emitted by the performance element, adapting its internal process model according to some pre-determined objective function ("optimality criterion") (e.g., control success and failure; minimal energy, etc.). Two alternatives are discussed in the literature for solving this problem (Russell and Norwig 1995):

- a utility function on state histories is learned and used for decision making by selecting actions that maximize the expected outcome,
- an action–value function, describing the utility of taking a given action in a given state, is learned (Q–learning).

The critic element is thus crucial to the success of learning as it generates for the learning algorithm the essential reinforcement signal. An interesting extension would be to employ a knowledge–based approach for the critic element, e.g., a second fuzzy rule–based system. Intuitively, it seems to be simpler to come up with rules classifying actions in *good* and *bad* states, than to come up with entire control rules. With regard to knowledge acquisition such an approach would be favorable, since it is less labor intensive, but at the same time goal–oriented towards incorporating knowledge into the learning process.

7.7 Conclusion

We argue that, to obtain a less ad hoc design methodology for designing intelligent systems, attribute should be paid to the learning agent architecture which has long been discussed in the AI community. We have presented two original instantiations of this architecture and have experimentally validated their designs.

Our experiments present a preliminary study of the interaction of the different components in the agent. We intend to further study their mutual effects and experiment with alternative instantiations.

In the system instantiations presented here we have mainly focused on neural network and fuzzy system based techniques for realizing the individual components. Clearly, other techniques might equally well be used instead, e.g., believe networks, dynamic believe networks, decision trees, or symbolic processing techniques. Moreover, the individual components may be arbitrarily complex constituting any one instance of the architectures presented in Section 7.2. We leave such exploration open for future work.

Acknowledgments

The author is very grateful to the following people for assisting in one way or another in the preparation of this paper: Lotfi Zadeh, Joachim Weisbrod, Bernard Amy, Irena Markova (Iordanova), and Arnaud Giacometti.

References

Arao, M., Y. Tsutsumi, T. Fukuda, and K. Shimojima (1995, March). Flexible intelligent system based on fuzzy neural networks and reinforcement learning. In *Proceedings of 1995 IEEE International Conference on Fuzzy Systems*, Number 5 in 1, pp. 69–70. IEEE.

Barto, A., R. Sutton, and C. Anderson (1983). Neuro like adaptive elements that can solve difficult learning control problems. *IEEE Trans. Systems, Man & Cybernetics*.

Berenji, H. R. (1992, February). A reinforcement learning-based architecture for fuzzy logic control. *Int. J. Approximate Reasoning 6*, 267 –292.

Berenji, H. R. and P. Khedkar (1992, September). Learning and tuning fuzzy logic controllers through reinforcements. *IEEE Trans. Neural Networks 3*, 724–740.

Efstathiou, J. and R. Tong (1981). The problem of fuzzy relation decomposition. Technical report, ERL, University of California, Berkeley.

Eppler, W. (1993). *Pre-structuring of Neural Networks with Fuzzy Logic (in German)*. Ph. D. thesis, University of Karlsruhe (TH).

Giacometti, A. (1992, November). *Hybrid models for expertise (in french)*. Ph. D. thesis, Ecole National Supérieur des Télécommunications, Paris.

Hertz, J., A. Krogh, and R. Palmer (1991). *Introduction to the Theory of Neural Computation*. (Addison-Wesley).

Jacobsen, H.-A. (1992, Feb). Fuzzy inference in a hybrid expert system (in french). "Studienarbeit", University of Karlsruhe (TH) and LIFIA, Grenoble, France.

Jacobsen, H.-A. (1995, August). Adaptive fuzzy systems for control (in english). Master's thesis, University of Karlsruhe (TH), Karlsruhe, Germany.

Jacobsen, H.-A. (1998, May). A generic architecture for hybrid intelligent systems. In *IEEE International Conference on Fuzzy Systems*, Anchorage, Alaska.

Jacobsen, H.-A. and I. Iordanova (1994, September). Approach to extraction of fuzzy production rules from a connectionist component of a hybrid expert system. In *6th International Conference on Artificial Intelligence: Methodology, Systems and Applications*, Sofia, Bulgaria.

Jacobsen, H.-A., I. Iordanova, and A. Giacometti (1994, July). Extraction des regles floues dans une systeme hybride (in french). In *5th International Conference on Processing and Management of Uncertainty (IPMU)*, Paris, France.

Jacobsen, H.-A. and J. Weisbrod (1996, July). Reinforcement–driven adaptation of control relations. In *North American Conference on Fuzzy Information Processing*, Berkeley, CA. NAFIPS.

Jang, R. (1992). *Adaptive Network Fuzzy Inference System*. Ph. D. thesis, University of California, Berkeley.

Lee, C. C. (1990). A self-learning rule-based controller employing approximate reasoning and neural network concepts. *Int. J. Intell. Syst. 5*.

Moore, C. G. and C. J. Harris (1994). *Advances in Intelligent Control*, Chapter Indirect Adaptive Fuzzy Control. Burgess Science Press.

Nauck, D. and R. Kruse (1992, December). A neural fuzzy controller learning by fuzzy error propagation. In *NAFIPS92*, Puerto Vallarta, pp. 388–397.

Okamoto, W. and S. T. et al. (1995). Flins-fuzzy natural language communication system. In *Proceedings of 1995 IEEE International Conference on Fuzzy Systems*.

Riedmiller, M., M. Spott, and J. Weisbrod (1997). First results on the application of the fynesse. In *Proceedings of the IEEE Aerospace Conference*, Aspen.

Russell, S. and P. Norwig (1995). *A modern approach to artificial intelligence*. Englewood Cliffs, NJ: Prentice Hall.

Sulzberger, S. M., N. N. Tschichold-Gürman, and S. J. Vestli (1993, March). Fun: Optimization of fuzzy rule based systems using neural networks. In *Proc. IEEE Int. Conf. on Neural Networks 1993*, San Francisco, pp. 312–316.

Sutton, R. (1984). *Temporal Crdit Assignment in Reinforcement Learning*. Ph. D. thesis, University of Massachusetts.

Sutton, R. (1988). Learning to predict by the method of temporal differences. *Machine Learning*.

Tano, S. (1997). Potential of fuzzy symbols and computational inference for multi modal user interface. In *IFSA World Congress*, Prague.

Tano, S., Y. Namba, H. Sakao, T. Tomita, and H. Aoshima (1997). Design concept based on real–virtual–intelligen user interface and its software architecture. In *HCI'97*, pp. 901–90.

Tano, S., T. Oyama, and T. Arnould (1996). Deep combination of fuzzy inference and neural network in fuzzy inference. *Fuzzy Sets and Systems 82*(2), 151–60.

Weisbrod, J. (1995). Fuzzy control revisited — why is it working? In P. P. Wang (Ed.), *Advances in Fuzzy Theory and Technology, Vol. III*, pp. 219–244. Durham (NC): Bookwrights.

Zadeh, L. A. (1973). Outline of a new approach to the analysis of complex systems and decision processes. *IEEE Trans. on System, Man, and Cybernetics 3*, 28–44.

New Paradigm toward Deep Fusion of Computational and Symbolic Processing

Shun'ichi Tano

Graduate School of Information Systems,
University of Electro-Communications
Chofu, Tokyo 182-8585, JAPAN
Voice: +81-424-43-5601, Fax: +81-424-43-5681
E-mail: tano@is.uec.ac.jp

Abstract: The computational processing methods appeared to overcome the drawbacks of the symbolic processing method. Recently the serious limitations of the computational processing methods have been found through the development of the highly intelligent user interface systems. The simple solutions to the limitations are the return to the symbolism or the pursue of the hierarchical system architecture. However it is indispensable to deeply combine the symbolic and computational processing in order to realize the highly intelligent system. This paper analyzes the leading models, which use symbolic and computational processing, and clarifies the problems of them. The level of the combination is not deep, high and wide enough. Based on the analysis, we propose a new paradigm toward deep fusion of computational and symbolic processing and show the new model as the first step of the paradigm. The model is realized by "Symbol Emergence Method for Q-Learning Neural Network". We testified the validity of the new method.

8.1. Introduction

The computational processing methods such as fuzzy theory, neural network and statistical method appeared to overcome the drawbacks of the symbolic processing method; i.e. the knowledge based approach. Recently the serious limitations of the computational processing methods have been found through the development of the highly intelligent system. The simple solutions to the limitations are the return to the symbolism or the pursuit of the hierarchical system architecture.

However it is indispensable to deeply combine the symbolic and computational processing in order to realize the highly intelligent system. In this new architecture, the symbolic processing and the computational processing should affect each other at anytime and at any abstract level. Although the fuzzy methodologies potentially play an important role to combine the symbolic and computational processing due to the inherent nature of fuzzy theory, there are not appropriate fuzzy methodologies for the purpose.

In this paper, I will overview the leading attempts toward the deep fusion of computational and symbolic processing and discuss the future of this emerging field.

In the following section 8.2, our experience of the development of the new user interface system called RVI-Desk is briefly described to give a concrete example showing the necessity of the symbolic and computational processing.

In the section 8.3, the software architecture is shown and the fusion of symbolic and computational processing is addressed.

In the section 8.4, we analyze the leading attempts such as, the fuzzy theory, the conceptual fuzzy set, the Q-learning on the neural network and the rule reasoning, the logic operations on the neural network, the combination of pattern and symbol, the neural network with the attention mechanism and our methods. We point out that all of the conventional methods should be regard as the merely hybrid system. Their combination of the computational and symbolic processing can be categorized as either the rigid parallel structure or the simple sequential structure. The inflexible structure limits the cooperation of the symbolic and computational processing. Therefore they actually can not improve the performance drastically but improve only a little.

In the section 8.5, we reconsider the requirements of the combination of the symbolic and computational processing by analyzing the role of the pattern (concept), the symbol (word) and the natural language (structure of sentence) in human's intelligent problem solving behavior.

In the section 8.6, we propose a simple model as the first step toward the fusion of computational and symbolic processing. Our model consists of two layers. The lower layer is a neural network where the Q-learning is simulated. The inputs are the state variables and the outputs are the Q-values for each action. It is tuned to memorize the Q-table. The upper layer watches the activity in the lower layer and find out the specific node group, which are activated all together only when some actions in lower layer get the high reward from the environment. Thus, the symbols are emerged. And then they are embedded in the lower layer to speed up the learning. Moreover, sometimes the emergent symbols are generalized and embedded in the different position. By the simulation, we demonstrate that the symbol emergence and its forced application in Q-learning can make a great improvement in the performance of the simple football game players.

In the last section, the summary is given.

8.2. Experience of the Development of Next Generation User Interface System

8.2.1 New Design Concept: RVI-concept

The new concepts proposed for the user interface can be categorized into the following three concepts by our analysis.

(i) Virtual World-centered UI [1]
Basic idea is to realize a virtual desk or a virtual office environment in a computer by the virtual reality technology and the computer graphics technology. In other words, they try to build a real world in virtual (computer) world.

(ii) Real World-centered UI [2]

A completely opposite way of thinking is to augment a real world by a computer power. The paradigm is refereed as terms of "back to real world", "ubiquitous computing" and "augmented reality".

(iii) Intelligent UI [3]

Intelligent processing, i.e. problem solving and learning, is usually applied in the industrial world to solve complex problems such the diagnosis of the furnace. Someone believes that the user interface should be intelligent in order to move from the direct manipulation to the indirect management. Recently software becomes too complex to understand the full specifications. So the shift toward the Intelligent UI is inevitable.

The key idea of our design concept is the combination of these three conflicting concepts at the adequate level. At the first glance, the three concepts look quit different, but look carefully, and you can see that they compensate each other. Moreover they can synergistically combined. Our design concept is "Fusion of Three Exclusive Concepts". This idea is so simple that it is applicable to any fields. We call it RVI-concept [6, 7].

8.2.2 Experimental System: RVI-DESK

For the feasibility study, the RVI-concept has been applied to the design of the desk environment. We developed RVI-desk based on RVI-concept and evaluated it [4,5].

Appearance of RVI-desk is shown in Fig.8.1. RVI-desk consists of:
- Monitor with touch sensor x 1
- Pen Pad x 3 or more
- Pen with Scanner x 1
- Microphone & Speaker x 1 set
- Keyboard x 1

Three workstations and six PCs are needed for the recognition and the synthesis of multi media data and the intelligent processing.

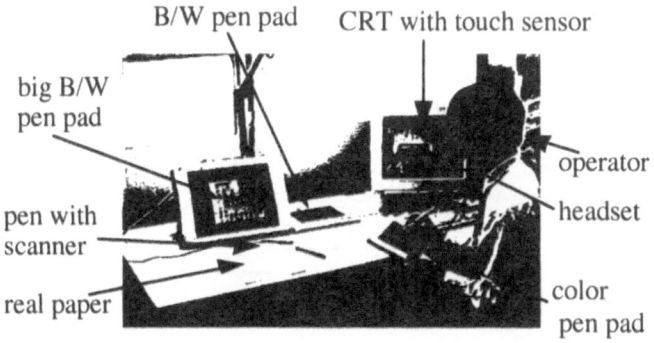

Fig. 8.1. Photograph of current RVI-desk

176

Two types of intelligent processing were realized in RVI-desk.

- Multi Media Input/Output Recognition

Recently the recognition algorithms have been greatly improved. Concerning speech recognition, accuracy and vocabulary are almost at level of practical use. But it is still difficult to use as a prime input media, except for Japanese handwriting. Actually Japanese handwriting can be recognized at quit high accuracy. So we have decided the pen input as primary input media and that the recognition results of other media are corrected by the semantic consistency. Of course, it is possible to use single modality such as speech through microphone and printed material through a pen with scanner. But, practically, single modal input except handwriting should not be used due to the low accuracy of recognition.

Intelligent processing is adopted to check the semantic consistency among the information form several modalities.

- Intelligent Multi Modal Agent

To realize the movement from the direct manipulation to the indirect management, we developed an agent whose face, as a symbol of an agent, is displayed in the EnvironmentViewer (CRT with touch sensor). The agent always listens and watches users' input. So the agent always checks the semantic consistency among the inputs from many modalities and corrects them. At the same time, the agent always looks for the command, which the agent can perform. When the agent succeeds in finding a command, the agent smiles and waits for allowance of the execution. Facial expression and the understood command are displayed in the EnvironmentViewer. Then the agent generates either the command sequence to control several applications or multi modal output to a user.

This agent is built by a knowledge-based approach. It has a knowledge base, which store information concerning applications that the RVI-desk has as well as the linguistic knowledge. Fig.8.2 shows the software architecture of RVI-Desk.

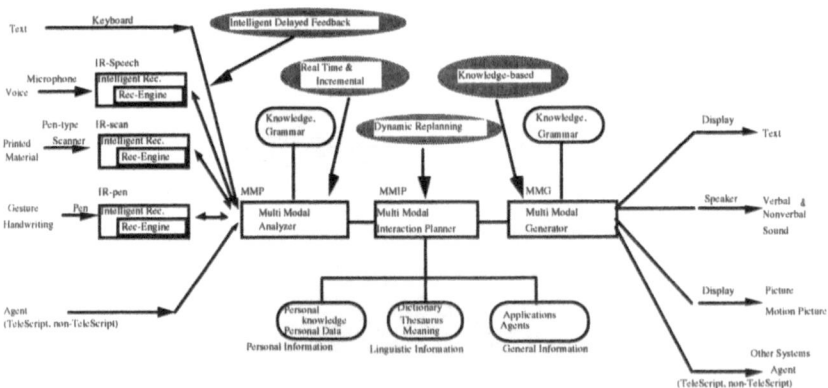

Fig. 8.2. Software architecture of RVI-desk

8.3. Software Architecture for Next Generation User Interface
- Fusion of Symbolic and Computational Processing -

The problem is how to realize a system with which a user can communicate through multi modalities, such as voice, handwriting, pen gesture, printed material, touch screen and keyboard. Eventually our RVI-concept leads a certain system, which is intelligent and can handle the multi modal input and output. So the architecture shown in Fig.8.3 will be a common architecture. The architecture shown in Fig.8.3 should be regarded as basic software for the future user interface.

How should we implement this architecture? Candidates are the computational AI, e.g. the neural systems, and the symbolic AI, e.g. the rule-based systems.

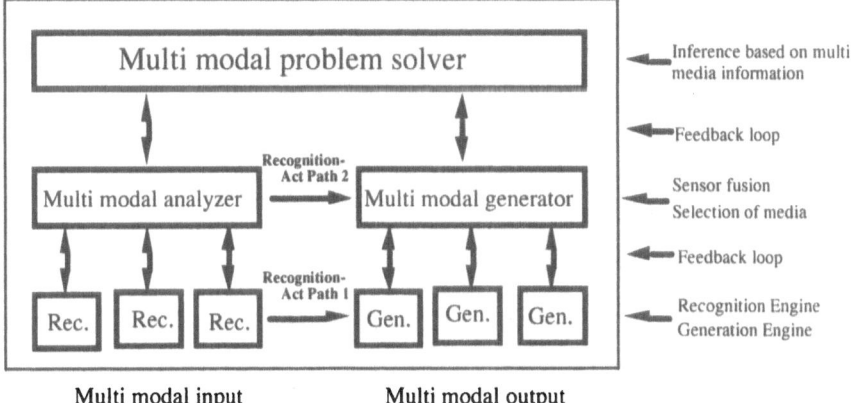

Multi modal input   Multi modal output

Fig.8.3. Basic software for next generation UI

Generally speaking, the former is suitable for recognition of raw data and the latter is suitable for high level inference. Actually, many systems adopt two layers structure where low level recognition is realized by a neural system and the correction and the problem solving in upper layer are realized by the logical inference mechanism. Our RVI-desk is not the exception (see Fig. 8.2). This approach can be regarded as the third state (e.g. Hybrid System) in Fig. 8.4.

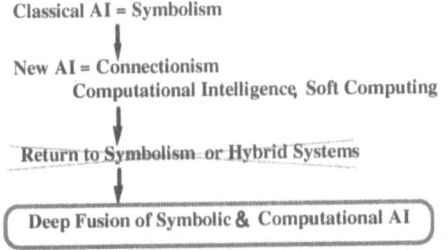

Fig. 8.4. History of symbolic & computational AI

But we found that symbolic AI is needed even in recognition of raw data for more accurate recognition and computational AI is needed even in high level problem solving for more robust inference and meta-level analogical reasoning (see Fig. 8.5). We started the study on the fusion of computational AI and symbolic AI. Note that it is not "hybrid" but "fusion."

	Stimulus-Response	Inference
Symbolism (Classical AI)	✕	○
Fusion of Symbolic & Computational AI	○ (Intelligent)	○ (Robust, Analogy)
Connectionism (Computational Intelligence) (Soft Computing)	○	✕ (△)

Fig. 8.5. Effects of deep fusion

8.4. Conventional Approaches and Problems

8.4.1 Overview

There are many research activities for the integration of symbol and pattern [8-12]. The related works are;
- Fuzzy Theory,
- Conceptual Fuzzy Set,
- NN(Q-learning) + Rule Representation,
- Logic on NN,
- Combination of Pattern and Symbol, and
- NN+Attention.

Please refer [16] for more detailed information. These researches try to combine the symbol and pattern based on the pattern processing. That is, they based mainly on the pattern processing or the computational processing first, and then try to take in the symbolic processing. We took the opposite way of thinking. We took in the symbolic processing first and then combined the computational processing. Our research are;
- FINEST: Extension of Symbolic and Computational Nature of Fuzzy Reasoning [17, 18] and
- FLINS: Fusion of Symbolic AI and Fuzzy Methodologies [19, 20].

8.4.2 FINEST: Extension of Symbolic and Computational Nature of Fuzzy Reasoning

8.4.2.1 Overview of FINEST

We developed FINEST (Fuzzy Inference Environment Software with Tuning) [17, 18]. It is actually a software environment for fuzzy inference with a mechanism to tune the inference method as well as fuzzy predicates. Since it has an improved fuzzy reasoning, it can be seen as an example of the extension of symbolic and computational nature of fuzzy reasoning.

FINEST has the following three special features.

(1) Improved generalized modus ponens

(2) Mechanism which can tune the inference method as well as fuzzy predicates

(3) Software environment for debugging and tuning

Concerning (1), the generalized modus ponens is improved in the following four ways: (a) aggregation operators that have synergy and cancellation nature, (b) a parameterized implication function, (c) a combination function which can reduce fuzziness, and (d) backward-chaining based on generalized modus ponens. The (a)-(c) extend the symbolic nature of the fuzzy reasoning.

8.4.2.2 Extension of Symbolic and Computational Nature of Fuzzy Reasoning

(1) Computational Nature of Fuzzy Reasoning

Consider the following fuzzy rules and facts.

$$Rule\ i: If\ x_1\ is\ A_{i1}\ and\cdot\cdot and\ x_n\ is\ A_{in}\ then\ y\ is\ B_i$$

$$Fact\ j:\ x_j\ is\ A_j^!\qquad (j=1,\cdots,n,\quad i=1,\cdots,m)$$

In FINEST, they are converted into a neural-network-like structure where fuzzy data are processed and flown.

(2) Extension of Symbolic Nature of Fuzzy Reasoning

The flow in the neural-network-like structure shows only the computational procedure. In other words, we can observe that the data are computed in some manner in the network, but we can not symbolically understand the meaning of the calculation and the calculated result flown in the network. The only exception is the fuzzy predicates. We can observe fuzzy sets flown in the network and at the same time we can understand the symbolical meaning, i.e., as the name of the fuzzy set.

To extend the symbolic nature of the fuzzy reasoning, it is necessary to clarify the symbolic meaning of the aggregation functions, the implication functions and the combination functions.

We have clarified and defined the symbolic meaning of these three functions.

(a) Extended Aggregation Function

Even though, in many cases, a rule is simply expressed in the form " If X and Y Then Z", the "and" operator has a vague meaning. It may have a strict "and" nature, or a weak one.

We defined a new aggregation operator '*and*' by adding a synergistic effect to an ordinary t-norm operator (denoted by 'basic(x,y)'). The following formula defines the *and* operator when the basic function 'basic(x,y)' is Dombi's t-norm.

$$*And* (x, y) = w \times synergy(x, y) + (1 - w) \times basic(x, y)$$
$$w = equal(x, y) \times high(x, y) \times \gamma$$
$$equal(x, y) = almost(0, x - y, \alpha)$$
$$high(x, y) = almost(1, x, \beta) \times almost(1, y, \beta)$$
$$almost(a, x, b) = exp(\ln 0. 5 \times (x - a)^2 / b^2)$$
$$synergy(x, y) = 1$$
$$basic(x, y) = \cfrac{1}{1 + \sqrt[p]{\left(\dfrac{1-x}{x}\right)^p + \left(\dfrac{1-y}{y}\right)^p}}$$

This operator has four parameters representing respectively the strength of the synergistic effect (γ), the area where this effect is required (α, β), and Dombi's t-norm parameter (p). Furthermore, the cancellation property, which is of the same nature as the synergistic effect, can be expressed as a special kind of synergistic effect.

(b) Extended Implication Function

There are various implication functions. They can be classified based on the relations that are generally considered to be satisfied between the premise "x is A' " and the conclusion "y is B' " deduced by a rule "IF x is A THEN y is B" using fuzzy inference. We have developed the parameterized implications whose parameters correspond the semantic meaning.

(c) Extended Combination Function

A combination operation is defined as a method of getting one result A''' when two fuzzy sets A' and A" are deduced by two inference processes.

Many systems use the max operator as a combination method, but this causes a constant increase of the fuzziness. To resolve the problems, we introduce two new parameters, equilibrium E, and dependence factors α and β.

An equilibrium parameter E is introduced to provide a tradeoff point, which is interpreted as neither a positive belief nor a negative belief. The meaning of the grade is divided at E. Values greater then E correspond to positive belief, whereas values lower than E correspond to negative belief.

The property of reinforcement is indispensable for combination operations. It is also important to take into account of the dependence of evidence. The parameters α and β show the dependence factors of the underlying derivation relation.

It covers the range of conventional combination functions, such as the max-based combination function, min-based combination function, voting-model-based combination function, probability-based combination and so on.

8.4.2.3 Evaluation of the Extension

As explained in the above sections, the symbolic meaning of the aggregation functions, the implication functions and the combination functions has been clarified. So now we can understand the symbolic meaning of all of the calculation and all of the calculated result flown in the network as well as the fuzzy predicates.

This extension enables to quantify the fuzzy meaning of sentences expressed in the form of fuzzy rules. For example, aggregation operators, implication methods, combination methods as well as fuzzy predicates can be tuned with FINEST, and as a result the nature of the sentences is made clear because the symbolic nature is clarified. The interpretation is, for example, "the 'and' in this rule has a strong synergistic nature," "the 'or' has a weak cancellation property," or "this rule expresses knowledge of the form 'the more ...., the more.....' ." It can be said that ordinary tools can quantify the meaning of fuzzy predicates such as "tall" and "big" because fuzzy predicates can be learned. FINEST, however, expands the range of quantification into the meaning of natural language sentences.

This work can thus be regarded as the first step of the deep fusion of symbolic and computational processing of the fuzzy inference.

8.4.3. FLINS: Fusion of Symbolic AI and Fuzzy Methodologies

8.4.3.1 Overview of FLINS

We developed a natural language communication system called 'FLINS', which is short for Fuzzy Lingual System [19, 20]. FLINS has three-layered fuzzy inference to understand the meaning of natural language. It can be seen as an example of the fusion of symbolic AI (Artificial Intelligence) and fuzzy methodologies.

8.4.3.2 Fusion of Symbolic AI and Fuzzy Theory

Fig.8.6 shows the structure of three-layered fuzzy inference developed for FLINS. It consists of three layers, i.e., basic inference layer, fuzzy inference layer, and fuzzy CBR layer.

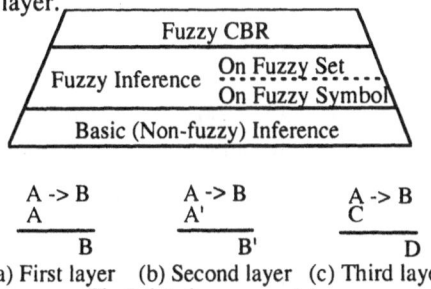

(a) First layer   (b) Second layer   (c) Third layer
Fig.8.6. Inference model

(1) Basic Inference Layer

The basic inference mechanism is an ordinary (non-fuzzy) inference, that is regular modus ponens shown in Fig.6 (a). In this base layer, the symbols are treated simply as labels.

(2) Fuzzy Inference Layer

The second layer is a fuzzy inference on fuzzy sets or fuzzy symbols. In this layer, a symbol is treated as either a fuzzy set (i.e., a sort of distribution over a universe of discourse) or a fuzzy symbol (i.e. words that can be calculated). For example, 'a tall boy' and 'a boy of 180 cm height' in natural languages can be matched in this layer although they can not be matched in the basic inference layer.

The following natural language proposition (NLP) is the canonical form of a standard fuzzy sentence in FLINS so far. This shows what kind of fuzziness FLINS can deal with.

$$(QA \text{ is } F \text{ is } \tau) * (QA \text{ is } F \text{ is } \tau) *...$$

where   Q : fuzzy quantifier : most
                 A : fuzzy quantity : foreigner
                 F : fuzzy predicate : tall
                 τ : fuzzy qualifier : true
                 * : and, or, implication,...

(3)Fuzzy CBR Layer

Top layer is a fuzzy case-based reasoning. It is the case-based reasoning (CBR) extended by fuzzy theory, which tries to match cases (which are also represented as texts) on the basis of their fuzzy relations, which are deduced by using the knowledge in 'Text Base'. This can be formalized as $(A \to B, C) \Rightarrow D$ where C is different from A as shown Fig. 8.6(c)

Cooperation of Three Layers

In the problem solving phase, the three-layered fuzzy inference mechanism is used in the bottom to the top manner (i.e. the ordinary inference, the fuzzy inference and the fuzzy CBR are evoked in this order) and *recursively*. When a user asks a question, the question is inputted to the basic layer where the question is processed by the ordinary (non-fuzzy) inference. When the question can not be solved by the basic layer, the question is passed into the fuzzy inference layer. Finally, it may be passed in the fuzzy CBR layer. In real problems, since it is often the case that some part of the question can be dealt by the basic layer, some part by the fuzzy inference layer and some part by the fuzzy-CBR, so the structure is not simple as explained above but very complicated. The calling sequence is illustrated in Fig.8.7. Note that the calling sequence is structured *recursively*.

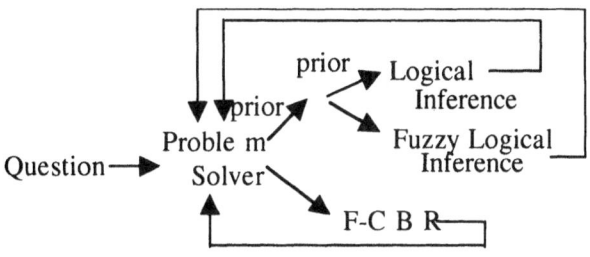

Fig.8.7. Calling sequence

8.4.3.3 Evaluation of the Fusion

The development of FLINS is a new challenge to apply the fuzzy theory in the natural language understanding system. Especially it is important of FLINS to combine the classical non-fuzzy logic, the fuzzy logic and the analogical reasoning.

The weak point of classical inference is compensated by the fuzzy inference and the weak point of fuzzy inference is compensated by the CBR. Moreover the loop of the compensation is structured recursively. As a result, the three-layered fuzzy inference realized the robust and high level logical inference.

8.4.4 Problems

The cooperation of the conventional approaches including ours is not close enough. For example, the difference between the symbol and the pattern is so clearly defined that they are processed in the completely difference manner and their role is prefixed. The combination can not be seen as fusion but hybrid. The problems can be analyzed from the following three point of view, i.e. the model structure, the information representation and the learning.

Model Structure

Conventional systems can be categorized into the sequential model and the parallel model. In the sequential model, the symbolic processing unit and the computational processing unit are sequentially combined. In the parallel model, they are combined in parallel.

In the sequential model, the output of the unit is an input of the other unit. Basically each unit has its own role and the role is exclusive. So it is impossible to help each other.

In the parallel model, they can interact each other through the input and the output. But it is still impossible to interact each other at the middle of the processing in the unit.

Information Representation

The information representation in the symbolic processing is completely different from that of the computational processing. That makes it impossible to interact each other.

Learning

Usually the designer gives the definition of the fuzzy set, the membership function, the meaning of the words and so on as prior knowledge. It does not cause the problem in case that the world is static. However the real world is highly dynamic. So the learning ability should be taken into account even in the combination of the symbolic processing and the computational processing.

8.5. New Paradigm toward Deep Fusion of Symbolic and Computational Processing

As shown in the previous sections, there are many research activities for the integration of symbol and pattern. But the cooperation between them is not close enough. For example, the difference between the symbol and the pattern is so clearly defined that they are processed in the completely difference manner and their role is prefixed. The combination can not be seen as fusion but hybrid.

I think the key feature is the mutual interaction at anytime, at anywhere and at any abstract level. The symbol and the pattern should be *synergistically* combined and the powerful mechanism should be emerged by this mutual interaction at anytime, at anywhere and at any abstract level [13-15].

Our current approach is shown in Fig. 8.8. Basic calculation model is a recurrent neural network and a self-organizing learning method. This model gives two processing views at the same time. That is, both of the stimulus-response reaction and the symbolic processing, including the language processing and the analogy based on the language metaphor, can be seen in this model through the different viewpoint.

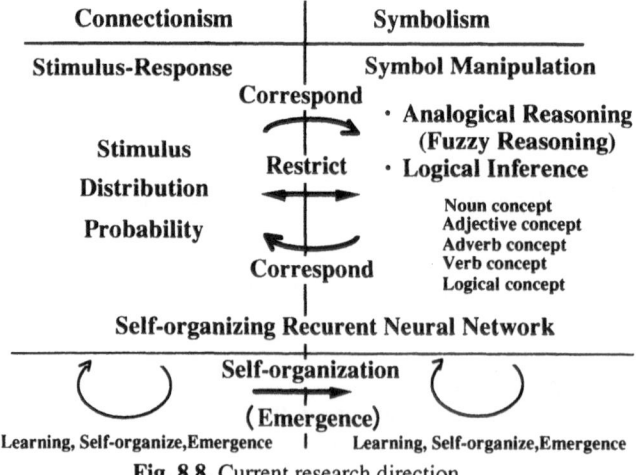

Fig. 8.8. Current research direction

Based on this model, we expect that it should learn according to the 2-phased learning curve shown in Fig.8.9.

In the first phase, it learns the structure of the fuzzy rule and the control ability is improved. In the second phase, it learns the common language structure and the competence of the problem solving are acquired.

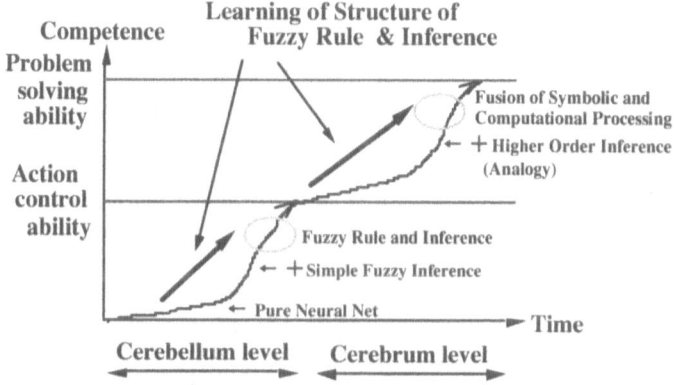

Fig. 8.9. Two levels of competence and algorithm

8.6. Prototype Model for the New Paradigm

We have developed the simple model and evaluated the performance as the first step toward the deep fusion of the symbolic and computational processing.

8.6.1 Approaches

Requirements
Based on the analysis above, we defined our goal to be a model that meets the following three requirements.

- The symbolic and computational processing should be tightly interwoven so as to utilize the advantages of each.
- Rather than simply be given a priori knowledge, the model should learn from the inputs, the outputs, and the rewards obtained from the environment.
- The learned knowledge should be generalized when possible, then used to improve performance.

Basic Concept
To meet these requirements, we structured our model to incorporate the following concepts.

Computational Processing: The basic model is that of a neural network with back propagation. That is, computational processing is the fundamental processing mechanism.
Learning without a priori knowledge: To learn rather than using a priori knowledge, we incorporated reinforcement learning, especially Q-learning.
Combined Q-learning and NN: The table for the Q-learning is represented by a neural network whose inputs are the attributes of the table and whose outputs correspond to the Q-value of the actions.
Symbolic Processing: As symbols gradually emerge from the NN, they are used to improve system inference performance and the learning ability.

Architecture
As shown in Fig. 8.10, our system is structured in two layers. The bottom

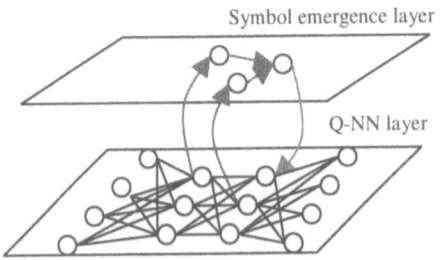

Fig. 8.10. System architecture

layer is the Q-NN layer in which Q-learning occurs on the neural network. The system learns based on the results of the actions the system selects, the data it receives about the environment, and the rewards it obtains from the environment. The Q-table, which is updated based on this learning, resides in the Q-NN layer.

The top layer is the symbol-emergence layer in which the activities in the Q-NN layer are constantly monitored. When an important concept is identified through this monitoring, it is embedded in the Q-NN layer as a node. The importance of a concept is judged based upon its relation with a good action. In other words, the system looks for concepts that lead to actions that bring high rewards.

These identified concepts are generalized so that they might be applied in different situations or in a different context.

8.6.2 Algorithm of Our Model

In this section, we describe the algorithm of our model in more detail. As explained in the previous section, our system consists of two layers. The bottom layer is the neural network for Q-learning. In other words, the bottom layer updates and stores the Q-table, which is shown in Fig. 8.11.

The system works by trying an action and checking the reward. Through this trial-and-error process, the system gradually obtains knowledge. This process is called "exploration". It works as follows.

X1	...	Xm	Action	Q
V(11)	...	V(1m)	A(1)	Q(1)
V(21)	...	V(2m)	A(2)	Q(2)
...	...	...	...	...
V(n1)	...	V(nm)	A(n)	Q(n)

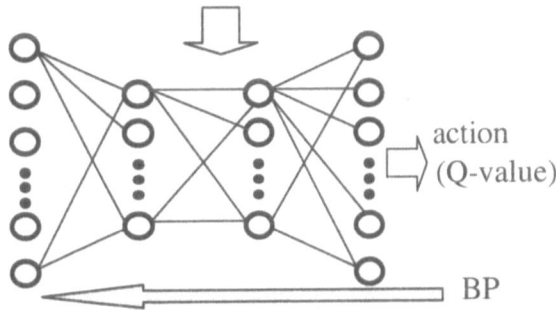

Fig. 8.11. Combination of NN and Q-table

Exploration Process

Step1: Sense environment. Feed sensed data X from environment, i.e. (x1, x2,...) to Q-NN input layer.

Step2: Propagate inputs through hidden layer until they reach output layer. Calculate Q-values of all actions, Q (X, a1), Q (X, a2) ,...

Step3: Select one action (A) by using roulette strategy.

Step4: Execute action A.

Step5: Estimate new status Y when action A was executed.

Step6: Calculate Q-values for Y by feeding Y to Q-NN.

Step7: Update Q-values by using the update formula of Q-learning.

Step8: Retrain Q-NN by using X and the updated Q-values as training data.

Although many trials are required, the system eventually learns a desirable series of action.

The system extracts the important nodes by monitoring the Q-NN. This extraction process works as follows. An example of symbol extraction is shown in Fig. 8.12.

Extraction Process

Step1: Assume that system received a reward when it executed action A.

Step2: Store list of activated nodes that affected action node A. For example, H2 and H3 in Fig. 8.12.

Step3: Store list of activated nodes that affect the nodes stored in Step 2. For example, H2: I2, I5 and H3: I6, I9.

Step4: Repeat Steps 2 and 3 until sufficient data have been collected.

Step5: Identify nodes that are often activated when action A is executed.

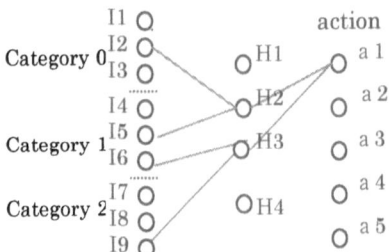

Fig. 8.12. Symbol extraction

The system then attempts to combine the extracted nodes to create an important concept. This combination process works as follows. An example is shown in Fig. 8.13.

Combination Process

Step1: Check input categories for extracted nodes.

H1 (category0, category1)

H2 (category0, category1)

H3 (category1, category2)

(Input nodes are grouped based on the semantic meaning. We call it the category.)

Step2: Judge which nodes from the same category set are similar.

Step3: Unify the similar nodes into one concept by creating a new node and connecting it to the nodes selected in Step2.

This combination process extracts an important concept and creates a new node for it in the Q-NN layer. Its task is to find new concepts.

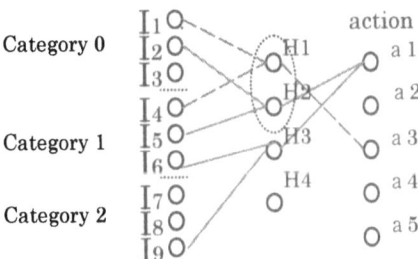

Fig. 8.13. Combination of nodes

The combined nodes can be regarded as describing an important concept in which the inputs come from the categories. Therefore, the concept may play an important role when the category set is different from the original one. Based on this idea, we designed the forced application mechanism. The system always attempts to generalize an extracted concept and to apply it. This can lead to a drastic improvement in both finding new concepts and in the speed of learning. The forced application process works as follows. An example is shown in Fig. 8.14.

Forced Application Process

Step1: Assume that when the system identifies an important concept, it combines the related nodes into a new node and embeds the new node. H1 and H2 are new nodes representing important concepts in the example shown in Fig. 8.14.

Step2: Change partially and probabilistically the input categories of the important-concept nodes. In Fig. 8.14, category 1 does not change, while category 0 is changed to category 2.

Step3: Embed new nodes in network. N1, N2, and S1 are embedded in the network shown in Fig. 8.14.

Step4: Connect new node to all nodes in the next layer at a low weight. In Fig. 8.14, S1 is connected to a1 to a5.

In the example shown in Fig. 8.14, an important concept that is valid in categories 0 and 1 is generalized into a concept that may be valid in categories 1 and 2.

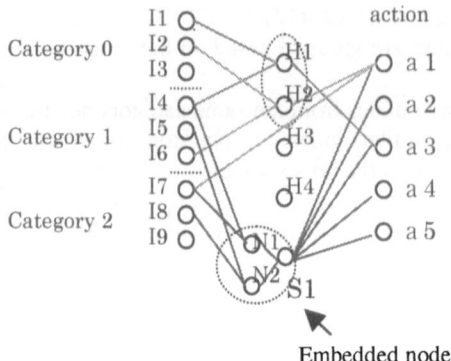

Fig. 8.14. Forced application of symbol

8.6.3 Simulations

To evaluate the feasibility and effectiveness of our algorithm, we tested it by using a simulated football game. The size of the field was 13 x 6, and each team had two players. The initial state of the simulation is shown in Fig. 8.15 (a).

Each player can see its teammate and the two opposing players. Their range of view is shown in Fig. 8.15 (b). For example, the player shown can see that his teammate is in direction 4 and not too far away. The two possible actions are "move" and "kick". The direction of the selected action is defined as shown in Fig. 8.15 (c).

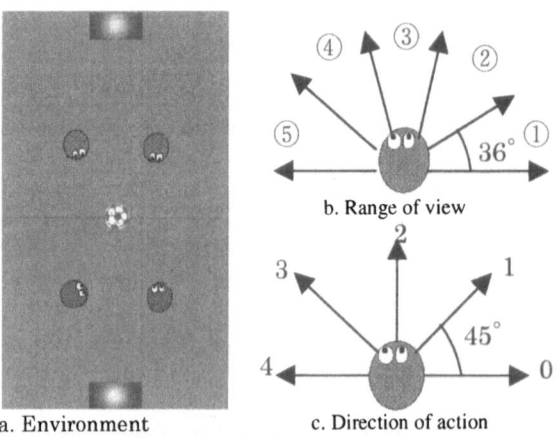

Fig. 8.15. Simulation conditions

When the game begins, the system does not have any knowledge. That is, a player does not even know that he gets a point when he kicks the ball into the opponent's goal. The players explore the game world by performing various actions in the various situations. Each player's behavior is determined by our system. The actual Q-NN layer for the simulation is shown in Fig. 8.16. A player receives the following rewards.

- For getting control of ball: +0.05
- For kicking ball into goal: +0.2
- For passing to teammate: +0.2
- For passing to opposing player: -0.2
- For kicking ball without effect: -0.01

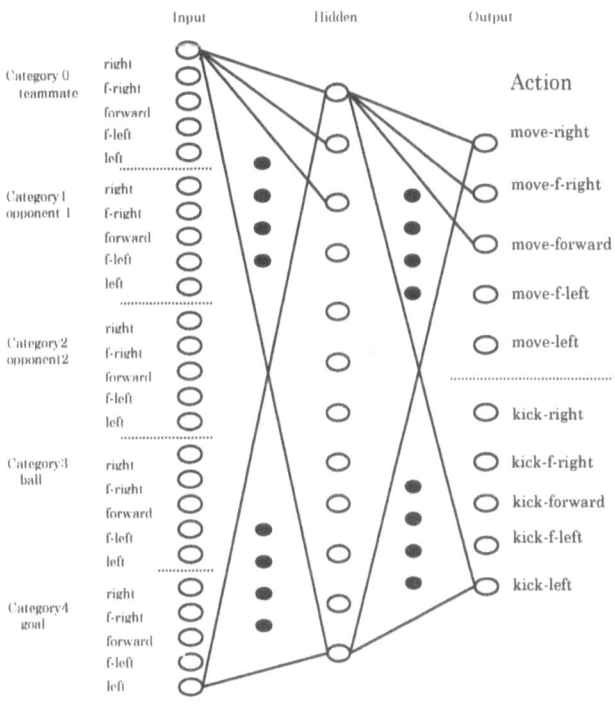

Fig.8.16. Network structure

8.6.4 Evaluation

Three types of team were used for our evaluation. One team was implemented using our methods, i.e., Q-learning + symbol emergence. One team was implemented using Q-learning only. The other team was implemented using a random walk, i.e., the players could not learn.

The estimated learning curves for these teams are shown in Fig. 8.17. The horizontal axis represents time, with one time unit corresponding to one move of a player. A game was 10,000-time units long. The vertical axis shows the average score per game.

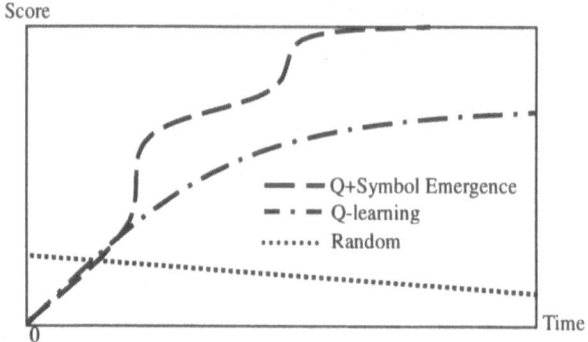

Fig. 8.17. Estimated learning curves

As "Q-learning + symbol emergence" and "Q-learning" obtained knowledge, the average scores of their games gradually increased. The performance of "Q-learning + symbol emergence" increased remarkably on two occasions. These jumps occurred when an important concept was identified. Because "Random" did not learn, the average score of its games did not increase. In fact, the scores actually decreased, probably because the opponent team also learns to minimize the losing points.

The results for one simulation are shown in Fig. 8.18. Games were played

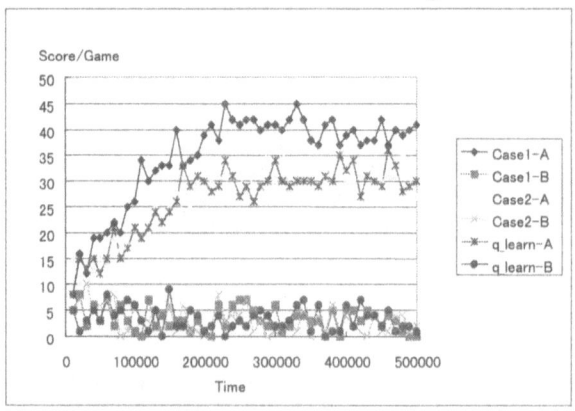

Fig. 8.18. Examples of learning curves

between teams A and B. Team "B" is always "Random". "Case1" and "Case2" are the games between "Q+Symbol Emergence" and "Random". "q_learn" is the game between "Q-learning" and "Random". The average score for team B was always very low. The average scores for teams A of Case1 and Case2 are improved as they gained experience. Although the scores of both teams improved, the improvement by team A of Case1 was remarkably better.

The reason for the remarkably better improvement by team A of Case1 is illustrated in Fig. 8.19. When a drastic change was observed, a forced application was successfully performed. Team A of Case1 was able to generalize the concept "there is no opponent in the direction of my teammate" to the concept "there is no opponent in the direction of the opponent's goal".

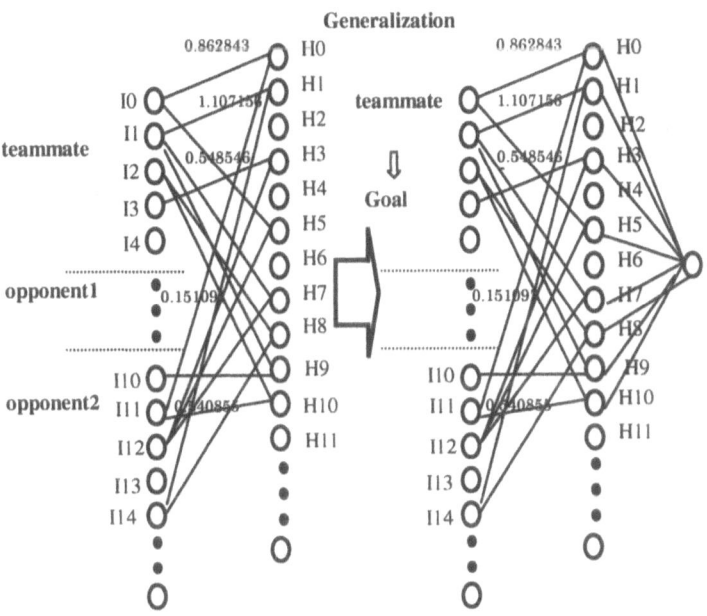

Fig. 8.19. Symbolization and application

Due to the forced application of this concept, the average score jumped dramatically immediately after the symbol for that concept emerged and became generalized at 100,000-time units (see Fig. 8.20). The weights of the generalized node were initially set very low as explained in step4 of the forced application process. The change in the weight after the node was generated at the 100,000-time unit is shown in Fig. 8.21. The increased weight means that the generated node was successfully utilized by the next layer, leading to the jump in performance shown in Fig. 8.20.

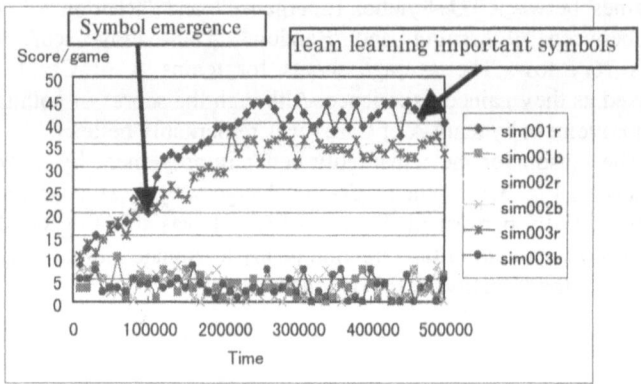

Fig. 8.20. Symbol emergence and learning curve

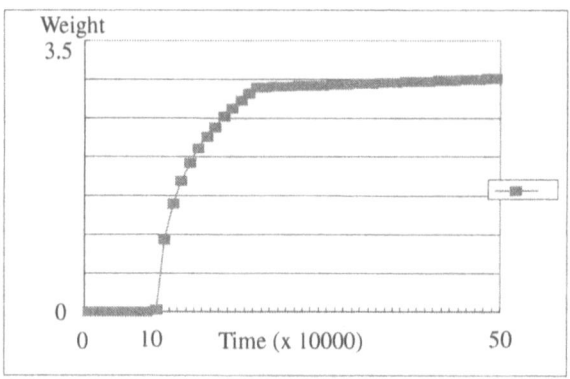

Fig. 8.21. Change in weight

8.6.5 Future Works

Several problems still remain. Because we use a three-layered neural network, the generated nodes are placed between the 2nd and 3rd layers and treated as special cases. We are now extending the network to a multi-layered one so that all nodes can be treated uniformly and to enable recursive generalization based on the generated nodes.

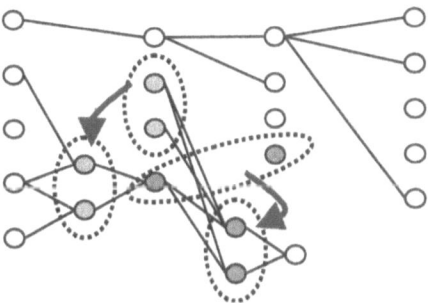

Fig.8.22. Extension to multi-layer network

8.7. Summary

Multimedia and network technologies make it possible to freely access various stores of multimedia information spread around the world. To maximize the use of this information, new information systems are needed. They must be highly intelligent and able to handle multimodal inputs and outputs, such as speech, gestures, and gazes.

Through the development of the experimental system, called RVI-desk, we found that it was indispensable deeply to combine the symbolic and computational processing in order to realize software architecture for the next generation user interface.

We think the key is to enable interaction between computational and symbolic processing anytime, anywhere, and at any level of abstraction. By synergistically combining symbols and patterns, powerful mechanisms should emerge. We call this approach "Deep Fusion of Computational and Symbolic Processing".

We have proposed a simple model as the first step toward fusing computational and symbolic processing. It consists of two layers. The lower layer is a neural network in which Q-learning is simulated. The inputs are the state variables, and the outputs are the Q-values for each action. It is tuned to update and store the Q-table. The upper layer watches the activity in the lower layer to identify the group of nodes that are activated when some actions in the lower layer obtains a high reward from the environment. In this way, new symbols emerge that are embedded in the lower layer to speed up the learning. When an important concept is learned, the corresponding symbol is generalized and embedded in a different place at a lower level.

Through simulation we demonstrated that symbol emergence and the forced application of these symbols in Q-learning greatly improves the performance of players playing a simple football game.

We have proposed an approach based on symbol emergence, a first step towards **"Deep Fusion of Computational and Symbolic Processing"**. Further research is needed.

References

[1] Kruger, W., et. al. The Responsible Workbench: A Virtual Work Environment, COMPUTER, Vol. 28, No. 7, pp.42-48, 1995.
[2] Wellner, P. Interactive With Papers on the DigitalDesk, Communications of the ACM, Vol. 36, No. 7, pp.87-97, 1993.
[3] Maes, P. Agent that Reduce Work and Information Overload, CACM, Vol. 37, No. 7, 30-40,1994.
[4] Tano, S. Research Trend of Next Generation User Interface, Journal of Japan Society for Fuzzy Theory and Systems, Vol. 8, No. 2, pp. 216-228, 1996 (in Japanese).
[5] Tano: Potential of Fuzzy Symbolic and Computational Inference for Multi Modal User Interface, IFSA-97, pp.407-412,1997.
[6] Tano, S., et. al. Design Concept Based on Real-Virtual-Intelligent User Interface and Its Software Architecture, HCI-97, pp.901-904,1997.
[7] Namba, Y., et. al. Complex Chained Function Structure for Human-Computer Interface, HCI International '95 Poster Session, pp. 32-32, 1995.
[8] R.Sun, T.Peterson, "Hybrid Learning Incorporating Neural and Symbolic Processes", FUZZ-IEEE'98, pp. 727-732, 1998
[9] T.Omori, N.Yamanashi, "PATON A Model of Concept Representation and Operation in Brain", Proc.of Int'l Vonfon NeuralNetwork94, pp.2227-2232, 1994
[10] I. Takeuchi, T. Furuhashi: A Study on Inference between Patterns and Symbols, 13th Fuzzy System Symposium, pp. 573-576, 1997 (in Japanese)
[11] T.Takagi,A.Imura,H.Ushida,T.Yamgaguchi, "Computational Fuzzy Sets as a Meaning Representation and Their Inductive Construction", International journal of intelligent systems Vol.10, No.11, pp.929-945, November 1995
[12] S.Ohsuga, "Symbol processing by Non-Symbol Processor", Proc.4 th Pacific Rim International Conference on Artificial Intelligence, Cairns, Australia, 1996
[13] S.Tano, "Synergetic Effect by Deep Fusion of Computational and Symbolic Processing", FUZZ-IEEE'98, pp. 744-749, 1998
[14] Y. Uemura , S. Tano: Analysis of symbolic and computational processing and a new fusion method, 14th Fuzzy System Symposium, pp. 179-180, 1998 (in Japanese)
[15] Y. Uemura , D. Futamura, S. Tano: Proposal of Symbolic and

Computational Processing and Initial Evaluation by Simulation, 15th Fuzzy System Symposium, pp. 471-474,1999 (in Japanese)

[16] Papers in the organized session "Deep Fusion of Computational and Symbolic Processing" of FUZZ-IEEE 98 at World Congress on Computational Intelligence (WCCI' 98), pp. 709-749, 1998.

[17] Tano, Miyoshi, Kato, Oyama, Arnould and Bastian: Fuzzy Inference Software - FINEST: Overview and Application Examples, IEEE International Conference on Fuzzy Systems - FUZZ-IEEE'95 , pp. 1051-1056, 1995.

[18] Tano, Oyama and Arnould: Deep Combination of Fuzzy Inference and Neural Network in Fuzzy Inference Software - FINEST, International Journal of Fuzzy Set and Systems, Vol. 82 No. 2, pp. 151-160, 1996.

[19] Tano, Okamoto and Iwatani: New Design Concepts for the FLINS-Fuzzy Lingual System: Text-based and Fuzzy-centered Architectures, International Symposium on Methodologies for Intelligent Systems-ISMIS '93, pp.285-294, 1993.

[20] Tano, S., et. al. Three-layered Fuzzy Inference and Self-wondering Mechanism as Natural Language Processing Engine of FLINS, IEEE International Conference on Tools with Artificial Intelligence - TAI'94, pp. 212-218, 1994.

Part III

Knowledge Representation

Fusion of Symbolic and Quantitative Processing by Conceptual Fuzzy Sets

Tomohiro Takagi

Department of Computer Science, Meiji University 1-1-1 Higashi-Mita, Tama-ku, Kawasaki-shi Kanagawa-ken 214-8571, Japan takagi@cs.meiji.ac.jp

Abstract: The real world consists of events and continuous numeric values, while people represent and process their knowledge in terms of symbols. Fuzzy sets provide a strong notation connecting the symbolic representation to the real world. In this paper, we discuss Conceptual Fuzzy Sets (CFS), a new type of fuzzy sets which conform to Wittgenstein's ideas[7]. In CFS the meaning of a concept is represented by the distribution of activation of labels in associative memory, and is capable of simultaneous symbolic and quantitative processing. In particular, a multi-layered structured CFS represents the meaning of the same concept as it is used in various expressions in each layer. As the propagation of activations corresponds to reasoning, multi-layered reasoning in CFS has following features; 1) capable of simultaneous top-down and bottom-up processing, 2) capable of context sensitive knowledge processing.

9.1 Introduction

The real world consists of a very large number of instances of events and continuous numeric values. On the other hand, people represent and process their knowledge in terms of abstracted concepts derived from generalization of these instances and numeric values. Logic based paradigms for knowledge representation use symbolic processing both for concept representation and inference. Their underlying assumption is that a concept can be defined precisely. However, as this assumption hardly holds for natural concepts, it follows that symbolic processing cannot deal with such concepts. Thus symbolic processing has essential problems from a practical point of view of applications in the real world. In contrast, fuzzy set theory can be viewed as a stronger and more practical notation than formal, logic based theories because it supports both the logic based world and the real world. Therefore, fuzzy set theory is a key methodology for the fusion of symbolic processing and quantitative processing.

However, simple concept formation using ordinary fuzzy sets cannot express context dependent meaning which is essential to connect the symbolic and quantitative processing. For example, in case of controlling a car the amount of steering to the "right" changes depending on the size of a car and road conditions. That is, we should deal with diversity of the meaning as well as the vagueness of the amount even for one symbol.

All the problems relate to the representation of **the meaning** of a concept. According to Wittgenstein[7], the meaning of a concept is represented by the totality of its uses. In this spirit we proposed[8] the notion of Conceptual Fuzzy Sets:(henceforth referred to as CFS), which is discussed in this paper, to solve the above problem. In the CFS the meaning of a concept is represented by the distribution of activation of labels naming concepts. Numerical membership functions are not necessary. Since the distribution changes depending on the activated labels to indicate a situation, CFS can represent various context dependent meanings.

Further, since the distribution of activation determined by the propagation of activation in CFS represents the meaning of a concept, the propagation of activations corresponds to reasoning. In particular, a multi-layer structured CFS represents the meaning of a concept in various expressions in each layer. Therefore, it follows that due to the capability of naturally realizing information processing in multi-layered structures, the CFS have the following features:

1) Since CFS are realized as an associative memory, it can carry out both bottom-up processing from the lower layer to the upper layer, and top-down processing from the upper layer to the lower layer simultaneously.

2) Because CFSs are realized and connected using an associative memory, CFS can carry out information processing both in the upper layer and lower layer simultaneously exchanging information. Thus they provide us easily with a framework where the processing in the upper layer supervises the processing in the lower layer.

In this paper, we discuss a new type of fuzzy sets named Conceptual Fuzzy Sets (CFS) to connect the symbolic and quantitative world. In section 2 we discuss CFS and their fundamental properties. In section 3, we discuss two aspects of the fusion of symbolic and quantitative processing by CFS.

9.2 Conceptual Fuzzy Sets

9.2.1 Conceptual Fuzzy Sets for Concept Representation

9.2.1.1 Realization of Conceptual Fuzzy Sets

A label of a fuzzy set represents the name of a concept and a fuzzy set represents the meaning of the concept. Therefore, the shape of a fuzzy set should be determined from the meaning of the label depending on various situations (Fig. 9.1). According to the theory of meaning representation from use proposed by Wittgenstein, the various meanings of a label (word) may be represented by other labels (words) and we can assign grades of activation showing compatibility degrees between different labels (Fig. 9.2).

The CFS[8], achieves this by the distributions of activations. A CFS is realized as an associative memory, in which a node represents a concept and a link represents a strength of the relation between two (connected) concepts. The activation values agreeing with grades of membership are determined through associative memory. In CFS the meaning of a concept is represented

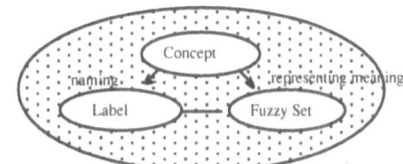

Fig. 9.1. A fuzzy set as a meaning representation

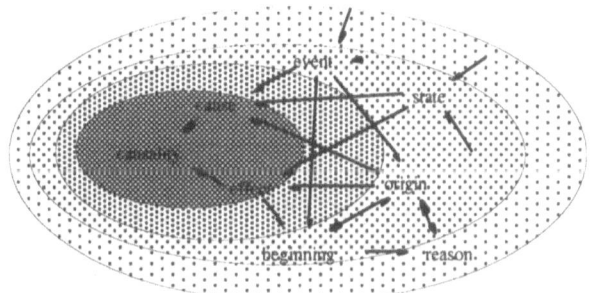

Fig. 9.2. A fuzzy set as a meaning representationExample of meaning representation according to Wittgenstein

by the distribution of activation values of other nodes. The distribution is evolved by the activation of the node representing the concept in interest. Fig.9.3 shows the image of CFS. In CFS a long-term memory is used for the network representing knowledge and a short-term memory is used for the distribution of activation values representing the meaning of a label of a fuzzy set in interest.

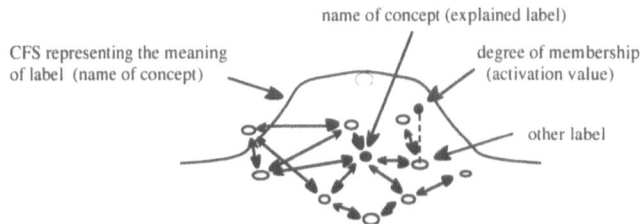

Fig. 9.3. A conceptual fuzzy set represented by associative memories

Activations of nodes produce a reverberation and the system energy is stabilized to a local minimum where corresponding concepts are recollected as a result. The recollections are carried out through a weight matrix encoded from stimulus-response paired data. In this paper we use Bidirectional Associative Memories (BAMs)10,11 because of the clarity of constraints for their utilization. At the association in BAMs reverberations are carried out according to:

$$Y_t = \phi(M \cdot X_t), \quad X_{t+1} = \phi(M^T \cdot Y_t). \tag{9.1}$$

where, $X_t = [x1, x_2, \ldots, x_m]^T$, $Y_t = [y_1, y_2, \ldots, y_n]^T$ are activation vectors on x and y layers at the reverberation step t, and $\phi(\cdot)$ is a sigmoid function of each neuron. BAMs memorize corresponding pairs of elements at each layer in terms of a synaptic weight matrix, M, to memorize CFS, and calculated from corresponding input/output pairs of A_i'/B_i' (transformed bipolar vector of input/output A_i/B_i) with coefficient α_i:

$$M = \sum_i \alpha_i A_i' B_i' \tag{9.2}$$

Example 2.1. CFS representing "fat"

In Fig.9.4 the BAM consists of two layers whose upper layer includes "fat" and "tall", and lower layer include nodes such as "Dan" and "George". The activation of node "fat" makes the distribution of activations of nodes in the lower layer. In this example the fuzzy set "fat" is given as follows.

$$fat = \{0.4/Dan, 0.9/George, 0.3/Mark, 0.0/Paul\}$$

The ratio of black portion in each node represents the grade of activation in [0,1] which agrees with the grade of membership to "fat". Black arrows indicate promoting links and gray arrows indicate depressive links. Each node employs sigmoid function.

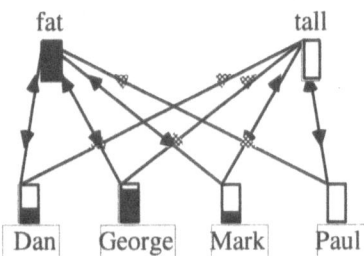

Fig. 9.4. The conceptual fuzzy set "fat"

In this example, an associative memory is used to memorize the membership function which determines membership degrees of the elements "Dan", "George", etc. from a non-numeric domain.

9.2.1.2 CFS Representing a Composed Concept which has Multiple Meanings Depending on Situations

Since the distribution changes depending on the activated labels which indicate conditions, the activations resulted through CFS show a context dependent meaning. When more than two labels are activated CFS is realized by the overlapping propagations of activations. In CFS notations, operations and their controls are all realized by the distributions of activation and their propagations in associative memories.

We can say that the distribution determined by the activation of a label agrees with the region of thought corresponding to the word expressing its meaning. Since situations are also indicated by activations, the meaning is expressed by overlapping the regions of thought determined by these activations. Fig. 9.5 illustrates the different meanings of the same label, L1, in different situations, S1 and S2.

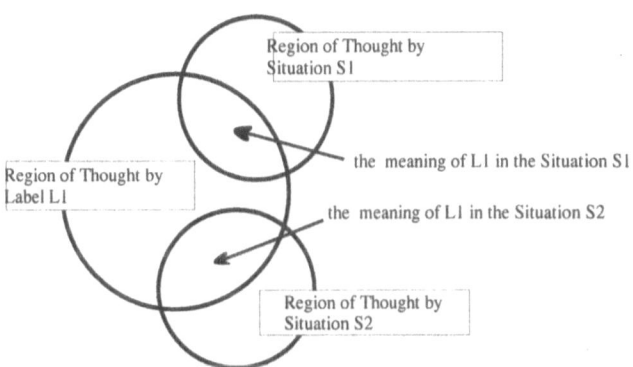

Fig. 9.5. Different meanings in different situations

Example 2.2. "Tall " Depending on "American Height" or "Japanese Height"

Let us consider the concept "tall", and its meaning according to whether it is applied to an American or Japanese person. The meaning of concept "tall" changes in these two situations. The distribution of activation of other labels explains the meaning of "tall" depending on these contexts. Fig. 9.6. shows the concept "tall American" which agrees with the meaning of "tall" in case of an American person. The activations of nodes which express "American" and "tall" make the distribution of activation in the middle layer which consists of numerical values. Fig. 9.7 shows the distribution representing "tall Japanese" which is obtained by the activations of "Japanese" and "tall" nodes. In these figures and throughout the remainder of this paper, "American" and "Japanese" refer to "American height" and "Japanese height" respectively.

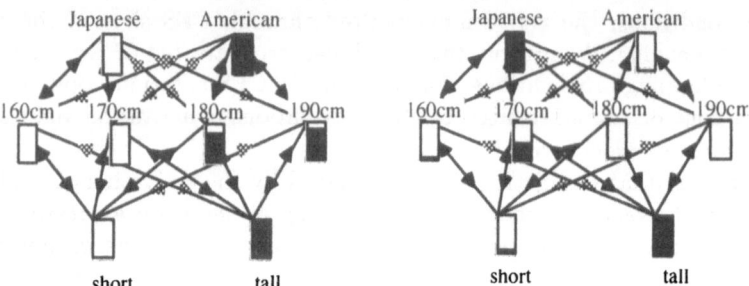

Fig. 9.6. CFS representing "tall" American

Fig. 9.7. CFS representing "tall" Japanese

9.2.1.3 Explicit Representation of a Concept which cannot be Realized by Logical Representation:

Denotative notation of fuzzy sets cannot provide the grade of membership for a new element which was not already included in the definition. In the case of defining fuzzy sets in terms of attributes, explicit algorithms are necessary to determine the membership values from the attribute values and such algorithms are difficult to realize. Thus the membership grade of the new element cannot be determined by the attribute based definition either.

CFS can provide the membership value for the new element in denotative representation. The propagation of activations determined by the activation of the node which represents the label of a fuzzy set activate the new element and its activation expresses its membership value. We do not need explicit descriptions of either relations between attributes and membership values or of logical decomposition.

9.2.1.4 Summary of Properties of Conceptual Fuzzy Sets

The following features of CFS allow for solving the shortcomings of purely symbolic knowledge representation paradigms.

1) CFS can realize non-numeric membership functions to determine the membership grades of non-numeric elements. Therefore, CFS can obtain the membership grade for a non-numeric new element.
2) Since CFS can employ a multi-layered distributed structure, many kinds of expressions such as denotative and connotative can be mixed. Inference is performed by passing through layers and propagating activations.
3) CFS can represent the context dependent meaning of a concept.

4) CFS can explicitly represent the concept whose logically explicit representation is impossible.

The CFS has essential features listed above to solve the problems of ordinary fuzzy sets. Moreover it has the following advantages:

1) The associative memory can indicate the output depending on a situation which is not exactly the same as the stored knowledge. No explicit procedures to calculate a matching degree and to search for the best match are necessary, because these are carried out by the characteristics of associative memories.

2) Combination of long term memories (network structure) and short term memories (distribution of activation values) reduces the complexity of the knowledge representation structure. The structure becomes too complex in ordinary knowledge representation based only long term memories: all the information must be compiled in the structure. It is impossible to classify all cases especially when the number of cases is very large. In contrast, short term memories can encode continuous changes.

9.2.2 Construction of CFS by Learning[12]

9.2.2.1. Inductive Construction of CFS

We construct CFS inductively using Hebbian learning. CFS is realized using associative memories in which a link represents a strength of the relation between two concepts. Hebbian learning modifies the strength m_{ij} of links by the product of the activations of two nodes x_i and y_j according to:

$$m_{ij} = -m_{ij} + x_i y_j \qquad (9.3)$$

In this case the correlation matrix is obtained directly from instances such as

"TheheightofMarkis175cm.Heistallwithagrade0.8"

"TheheightofGeorgeis160cm.Heistallwithagrade0.2"

Example 2.3. Inductive learning of "tall"
The learning vectors to construct CFS from three instances of person A, B and C are

		160cm	170cm	180cm			short	tall	
person A	(	1	0	0	)	(	0.8	0.3	)
person B	(	0	1	0	)	(	0.2	0.7	)
person C	(	0	0	1	)	(	0.1	0.8	)

The associative memory in this example consists of two layers. The upper layer includes nodes such as "tall" and "short". The lower layer includes nodes such as "160cm", "170cm" and "180cm". The obtained correlation matrix M is

	short	tall
160cm	0.15	-0.35
170cm	-0.22	0.01
180cm	-0.09	0.31

Fig. 9.8 shows the result of simulation to construct the concept "tall" figured by the activation of "tall" node in the CFS obtained by Hebbian learning.

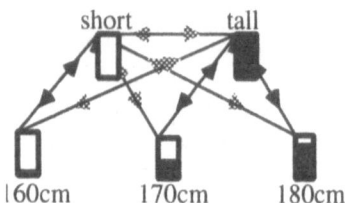

Fig. 9.8. CFS representing "tall"

If we exchange the input and output vectors, the CFS obtained is the same as in Fig. 9.8.

Since the proposed learning method makes negative correlation for the pairs of elements which are not relating to the concept in question, the obtained CFS does not activate unnecessary elements. Therefore, necessary elements are activated, unnecessary elements are not activated and uncertain elements are activated with an intermediate amount. For this reason the proposed method can provide us with a desirable CFS even in support sets which contain verbose elements.

9.2.2.2. Composition of Pieces of Knowledge

A complex CFS is realized by composing several pieces of associative memory structured individually. If C_1, C_2, ..., C_n denote individual CFSs and M_1, M_2, ..., M_n are their corresponding correlation matrices then we can combine them to obtain a CFS C, whose correlation matrix M is given by:

$$M = \text{norm}(M_1 + M_2 + \ldots + M_n) \tag{9.4}$$

, where "norm" stands for normalizing process for the maximum and minimum values in

$$M_1 + M_2 + \ldots + M_n.$$

9.2.2.3. Features of the Construction Method

The inductive learning method presented has the following features:

1) The knowledge itself and the procedure to use it are integrated and realized in a simple formula. Both are built through a learning process implicitly instead of making explicit procedure.
2) The composition of knowledge is realized by a simple addition of correlation matrix. For this reason we can build the whole representation of a complex concept from pieces of knowledge bypassing the requirement for a structure (such as a tree) usual in ordinary knowledge representation frameworks.
3) Like neural network methods it can construct a concept robustly from noisy or error containing data.
4) Unlike neural network methods it provides us with an explicit knowledge representation.
5) It extracts structure from verbose examples.

9.3 Fusion of Symbolic and Quantitative Processing

9.3.1 Approximate Reasoning by Means of CFS [9]

As we see above, CFS represent the meaning of a concept in multiple layers. The meaning of the concept is translated into the expression indicated by the distribution of activation in each layer. Since the representation of the meaning in the input layer is translated into a representation in the output layer, the propagation of activation corresponds to reasoning (Fig. 9.9). CFS can realize many kinds of reasoning which behave consistently with other reasoning methods (slight differences are due to different notation).

In particular, rule based approximate reasoning is realized as follows. Consider a rule of the form IF x is A then y is B. A layer consists of nodes representing premises $A1$, $A2$, ..., Am, describing x. Another layer consists of nodes representing the consequences $B1$, $B2$, ..., Bn, describing y. These layers are connected by a weight matrix M calculated from correspondences of premise Ai and consequence Bj. If the input is $x = x*$, the concepts $A1$, $A2$, ..., Am are activated with the activations being equal to the corresponding membership values of $x*$. The propagation of activation determined by the activation of the premise layer produces the distribution of activations in the consequence layer, that is $B1$, $B2$, ..., Bn. As each activation corresponds to the truth value of each concept, approximate reasoning is realized .

As CFS behave beyond the limitation of logic based notation, the following reasoning can be realized in CFS (Fig. 9.10):

1) Propagations which arise from the activation of an abstracted concept show its meaning in the concrete layer. This corresponds to answering the question asking the meaning of the concept.
2) In contrast, the activation of a lower concept determines the activations of an upper concept and it corresponds to recognition or understanding.

210

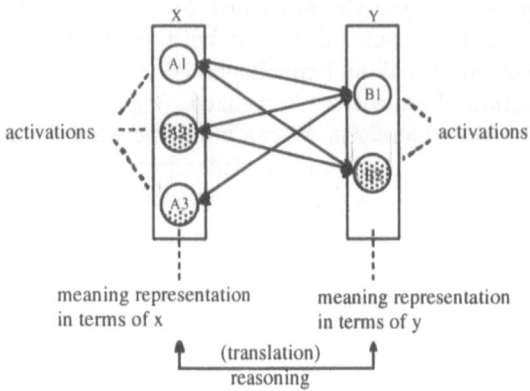

activations   activations

meaning representation   meaning representation
in terms of x   in terms of y

(translation)
reasoning

Fig. 9.9. Approximate reasoning in DFS

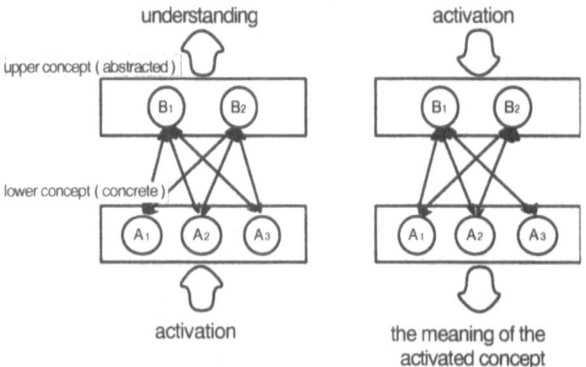

understanding   activation

upper concept (abstracted)

lower concept (concrete)

activation   the meaning of the
                                              activated concept

Fig. 9.10. Meaning representation in multiple layers

Further, due to its bidirectional features, the reasoning in CFS has various characteristics which cannot be achieved by the logic based paradigm.

9.3.2 Fusion of Top-Down and Bottom-Up Processing

Usually natural language processing consists of two steps: (1) parsing and (2) semantic analysis. A lot of meaningless results are obtained by parsing alone. If semantic information could be used simultaneously in the step of parsing it would lead to a more efficient parsing. In image processing, recognition is carried out using characteristic values which are already obtained by low image processing. The fusion of referring a model of an object or the context with the image processing makes the image recognition more efficient. We can say that people simultaneously realize both image processing and recognition.

For the reasons indicated above substantial work has been focused on replacing serial processing by parallel processing[2]. However, this work fails to achieve a real fusion of bottom-up and top-down processing supported by simultaneous information exchange and parallel processing, as it makes use of external procedures (such as for deciding the priority of layers or looping algorithms).

CFS can realize the parallel processing to support the fusion of bottom-up and top-down processing in terms of combining the semantic information processing in upper layer and local processing in lower layer. For example, in image recognition, the upper layer describes the knowledge on a context while the lower layer describes primitive concepts. The concepts in the upper layer are

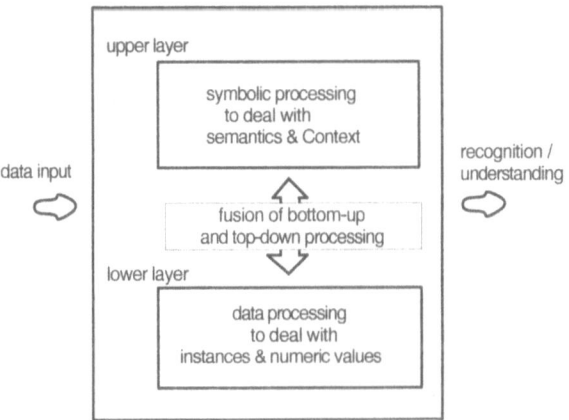

Fig. 9.11. Fusion of top-down and bottom-up processing

explained by the primitives in the lower layer. The characteristic values activate the primitives in the lower layer. This results in the activation of the concept in the upper layer. At that time the context described in the upper layer depresses the meaningless patterns of distribution of activation and promotes the meaningful patterns of activations in lower layer. Thus the primitives activated are those affected by the characteristic values and also satisfying the context. This **context sensitive processing** provides us with an accurate result. It uses the context to eliminate vagueness which may come from noisy and vague data and which could otherwise cause misunderstandings.

Example 9.3.1. Recognition of "THE CAT"

We recognize the words "THE CAT" in Fig. 9.12. Actually the characters in the middle of THE and CAT have exactly the same shape, and the shape can be recognized as either A or H. Therefore if the recognition of the characters is carried out before the recognition of words, it cannot be decided what the character is: A or H. Our actual response recognizing THE CAT indicates the *simultaneous* processing of character recognition and word recognition (context). CFS can realize this recognition supported by the fusion of bottom-up recognition process (from the left to the right) and top-down context sensitive processing(from the right to the left) as in Fig. 9.13.

Fig. 9.12. THE CAT

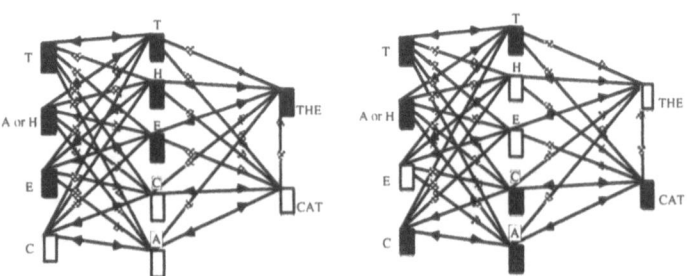

Fig. 9.13. The recognition of THE CAT using CFS

The CFS in Fig. 9.13 consists of the nodes indicating each character in the lowest layer, alphabets as results of character recognition in the middle layer, and correct words as a context in the upper layer. The lower half of CFS indicates how each character looks like and the upper half indicates the alphabets constructing word. Although the character T, E and C are recognized without vagueness and are connected to corresponding places in the alphabets in the middle layer, the characters of interest which have the shape between A and H are connected to both alphabets to indicate the possibility to be recognized as A or H.

The activation of T, E and the ambiguous character in the lowest layer carry out the recognition. As a result of the propagation of activations, T, H and E are activated in the middle layer and node "THE" is activated in upper layer. The simultaneous recognition indicates that the character in the middle of the word is H and the word is "THE". It should be noticed that context sensitive recognition supported by the upper layer and bottom-up recognition from the lower layer are processed simultaneously.

Example 3.2. Recognition of facial expressions

A facial expression is a vague concept: it is difficult of explicitly describing a facial expression; any descriptions have vague boundaries. In this example, the recognition of facial expression is discussed using multi-layered reasoning by means of CFS. The CFS for facial expressions consists of three layers: the upper layer contains facial expressions, the middle layer contains characteristics of the components of a face and the lower layer contains attributive

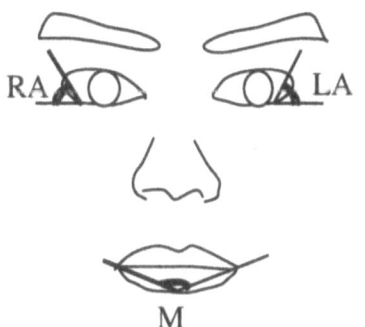

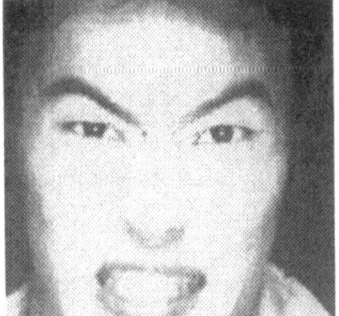

Fig. 9.14. Face characteristic value   **Fig. 9.15.** Object image

characteristic values. The facial expressions are described in terms of the following characteristics:the condition of both eyes (UP:upward, HZ:horizontal, DW:downward), and of the mouth (UP, HZ, DW). The above characteristics are described by the following characteristic values: the angle of the edge of both eyes (RA, LA) and the angle of mouth (M) in Fig. 9.14. Fig. 9.15 shows the object face. The recognition of facial expressions is carried out by activating the node in the lowest layer describing characteristic values.

We can say that humans recognize objects using generous (global) characteristics instead of detecting precise numerical characteristic values. Also, the context constructed by several patterns of facial expressions improves the efficiency and accuracy of recognition. In this section we illustrate the context sensitive image processing by describing general patterns of facial expressions in the middle and upper layers. Fig. 9.16 shows the constructed CFS to recognize facial expressions. The general patterns of facial expressions are described by promoting links connecting the characteristics to represent the facial expressions in the middle layer. These patterns are connected to the node in the upper layer standing for facial expressions. The patterns in the middle layer are connected by depressing links. We investigated the recognition using vague characteristic values, which are described by fuzzy sets,

214

to simulate the recognition process by humans **without using accurate characteristic values**. The object face is recognized as "Angry" and the result is in agreement with our recognition.

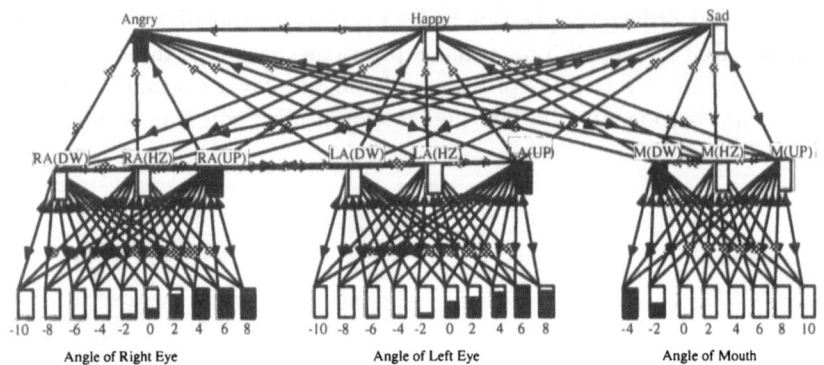

Fig. 9.16. Recognition of facial expressions by means of multi-layered reasoning

In contrast, the recognition using simple logical notation was "Happy" as shown in the following process: facial expression are determined by:

Angry = (Angle of right eye is big) and (Angle of left eye is big)
and (Angle of mouth is big)

Happy = (Angle of right eye is small) and (Angle of left eye is small)
and (Angle of mouth is small)

Sad = (Angle of right eye is medium)
and (Angle of left eye is medium) and (Angle of mouth is big)

Each truth value is calculated as:

$$\mathrm{Tv(Angry)} = \min(1.00, 1.00, 0.62) = 0.62$$
$$\mathrm{Tv(Happy)} = \min(0.73, 0.82, 1.00) = 0.73$$
$$\mathrm{Tv(Sad)} = \min(0.92, 0.82, 0.62) = 0.62$$

Taking the facial expression which has maximum truth value produces the result "Happy".

We also investigated the face recognition of 28 people.

CFS: 14.3% fail
logic based: 21.4% fail

The results show the advantage of context sensitive recognition which is supported by the fusion of bottom-up and top-down processing, in particular, when the recognition starts with error containing vague characteristic values. It also implies the possibility of CFS for image understanding to eliminate the need for precise image processing

9.3.3 Multi-layered Reasoning

Consider a simple example of predicting the currency exchange rate. In the case of a war happening, we use concrete examples from past experience, such as the Gulf War, to predict a precise value. At the same time, we refer the macroscopic knowledge such as "dollar rises in case of emergency" and make rough prediction such that dollar rises up. We can say that the abstracted knowledge described in the upper layer supervises the generous reasoning path and corrects the result of reasoning in the lower layer in terms of concrete, but sometimes uncertain, knowledge such as numeric data and event data.

In general, quantitative processing or neural network deal with numeric data and are not capable of integrating symbolic semantics. In contrast, symbolic processing suits intellectual information processing, but does not suit numeric processing. Since both processing methods take completely different approaches to knowledge processing and knowledge acquisition, the effective integration of these methods, while desirable, is difficult to achieve in a way of which combines their best features.

A reasoning in a multi-layer structured CFS realizes, to some extent, the integration of these two paradigms. The upper layer is meant to carry out symbolic processing using abstracted concepts while the lower layer to process numeric data and instances. If only the reasoning in the lower layer is used, it gives us precise results, but possibly a wrong reasoning path from macroscopic view point. On the other hand, the reasoning in upper layer alone cannot provide a precise result. Bidirectional association connecting two layers enable us to fuse the simultaneous processing in upper and lower layers to obtain a semantic guide supported by the upper layer and the precise processing supported by lower layer. The correspondences of concepts in upper layer represent the abstracted knowledge and the correspondences of examples or numeric data in the lower layer represent concrete knowledge. Since the concepts in the upper layer are connected with examples in lower layer, these connections result in the fusion of two differently abstracted layers. In the case when more than two layers exist various abstracted processes are carried out at the same time.

The reasoning in a multi-layer structured CFS is carried out according to the following procedure: The activation of the node in premises activates the corresponding several nodes in consequences in the lower layer. At the same time, the result of the semantic information processing in the upper layer propagated by the activation of the node in the premises in lower layer affects the consequences in the lower layer. As a result, the nodes affected by both the direct propagation in the lower layer and the semantic propagation in the upper layer remains to be activated. Finally, a concrete result is obtained in the lower layer and abstracted results are obtained in the upper layer simultaneously. We call **Semantic Guide Line** the supervision of the processing in lower layer by the intellectual information processing in upper layer.

Example 3.3. Decision regarding the amount to steering

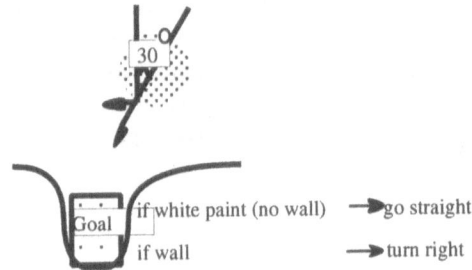

Fig. 9.17. Parking conditions

When driving a car the amount to steering changes depending on situations. In the case that parking spaces are indicated by a painted line, we usually park the car passing the line. If the spaces are surrounded by borders or walls (as in a garage), another trajectory is considered (to avoid the collision with the wall as in Fig. 9.17).

Consider the case that we decide the amount to steering besides parking space and the direction of the car is placed at 30 degree with the direction of parking space as indicated in Fig. 9.17.

We decide the amount to steering using generous rule such as "steer to right to make right turn". The "right" is a concept generalized from various driving experiences and:

1) This kind of symbolic representation is effective to describe explicit and semantic knowledge.
2) However, its indications are vague and can not determine the amount to steering precisely.
3) Its meaning changes depending on the situations such as the position of a car.

On the other hand, cases such as "when the car makes x degree, we steered y degree" are described by concrete numeric values and:

1) The concrete experience indicates the precise amount to steering.

2) However, purely quantitative correspondence of conditions and actions does not suit logical information arising from varieties of conditions.

The CFS fuse both representations consisting of two layers. The lower layer memorizes the correspondences of the numerically described direction of the car and decided amount of steering. Since the lower layer consists of superficial numeric correspondences, it does not recognize the difference between the cases "with wall" and "without wall". In the upper layer, the conditions described by the symbolic notation such as "direction of the car" correspond to the actions such as "with wall" or "without wall". The correspondences of symbols are equivalent to the semantic control rules generalized from experiences . The nodes in the lower layer represent: direction of the car (left nodes) and decided amount of steering (right nodes). The nodes in the upper layer represent: the concept associating with the degree of the car such as "about 45 degree" and "about 90 degree (parallel to the front wall), two nodes on the left, and the conditions "wall" and "no wall" , the remaining two nodes on the left. The nodes on the right side of the upper layer represent the resulted actions such as "Turn left","Go Straight" and "Turn Right". Further, the concepts of the upper layer are connected to the concrete nodes of the lower layer, thus realizing meaning representation.

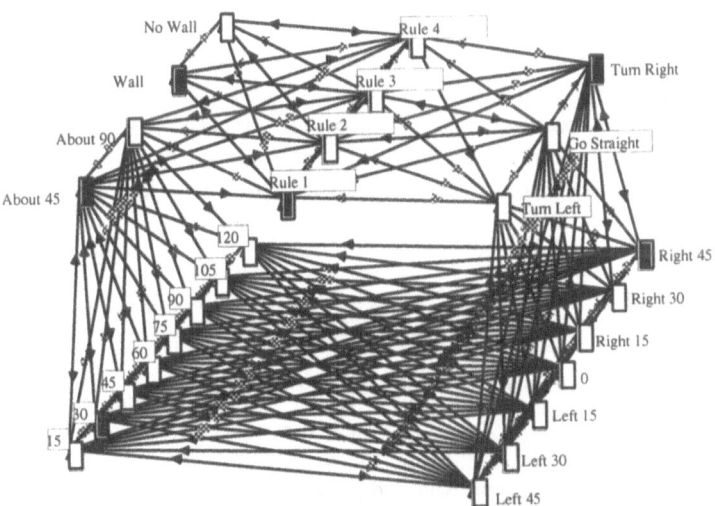

Fig. 9.18. Decision of the amount to steering by two-layered reasoning

Fig. 9.18 also shows the conditions and the decided action when the car is placed in 30 degrees with a parking space having a wall. The condition "30 degrees" results in two kinds of actions depending on the cases "with wall" and "without wall". Because the lower layer simply memorizes both actions

"15 degree to left" and "45 degree to right" corresponding to the conditions 30 degrees, the correct result cannot be recollected by using only the lower layer.

In the upper layer the recognition of a close wall activates "Turn Right" and it produces the activation of "turn right by 45 degrees" in the lower layer. The results of this multi-layered reasoning are "Turn right" in the upper layer and "turn right by 45 degrees" in the lower layer. This process of determining the actions indicates the successful supervision by the macroscopic views in the upper layer of the lower layer. Moreover, the results of the reasoning are equivalent to the meaning of "right" depending on different conditions.

9.4 Conclusions

Fuzzy set theory can be viewed as a stronger and more practical notation than purely symbolic information processing paradigms, connecting the logic based world and the real world. The duality abstract/concrete of the real world is reflected in the intelligent/lack of intelligence duality at the intellectual level. To cope with this duality a knowledge representation paradigm must be able to hierarchically represent both aspects.

In this paper we discussed Conceptual Fuzzy sets (CFS) based on the meaning representation of a concept for the fusion of symbolic and quantitative processing. The distributed multi-layered structure of CFS provides several advantages when compared with logic based knowledge representation. CFS is constructed inductively providing a suitable knowledge representation of context dependent complex concepts. We also discussed Context Sensitive Knowledge Processing in CFS. Multi-layer structured CFS can realize it, since the propagation of activations corresponds to reasoning, which are capable of simultaneous top-down and bottom-up processing.

References

1. L.A. Zadeh, "A Fuzzy-Algorithmic Approach to the Definition of Complex or Imprecise Concepts," Int. J. Man-Machine Studies, Vol.8, pp.249-291 (1976)
2. R.A.Brooks, "A Robust Layered Control System for a Mobile Robot," IEEE Journal of Robotics and Automation, 2- (1986)
3. J. Russmussen, "Skills, Rules, and Knowledge: Signals, Signs, and Symbols, and Other Distinctions in Human Performance Models," IEEE Trans. on System, Man and Cybernetics, SMC-13-3, pp.257-266 (1983)
4. G.N. Saridis, "Intelligent Robotic Control," IEEE Trans. on Automatic Control, AC-28-5, pp.547-557 (1983)
5. T. Sawaragi, T. Norita and T. Takagi, "Fuzzy Theory," Journal of the Robotics Society of Japan, Vol.9 No.2, pp.238-255 (1991) (in Japanese)
6. T. Sawaragi, S. Iwai and O.Katai, "Self-Organization of Conceptual Generalities and Pattern-Directed Learning," Automatica, 26-6, pp.1009-1023 (1990)
7. Wittgenstein, "Philosophical Investigations," Basil Blackwell, Oxford (1953)

8. T. Takagi, A. Imura, H. Ushida and T. Yamaguchi, "Conceptual Fuzzy Sets as a Meaning Representation and their Inductive Construction," International Journal of Intelligent Systems, Vol.10, pp.929-945 (1995)

9. T. Takagi, A. Imura, H. Ushida and T. Yamaguchi, "Multilayered Reasoning by Means of Conceptual Fuzzy Sets," International Journal of Intelligent Systems, Vol.11, pp.97-111 (1996)

10. B.Kosko, "Adaptive Bidirectional Associative Memories," Applied Optics, Vol.26, No 23, pp. 4947-4960 (1987)

11. B.Kosko, "Neural Network and Fuzzy Systems," Prentice HALL (1992)

12. T. Takagi, A. Imura, H. Ushida and T. Yamaguchi, "Inductive learning of Conceptual Fuzzy Sets," 2nd International Conference on Fuzzy Logic and Neural Networks IIZUKA'92, VOL.I, pp.375-380 (1992)

13. S. Yamamoto, T. Yamaguchi, T. Takagi, "Fuzzy Associative Inference System and its Features," IEEE International Conference on System Engineering, pp.155-158 (1992)

14. T. Yamaguchi, M. Tanabe, K. Kuriyama and T. Mita, "Fuzzy Adaptive Control with An Associative Memory System," IEE CONTROL91 No.332, Vol.2, pp.944-947 (1991)

15. Kobayashi and Hara, "The Recognition of Basic Facial Expressions by Neural Network," International Joint conference on Neural Network, pp 460-466 (1991)

Novel Knowledge Representation (Area Representation) and the Implementation by Neural Network

Masafumi HAGIWARA and Naruhiro IKEDA[*]

Department of Information and Computer Science
Faculty of Science and Technology
Keio University

Abstract: This chapter presents a new paradigm to represent knowledge and the implementation by neural network. Knowledge representation is fundamental and important matter to construct intelligent systems. Local representation and distributed representation are widely known, however, they have their own shortcomings. For example, the local representation is not robust and is not fit to biological findings. The distributed representation is difficult to treat inference in spite of having similarity to brain. Since the newly proposed area representation (AR) method is, so to speak, an intermediate method between them, it can preserve advantages of each method. The AR method can express hierarchical knowledge by employing a new inclusion relation in which an upper level concept includes the lower level concepts. The neural network implementing the concept of the AR consists of Kohonen feature maps and it employs a new learning algorithm named neighborhood Hebbian learning. Each map is connected and forms multidirectional associative memory.

10.1 Some Paradigms to Create Intelligent Systems

To create highly intelligent systems has been one of the dreams of human beings. A lot of studies have been made to achieve such a target. AI approach[1-2] is based on logical processing in general and a lot of expert systems have been developed.

AI has been studied through "times of inference" of 1960's and "times of knowledge" of 1970's and it has been used practically in real world. Especially since mid 1980's, it has become one of elemental technologies embedded in a system.

Studies on neural networks[3-4], fuzzy logic[5-6] and evolutionary computation[7-8] are the other approaches[9]. One of the important purposes of neural network is to create intelligent systems by mimicking human brain. Fuzzy logic is developed to make use of subjectivity, experience and intuition of human

---

[*] He is now working for NTT.

beings. Evolutionary computation aims at extraction of hidden mechanism in evolution.

10.2   Knowledge Representation --- Local Representation and Distributed Representation

The most important thing to create intelligent systems by any approach is how to represent knowledge because an intelligent system has to store and process knowledge: treating knowledge plays a crucial role in such a system.

Knowledge representation methods can be divided into two categories: local representation and distributed representation. Fig.10.1 shows the idea of each representation method. The local representation method expresses a concept by a node or an address: a concept is stored in a single node. The distributed representation method expresses a concept by a pattern of activity of many nodes: a concept is stored in plural nodes.

AI approach such as semantic network, frame model and blackboard model is based on the local representation method. Several neural networks based on the local representation method have been proposed: Rumelhart[3] expresses upper level knowledge by combination of the lower level micro features. He proposed another neural network named IAC (interactive activation and competition) model. There are more models based on the local representation: an analogical reasoning system by association [10].

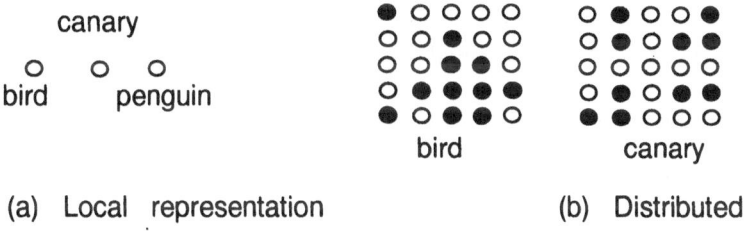

(a) Local representation   (b) Distributed

Fig.10.1. Local and distributed representations.

10.3   Distributed Representation

10.3.1 Advantages of Distributed Representation
The distributed representation method has the following advantages over the local representation.
1) Robustness: Since the distributed representation expresses knowledge in a plural number of nodes, it is much more robust than the local representation.
2) Efficiency for knowledge representation: The local representation can express the number of concepts which is equal to the number of nodes. On the other hand, the distributed representation can express much more number of concepts because concepts can be expressed by the activation pattern of

many nodes.
3) Expression ability for similarity of concepts: Since the distributed representation expresses concepts by an activation pattern of nodes, it can also express the similarity among concepts.

Several neural network models based on the distributed representation have been proposed to make use of the above mentioned advantages. Ritter and Kohonen[11] proposed a semantic map to model representation of concepts and words in a brain using Kohonen feature map[12]. Miikkulainen[13] proposed a distributed feature map to model lexicon. He proposed a model of an episodic associative memory named trace feature map [14]. Schyns[15] proposed a modular neural network to model concept acquisition. Omori et al. proposed a new neural network named PATON to model concept representation and operation in brain[16]. In the PATON, the pattern layer and the symbol layer are controlled by output of the attention layer. Furuhashi et al.[17] proposed an associative neural network to acquire vague patterns and symbols using multidirectional associative memory[18].

This chapter explains a novel knowledge representation method named area representation method and the implementation by neural network[21-22]. The new knowledge representation method is named area representation (AR), which can preserve the merits both in the conventional knowledge representation methods: local representation and distributed representation.

10.3.2 Shortcomings of Distributed Representation

The local representation method expresses knowledge in a single node. The distributed representation method expresses knowledge in a plural number of nodes.

Although the distributed representation method has important and desirable merits and capabilities as mentioned in **10.3.1**, it has the following shortcomings.
1) Storage of hierarchical knowledge is difficult.
2) Part/whole problem: it is difficult to represent a whole concept by adding the partial concepts.
3) To determine a suitable distributed representation is difficult.

As for 1) and 2), we solved the problems by employing a new inclusion relation based on the area representation (AR). It will be explained in the next section. And for 3), we employ Kohonen feature map algorithm to represent concepts distributedly.

10.3.3 Area Representation

Fig.10.2 shows the basic idea of the area representation (AR). The AR represents a concept in an activation pattern in the area using some neurons. The AR method can be considered as an intermediate method between the conventional knowledge representation methods preserving the advantages of each method.

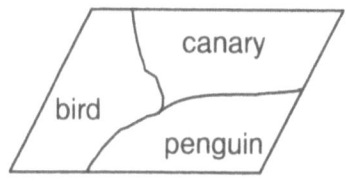

Fig.10.2. Basic idea of area representation.

(a) Conventional inclusion relation

(b) New inclusion relation

Fig.10.3. Conventional and the new inclusion relations.

10.4 A New Inclusion Relation Based on Area Representation

Fig.10.3 shows the conventional and the new inclusion relations.

Fig.10.3(a) shows the conventional inclusion relation[19] which is widely used in AI field. In order to store hierarchical knowledge, only the properties which are common in the lower level concepts are regarded as those of the upper level concepts: an upper level concept is represented by the common region of the lower level concepts. Properties only for a lower level concept are attached to the concept and those common to the lower level concept are inherited from the upper level concept. This contributes to reduction of memory space: the conventional inclusion relation has priority for the implementation for computer.

Now, let's think about a bird, for example. Do we regard a bird by considering the common properties that various kinds of birds have? No. We simply call various kinds of birds bird. This consideration makes us propose a new inclusion relation scheme based on the AR.

Features of the AR and the new inclusion relation are summarized as:
1) An upper level concept includes the lower level concepts. This idea is shown in Fig.10.3(b). This idea enables storing of hierarchical knowledge. In addition, it can solve the part/whole problem: an upper level concept is represented by whole area of the lower level concepts.

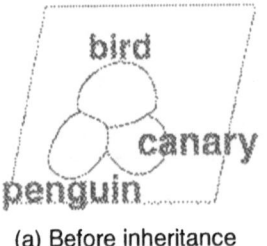
(a) Before inheritance

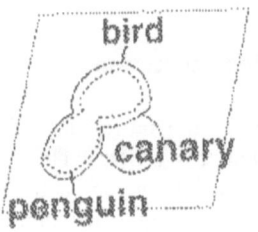
(b) *Penguin* region is extended

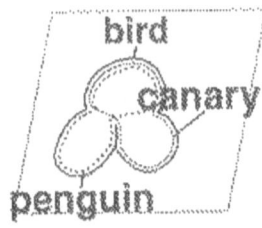
(c) *Canary* region is extended

Fig.10.4. Storing process based on AR.

2) A concept is represented by a plural number of neurons or nodes.

In the case of the conventional knowledge representation, it should be noted that there exist strange areas, for example in Fig.10.3(a), there exists such a region as "an area which belongs to *penguin*, but not belongs to *bird*": the part/whole problem can not be solved by the conventional inclusion relation.

10.5 Storage and Recall of Hierarchical Knowledge Based on Area Representation

10.5.1 Storing Process

Here, we explain the storing process based on the AR method using Fig.10.4.

First, as shown in Fig.10.4(a), knowledge entities[1] are inputted and stored in some regions based on AR. An example of the implementation explained later uses Kohonen self-organizing feature map algorithm[12] to represent knowledge entities in maps (neural sheets).

Now, let's consider the case where a knowledge entity expressing a hierarchical relation, namely knowledge having an *is-a* relation, is inputted. In this case, the area of the upper level concept is extended to include the areas of the lower level concepts. As a result, the lower level concepts can inherit the properties that the upper level concept has.

---

[1] In this chapter, we treat knowledge expressed as triples such as (*bird, can, fly*) and call it knowledge entity. Knowledge entities used in this chapter can be expressed as (*node, relation, attribute*). At the same time, we call a word constructing knowledge entities, such as *bird, penguin, can, fly* and so on, concept.

Fig.10.4(b) shows an example when a knowledge entity (*penguin, is-a, bird*) is inputted. The *bird* area includes the *penguin* area and therefore the hierarchical relation is represented. On the other hand, the *penguin* area is extended to include the original *bird* area and therefore the concept of *penguin* can inherit from the properties of the upper concept *bird*. When knowledge entities having contradiction such as (*bird, can, fly*) and (*penguin, cannot, fly*) exist, the property concerning the lower level concept has the priority: this idea is the same which is used in semantic network[1].

Fig.10.4(c) shows the case where a knowledge entity (*canary, is-a, bird*) is inputted. The *bird* area is extended to include *canary* area and the hierarchical relation, *canary* belongs to *bird*, is expressed. At the same time, *canary* area is extended to include the original *bird* area and therefore the concepts of *canary* can inherit the properties of the upper concept *bird*. As a result, the *bird* area becomes the area containing the original *bird* area, *penguin* area and *canary* area: A hierarchical relation shown in Fig.10.3(b) is represented.

10.5.2 Recall Process

Recall of the stored knowledge entities is explained here. Let's consider the case where some neuron in *penguin* area received stimulation. In this case, first, neurons in the *penguin* area are activated and the knowledge entities concerning *penguin* are recalled. Then the neurons in the original *bird* area shown in Fig.4(a) are activated because the area has relation to the *penguin* area owing to the formerly inputted (*penguin, is-a, bird*) knowledge entity. As a result, knowledge entities concerning *bird* can be recalled. In this manner, recall by inheritance is realized.

When some neurons in *bird* area receive stimulus, knowledge entities concerning *bird* are recalled. Then *canary* area and *penguin* area are activated and knowledge entities concerning them are recalled. This phenomenon is similar to our association such that we recall knowledge on *canary* when we think about *bird* and associate *canary*.

10.6   Neural Network Implementing Area Representation

10.6.1 Construction and Learning of the Network

An example of a neural network implementing the area representation (AR) is shown in Fig.10.5. The network consists of the input layer and some (three in this case) map layers. All of the neurons in the input layer are connected to all of the neurons in the map layers; all of the neurons in a map layer are fully connected to the neurons in the other map layers. As a result, the network works as a multidirectional associative memory[18].

As mentioned in the previous section, the map layers are constructed by Kohonen self-organizing feature map[12]. Since the Kohonen's map has desirable physiological properties: such that similar input is mapped to similar area in a map, it is suitable to employ the algorithm in the neural network implementing AR.

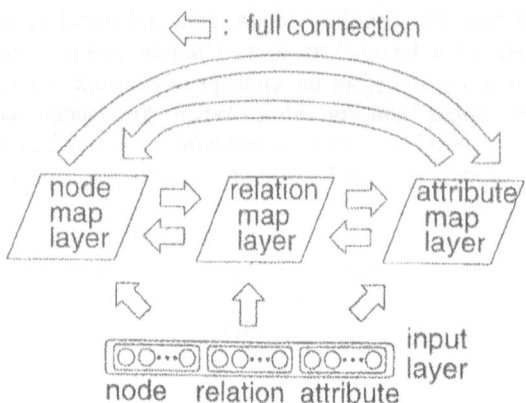

Fig.10.5. An example of a neural network implementing the area representation (AR).

There are three phases in the learning of the network: the map formation phase, the inter-map weight learning phase and the inheritance learning phase.

10.6.2 Map Formation Phase

In this learning phase, each map is formed to represent concepts using the Kohonen self-organizing feature map algorithm[12]. The input vector is constructed by concatenating some vectors expressing concepts. This chapter treats knowledge used in semantic networks: knowledge composed of three elements: node, relation and attribute (also see the footnote in **10.5.1**). Therefore, three maps exist in the network: a map for node concepts, a map for relation concepts and a map for attribute concepts.

The elements in the input vector for the corresponding concept to a map are emphasized and the other elements are just concatenated as contextual information. In other words, the node map receives the input vector in which the elements correspond to the node are emphasized: the elements for relation and those for attribute are added as additional contextual information. The relation map and the attribute map receive the input vectors in which the corresponding elements are similarly emphasized.

Therefore, for example, the knowledge entity for bird (*bird, can, fly*) and that for (*bird, has, wings*) are differently stored because the contextual information differs. In the network, each element expresses one concept for simplicity.

Now we explain the algorithm for the map formation phase. It can be written into a step by step procedure.

1) Knowledge entity is randomly selected and it is denoted as pattern *p*.

$$a^{(p)} = \left(a_1^{(p)} \middle| \cdots \middle| a_m^{(p)} \middle| \cdots \middle| a_N^{(p)} \right) \tag{1}$$

Here, | expresses concatenation of vectors. The input vector to the *m*th map is expressed as

$$x_m^{(p)} = \frac{b_m^{(p)}}{\left\| b_m^{(p)} \right\|} \tag{2}$$

$$b_m^{(p)} = \left(a_1^{(p)} \middle| \cdots \middle| \alpha\, a_m^{(p)} \middle| \cdots \middle| a_N^{(p)} \right), \tag{3}$$

and $\alpha\,(>1)$ is the emphasizing factor. $a_m^{(p)}$ means the concept to be stored and the other vectors mean contextual information.

2) Output of the *i*th neuron in the *m*th map layer is expressed as

$$y_{mi} = w_{mi} \cdot x_m^{(p)}. \tag{4}$$

Here, w_{mi} is the weight vector between the input layer and the neurons in the *m*th map layer. In the same way, outputs of all of the neurons in map layers are calculated.

3) The neuron having maximum output in each map is regarded as the *winner neuron* i^* and the weights of neurons near the winner neuron are learned by the following rule:

$$\Delta w_{mi} = \varepsilon\, h_{mi\,i^*} \left(x_m^{(p)} - w_{mi} \right) \tag{5}$$

Here, ε is the learning constant. The neighborhood function $h_{mi\,i^*}$ and the radius σ are expressed respectively as

$$h_{mi\,i^*} = \exp\left(-\frac{d(i,i^*)^2}{\sigma^2} \right) \tag{6}$$

and

$$\sigma = \sigma_i \left(\frac{\sigma_f}{\sigma_i} \right)^{t/t_{max}}. \tag{7}$$

Here, $d(i, j)$ means the Euclidian distance between the *i*th neuron and the *j*th neuron, t_{max} means the maximum learning times, and σ_i and σ_f mean the initial and the final radius values of neighborhood function, respectively.

10.6.3 Inter-map Weight Learning Phase

The weights between maps are learned in order to enable association in the map layers. The map formation learning and the inter-map weight learning are independent and can be performed in parallel.

The first candidate for the inter-map weight learning rule might be Hebb rule. However, weights learned by Hebb rule tend to increase endlessly[20]. Therefore we have proposed a modified Hebb rule named neighborhood Hebb rule[21-22].

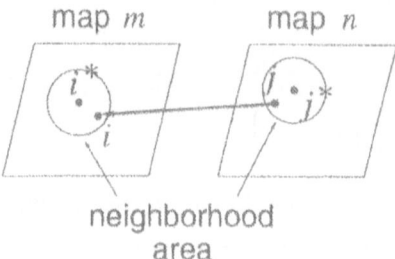

map m　　　map n

neighborhood
area

Fig.10.6. Neighborhood Hebb rule.

Fig.10.6 illustrates the neighborhood Hebb rule. In the rule, only the weights between the neurons neighboring the winner neurons are updated. The neighborhood Hebb rule is effective to learn many relations concerning a lot of concepts without diverging values of weights.

Based on the rule, the weight from the jth neuron in the nth map to the ith neuron in the mth map $v_{n\,j\to mi}$ is learned as

$$\Delta v_{n\,j\to mi} = \frac{\varsigma}{1+\exp\left(-\dfrac{t-\theta_t}{T_t}\right)} h_{mi\,i*} h_{n\,j\,j*}\, y_{n\,j}\left(\beta\, y_{mi} - v_{n\,j\to mi}\right). \tag{8}$$

Here, ς and β are the constants, and θ_t and T_t are the parameters which determine the shape of the sigmoid function, t is the number of learning times. The fraction in the right side of eq.(8) is the learning constant. The sigmoidal function in the right side of eq.(8) is added to increase the value monotonically: update proceeds largely after concepts are roughly mapped in map layers. $h_{mi\,i*}$ and $h_{n\,j\,j*}$ are the neighbor-hood functions expressed by eq.(6). $(\beta\, y_{mi} - v_{n\,j\to mi})$ means that the weight vector $v_{n\,j\to mi}$ should be approached to the input vector y_{mi} and the learning should be proportional to the output $y_{n\,j}$ of the jth neuron in the nth map.

10.6.4 Inheritance Learning Phase

After the map formation phase and the inter-map weight learning phase have been finished, inheritance learning is executed whenever a knowledge entity having an *is-a* relation is inputted. In the inheritance learning phase, the following items are learned:

a) Inheritance from upper level to lower level: The lower concept inherits the properties of the upper concept.
b) Upper-lower hierarchical relation: Hierarchical relation is expressed in a map by the new inclusion relation explained in **10.4**.

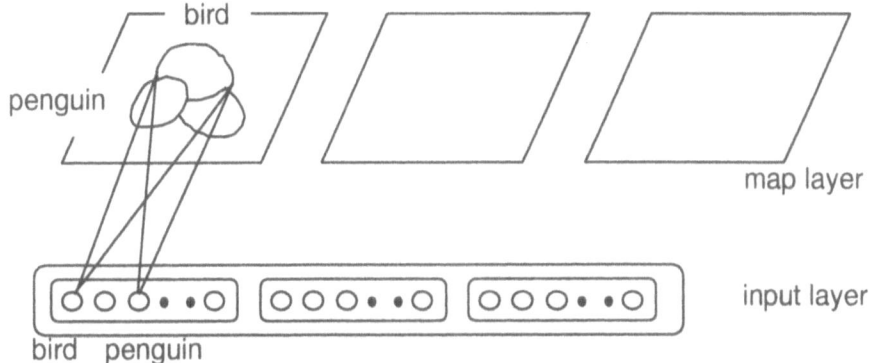

Fig.10.7. Inheritance learning (1).

Here we explain each item.

a) Inheritance from Upper Level to Lower Level

In order to inherit properties from the upper level concept, after a neuron for a lower level concept in the input layer received stimulation, the neurons for the corresponding upper level concept in the map layer also should be activated.

Here we explain the mechanism using Fig.10.7 as an example. We should note here again that each neuron in the input layer expresses its own concept for simplicity.

Now let's consider the case where the knowledge entity (*penguin, is-a, bird*) is inputted. If the neurons in the *penguin* area can stimulate those in the *bird* area, the properties of the upper concept (*bird*) can be inherited as those of the lower concept (*penguin*). To realize such a mechanism, the weights from the *penguin* neuron in the input layer to the neurons in the *bird* area in the map layer are learned to approach the weights from the *bird* neuron in the input layer to the neurons in the *bird* area in the map layer. It is shown in Fig.10.7.

Assume that a knowledge entity expressing hierarchy is stored in the mth map layer. Also assume that the uth neuron and lth neuron in the input layer correspond to the upper and the lower concept, respectively. In this case the learning rule is expressed as the followings.

1) The uth neuron corresponding to the upper concept in the input layer is stimulated and the activation is transmitted to the map layer. The neighborhood area of the winner neuron is considered as the area of the upper concept.

2) Let w_{miu} and w_{mil} be the weights from the neuron corresponding to the upper concept in the input layer to the neurons in the mth map layer and that corresponding to the lower concept in the input layer, respectively. The weight is learned based on the equation.

$$\Delta w_{mil} = \xi\, r_{mi\,i*} \left(\gamma\, w_{miu} - w_{mil} \right) \qquad (9)$$

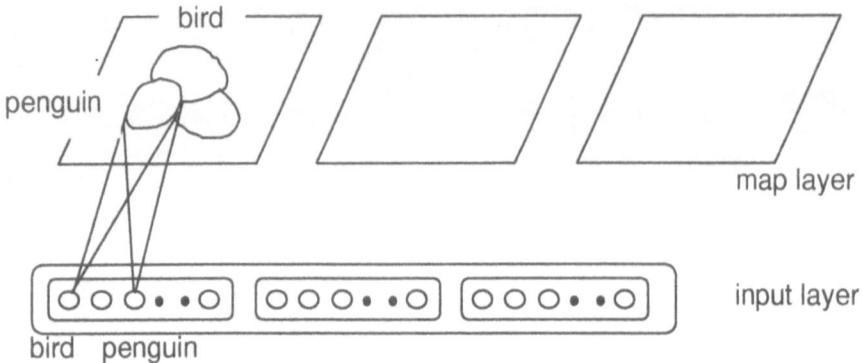

Fig.10.8. Inheritance learning (2).

Here, ξ is the learning constant, $\gamma\,(<1)$ is the constant and is equal to the maximum value of w_{mil} because maximum value of w_{miu} is 1.0. The neighborhood function and the radius are expressed respectively as

$$r_{mi\,i*} = \exp\left(-\frac{d(i,i^*)^2}{\rho^2}\right) \tag{10}$$

and

$$\rho = \rho_i\left(\frac{\rho_f}{\rho_i}\right)^{t/t_{i\,max}}. \tag{11}$$

Here, $d(i, j)$ means the Euclidian distance between the ith neuron and the jth neuron, $t_{i\,max}$ means the maximum learning times for the inheritance learning, and ρ_i and ρ_f mean the initial and the final radius values of neighborhood function, respectively.

b) Upper-lower Hierarchical Relation

In order to represent the hierarchical relation that an upper concept includes the lower concepts, similar learning should be performed between the input layer and the map layer. In this case, the area for a lower concept should be activated by the stimulation of the upper concept.

Taking Fig.10.8 as an example where the knowledge entity (*penguin, is-a, bird*) is inputted. If the neurons in the old *bird* area can stimulate those in the new *bird* area, the properties of the lower concept (*penguin*) can be attached to those of the upper concept (*bird*). To realize such a behavior, the weights from the *bird* neuron in the input layer to the neurons in the *penguin* area in the map layer are learned to
approach the weights from the *penguin* neuron in the input layer to the neurons in the *penguin* area in the map layer.

As a result, an upper level concept can be represented to include the lower level concepts and the association of knowledge from *bird* to *penguin* is made possible. When the similar learning concerning (*canary, is-a, bird*) and (*robin, is-a, bird*) is performed, the relation of inclusion shown in Fig.10.3(b) is realized.

10.6.5 Recall Process

The neural network explained in this chapter can recall all of the properties on the stimulated concept by the weights between the input layer and the map layer and those among map layers.

Inhibition of neuron[23] is introduced during recall. Owing to the inhibition, only the neurons in the most strongly activating area can be active: it is difficult for the other neurons to be activated. Therefore only one knowledge entity can be recalled at the same time.

In addition, in order to recall all of the relevant knowledge entities, refractory is also introduced. Refractory is a phenomenon that once a neuron activates, it can not activate for short period of time. Using the ideas of the inhibition and refractory, different knowledge entities can be recalled successfully.

Let's assume that a neuron corresponding to a lower level concept in the input layer receives stimulation. The knowledge entities concerning the lower level concept is recalled for the beginning because the most activated area suppresses the other areas. Gradually many neurons in the area become the refractory state. As a result, the most activated area moves to the other area which belongs to the upper level concept because of the inheritance learning. By the mechanism explained so far enables knowledge inheritance from the upper concepts.

The algorithm for the recall process is summarized as follows.

1) Calculation of output of neurons:

The total input to the ith neuron in the mth map layer is

$$u_{mi} = \boldsymbol{w}_{mi} \cdot \boldsymbol{x}_m + \sum_n \sum_j v_{nj \to mi} \, y_{nj} \,. \tag{12}$$

The output is normalized to 1.

$$z_{mi} = \frac{u_{mi}}{\max_i u_{mi}} \,. \tag{13}$$

2) Determination of the most activated area:

2-a) Activation of each neuron in map layers is calculated. The area activity A_{mi} is the activity of area centering the ith neuron in the mth map.

$$A_{mi} = \sum_k \lambda(i, k) \, z_{mk} \tag{14}$$

$$\lambda(i,k) = \frac{1}{1 + \exp\left(\dfrac{d(i,k) - \theta}{T}\right)} \tag{15}$$

Here, θ and T are the parameters to determine the shape of the sigmoid function. We should note that a Gaussian shaped function can be used in eq.(15) .

2-b) The most activated neuron i^+ in each map is regarded as the center of the activation area.

$$A_{m i^+} = \max_i A_{m i} \qquad (16)$$

2-c) All of the neuron are inhibited according to the distance from the center of the activation.

$$y_{m i}(t) = \lambda(i, i^+) z_{m i} \qquad (17)$$

3) The winner neuron in each map becomes the refractory state for the following R steps

10.7 Computer Simulation Results

Computer simulations were carried out to confirm the validity of the area representation (AR) and the neural networks. The parameters are summarized in Table 10.1. These parameters were determined experimentally: they are not necessarily optimum.

The knowledge entities stored in the network are shown in Fig.10.9. 14 knowledge entities such as (*bird, has feathers*) are stored in the proposed network. As mentioned in the footnote in **10.5.1**, since each knowledge entity is composed of three concepts, there are three maps in the network: node map, relation map and attribute map. The first concept in each knowledge entity such as *bird* is inputted to the node map, the second concept such as *has* is inputted to the relation map, and the third concept such as *feathers* is inputted to the attribute map.

Table 10.1. Parameters used in simulations.

number of maps	3	ζ	0.25
size of maps	15×15	ρ_i	5.0
t_{max}	1000	ρ_f	1.0
t_{imax}	t_{max}	ξ	0.15
α	1.50	θ	4.0
β	0.02	T	0.0625
γ	0.90	θ_T	$t_{max} \times 0.75$
σ_i	8.0	T_T	$t_{max}/16$
σ_f	1.0	R	25
ϵ_e	0.25		

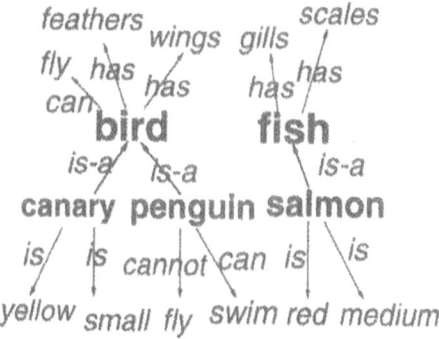

Fig.10.9. Knowledge entities stored in the network.

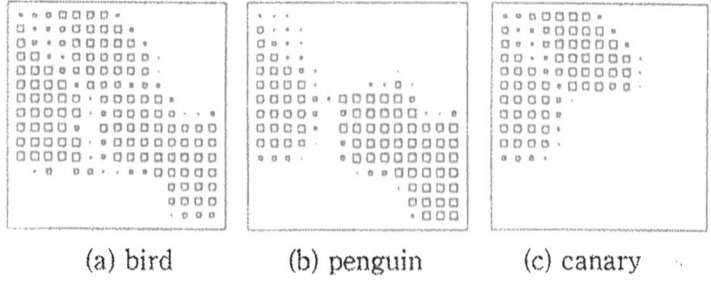

(a) bird   (b) penguin   (c) canary

Fig.10.10. Responses of the node map for *bird*, *penguin* and *canary*.

10.7.1 Representation of Hierarchical Relation

First, we examined how concepts are represented in the map layer.

Fig.10.10 shows the responses of the node map when elements, *bird*, *penguin* and *canary* are stimulated in the input layer. The size of ☐ expresses the activity of neuron. In this figure, the *bird* area includes *penguin* and *canary* areas because there exist knowledge entities expressing inheritance ((*canary*, *is-a*, *bird*) and (*penguin*, *is-a*, *bird*)) in Fig.10.9.

10.7.2 Recall of Stored Knowledge Entities

The *penguin* element in the input layer was stimulated continuously to recall stored knowledge entities. Before this simulation, we examined the activity pattern for each concept. Using the patterns, we can determine what concept is represented in a map by calculating the correlation between the pattern of response and the examined typical response for each concept.

234

Table 10.2 Recalled knowledge entities (values are normalized).

t	node map					relation map			
	salmon	fish	canary	penguin	bird	is	has	can	cannot
1	0.02	0.03	0.03	1.00	0.89	0.00	0.00	1.00	0.26
12	0.01	0.14	0.00	1.00	0.86	0.00	0.09	0.66	1.00
22	0.00	0.00	0.82	0.82	1.00	0.11	0.09	1.00	0.03

t	attribute map									
	red	medium	gills	scales	swim	yellow	small	fly	wings	feathers
1	0.00	0.00	0.00	0.00	1.00	0.00	0.00	0.15	0.08	0.05
12	0.00	0.00	0.00	0.00	0.41	0.00	0.00	1.00	0.00	0.03
22	0.00	0.00	0.00	0.00	0.22	0.00	0.12	1.00	0.01	0.41

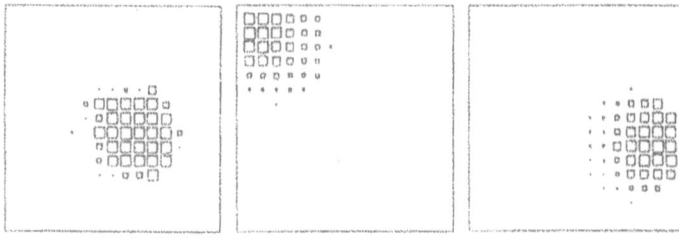

(a) node   (b) relation   (c) attribute

Fig.10.11. Response pattern at *t*=1. (*penguin, can, swim*) is recalled.

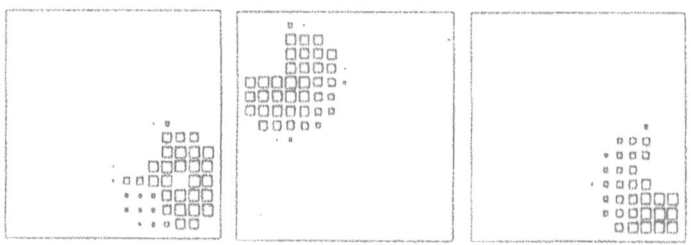

(a) node   (b) relation   (c) attribute

Fig.10.12. Response pattern at *t*=12. (*penguin, cannot, fly*) is recalled.

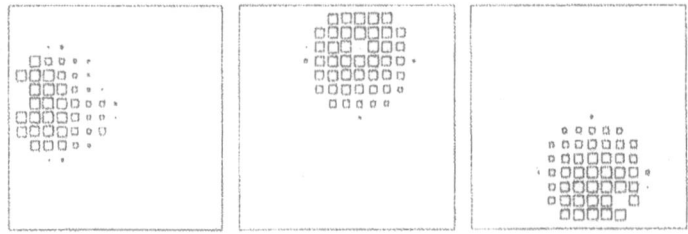

(a) node   (b) relation   (c) attribute

Fig.10.13. Response pattern at *t*=22. (*bird, can, fly*) is recalled.

Table 10.2 shows the recalled knowledge entities. For example at $t=1$, the concept of *penguin* has the highest activation value in the node map, the concept of *can* has the highest activation in the relation map, and the concept of *swim* has the highest activation in the attribute map. As a result, we can see that knowledge entity (*penguin, can, swim*) is recalled at $t=1$. Figs.10.11, 10.12 and 10.13 show the response patterns. As explained in **10.6.5**, since a winner neuron can not be activated for the following R steps, another neuron becomes a winner at the next time because of introduction of the refractory state. Owing to such a mechanism, no neuron can win successively, and therefore the network does not fall into a steady state until all of the corresponding knowledge entities are recalled. At $t=12$, the areas shown in Fig.10.12 are activated and we can see from Table 10.2 that (*penguin, cannot, fly*) is recalled. Since the recall process is dynamical like human beings, the other mechanism should be added to determine the timing of recall.

The knowledge entities concerning *penguin* explicitly in Fig.10.9 are (*penguin, can, swim*) and (*penguin, cannot, fly*). After recalling these entities, the network began to recall the knowledge entities concerning the upper concept *bird* because of the stored knowledge entities concerning inheritance (*penguin, is-a, bird*). It can be observed that the active area in the node map in Fig.10.13 is much different from those in Figs.10.11 and 10.12. From Table 10.2, we can see that (*bird, can, fly*) is recalled in Fig.10.13.

When there are contradictions in the recalled knowledge entities, the knowledge entities concerning the lower concept should take priority over those upper concept. This idea is widely used in the usage of semantic networks[1]. In this case, although (*bird, can, fly*) contradicts (*penguin, cannot, fly*), the knowledge entity concerning the lower level concept (*penguin, cannot, fly*) takes priority.

As explained so far, the network enables one-to-many associations, (*penguin, can, swim*) and (*penguin, cannot, fly*) concerning *penguin*, (*bird, can, fly*) and (*penguin, cannot, fly*) concerning *fly*. Therefore the network enables many-to-many associations [18] which are one of the remarkable features in human memory.

In addition, although both Fig.10.11(a) and Fig.10.12(a) express *penguin*, the areas differ each other because the concept *penguin* is stored in different contexts. This means that the network can reflect contexts.

10.8 Conclusions

A new paradigm to represent knowledge and the implementation by neural networks have been explained in the chapter. The AR represents a concept in an activation pattern in the area using some neurons. Since it is, so to speak, an intermediate method between local representation and distributed representation, it can preserve advantages of each method.

A new inclusion relation based on the AR method and improved Hebb rule named neighborhood Hebb rule are also explained. The new inclusion relation is effective to represent hierarchical relations and neighborhood Hebb rule is effective for stable learning. A neural network implementing the concept of the AR and the computer simulation results are also shown to express the validity.

References

1. P. H. Winston, Artificial Intelligence ---Third Edition, Addison-Wesley, 1992.
2. Y. Anzai, Pattern Recognition and Machine Learning, Academic Press, 1992.
3. D.E.Rummelhart, J.L.McClelland, and the PDP Research Group, Parallel Distributed Processing, The MIT Press, 1986.
4. J.Hertz, A.Krough and R.G.Palmer, Introduction to the Theory of Neural Computation, Addison Wesley, 1991.
5. J.C.Bezdek and S.K.Pal, Fuzzy Models for Pattern Recognition, IEEE Press, 1992.
6. C.H.Chen (ed.), Fuzzy Logic and Neural Network Handbook, McGraw-Hill, 1996.
7. D.E.Goldberg, Genetic Algorithms in Search, Optimization, and Machine Learning, Addison-Wesley, 1989.
8. D.B.Fogel, Evolutionary Computation -- Toward a new philosophy of machine intelligence, IEEE Press, 1995.
9. M.Hagiwara, Neuro, Fuzzy and Genetic algorithms, Sangyo-tosyo, 1994. (in Japanese)
10. M.Hagiwara and Y.Anzai: Connectionist model data base system with a template for association, Proc. IEE Japan, Vol.112-C, 3, pp.165-171, 1992-03. (in Japanese)
11. H.Ritter and T.Kohonen, Self-organizing semantic maps, Biological Cybernetics 61, pp.241-254, 1989.
12. T.Kohonen, Self-organized formation of correct feature maps, Biological Cybernetics 43, pp.59-69, 1982.
13. R.Miikkulainen, A distributed feature map model of The lexicon, The 20th Annual Conference of the Cognitive Science Society, pp.25-28, July 1990.
14. R.Miikkulainen, Trace feature map: a model of episodic associative memory, Biological Cybernetics 66, pp.283-289, 1992.
15. P.G.Schyns, A modular neural network model of concept acquisition, Cognitive Science, pp.2961-508, 1991.
16. T.Omori and N.Yamagishi, PATON: a model of concept representation and operation in brain, IEEE Int. Conf. on Neural Networks, pp.2227-2232, 1994.
17 I.Takeuchi, T. Furuhashi, Y. Hamada, Y. Uchikawa, A self-organizing network for acquisition of vague concept, 1996 the First Asia-Pacific conf. on Simulated Evolution and Learning, pp.473-480, 1996.
18. M.Hagiwara, Multidirectional associative memory, International Joint Conf. on Neural Networks, Washington, D.C., vol.1, pp.3-6, 1990.
19. R. Sun, An efficient feature-based connectionist inference scheme, IEEE Trans. on Syst. Man. Cybern., vol.SMC-23, no.2, pp.512-522, Mar. 1993.
20. The Society of Instrument and Control Engineers (ed.), Neuro, Fuzzy, and AI Handbook, Ohom-sha, 1994.
21. N. Ikeda and M. Hagiwara, A proposal of novel knowledge representation

(area representation) and the implementation by neural network, International Conference on Computational Intelligence and Neuroscience, vol. III, pp.430-433, 1997.

22. N. Ikeda and M. Hagiwara, A proposal of novel knowledge representation (area representation) and the implementation by neural network, Trans. on IEICE Japan, vol.J81-D-II, pp.1328-1335, 1998. (in Japanese)

23. E.R.Kandel, J.H.Schwartz and T.M.Jessell, Principles of Neural Science (third edition), Appleton & Lange, 1991.

A Symbol Grounding Problem of Gesture Motion through a Self-organizing Network of Time-varying Motion Images

Toshiro Mukai, Takuichi Nishimura, Takashi Endo and Ryuichi Oka

Tsukuba Research Center, Real World Computing Partnership,

Abstract : We applied a method for self-organizing network to gesture motion images. We extract both so-called common parts and singular parts of gesture by analysis of the network topology. We call these parts to elemental motion units. In this paper, we propose a method to extract elemental motion units from gesture motion images and a gesture recognition method of a large vocabulary on the basis of recognition of elemental motion units. When recognizing gestures in time-varying motion images, the usual adopted method has been to distinguish different kind of gestures from a series of movie or images. However when a gesture targeted for recognition has an extensive vocabulary, the recognition of that gesture with an extended version of the usual method is difficult. So we use elemental motion unit to recognize gestures with large vocabulary. We have already proposed the incremental path method that is one of self-organizing network method. This method is constructing an incremental network structure given an input sequence. We applied this method to gesture motion images, so that we extract common parts in some gestures and singular parts. We show detail of incremental path method in section 11.5 and Automated extraction method in section 11.6. At last we describe new gesture recognition method using this elemental motion units and conclusion.

11.1 Introduction

We applied a method for self-organizing network[Toyoura(1997)][Endo(1997)] to gesture motion images. We extract both so-called common parts and singular parts of gesture by analysis of the network topology. We propose a method to extract elemental motion units from gesture motion images and a gesture recognition method of a large vocabulary on the basis of recognition of the elemental motion units.

Human gesture motion image is an extremely useful means of communicating human intentions in a man-machine interaction [Yamamoto(1992)] [Nagaya(1995)] [Takahasi(1994)]. Unlike voice, gestures are a non-verbal means for expressing the meaning of human intentions. For this reason, gestures and voice can be used together to compensate each other. However, no attempt at capturing gestures as a time-varying motion image sequence has been made to create a satisfactory model of the whole image of a gesture.

Particularly, there has not been any attempt to decompose a sequence of gestures into elemental units such as what we call elemental motion units. This paper attempts to model the structure revealed in a time-varying motion image of gesture through a self-organizing network, and proposes a method to extract intersecting common features and singularity of a gesture by analyzing the topology which expresses the distance space of the network structure. Extracted intersecting common features and singularity of gestures are considered to be the elements composing a time-varying motion image of gesture. Furthermore, by focusing on gestures which express an extensive vocabulary, a gesture recognition method based on the recognition of these motion elements is examined.

11.2 Elemental Motion Units of a Gesture

When recognizing gestures in time-varying motion images, the usual adopted method has been to distinguish different kinds of gestures from a series of movie or images. However, when a gesture targeted for recognition has an extensive vocabulary, the recognition of that gesture with an extended version of the usual method becomes difficult [Nagaya(1995)]. This is likened to the difficulty associated with the recognition of continuous speech constituting extensive vocabulary through association of standard patterns composed of word-units [Nakazawa(1997)] [Ito(1995)].

To overcome this difficulty, we constructed a method in which what we call elemental motion units in gestures are extracted and a given gesture is recognized through its connection with elemental motion units. For example, a kind of gesture with motion units A, B and C is distinguished in terms of meaning from another kind of gesture with motion units A, B and C'. This corresponds to the use of demi-phonemes in continuous speech recognition.

11.3 Modeling of Gestures through IPM

With regard to time-varying motion images of a gesture, elemental units have not yet been defined. This makes a clear contrast with the situation in the area of speech recognition in which elemental units of demi-phonemes are justified through phonetics. Thus, it is not possible to express a simple topological network with already-known elemental units of gestures using the HMM model used in speech[Yamamoto(1992)][Sakaguchi(1995)].

Therefore, studying elemental motion units extracted from time-varying motion images of a gesture at the present time has to model the generation process of elemental motion its from the data of time-varying motion images of a gesture.

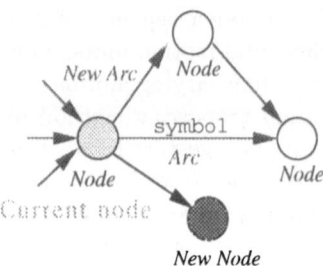

New Arc   *Node*

symbol

Arc

Node   *Node*

Current node

New Node

Fig. 11.1. Basic structure of the IPM network.

11.4 Adoption of IPM

The desirable design of a model that expresses the structure of time-varying motion images of a gesture should have an incremental structure as new input is introduced. This comes from the fact that the number of kinds of gestures introduced as inputs will increase whenever a new kind of gesture is introduced. We have already proposed the Incremental Path Method (abbreviated as IPM below), which is a method for constructing an incremental network structure given an input sequence. IPM is characterized by being able to construct a network where the trace of the network is identical to that of corresponding and identical input label series in a label series.

Let us now focus on the features of topology in the IPM network and suppose the common/singular parts of a network are elemental motion units that compose gestures. Considering the topology of the IPM network, singular parts are considered to express a particular type of singular characteristics of gesture, and common parts are considered to constitute a type of gesture but cannot uniquely determine the type of gesture independently. When the target gesture is of a large scale, the gesture can be determined through combinations of common parts.

For the above-mentioned reasons, we consider elemental motion units to be common/singular parts of the IPM network.

In this paper, we regard a time-varying motion image as a sequence of static images. We use the IPM method on quantified static images by handling time-varying motion images as a label sequence. The method applies the multivariate analysis to the nodes generated by the IPM to specify coordinates, maps the points to a 3-dimensional space to arrange the points corresponding to networks in a distance space, and visualizes their dynamic features.

11.5 IPM Network

Based on label sequences generated from time-varying motion images of gestures, we generate a network structure using the IPM method. The IPM method constructs a network using nodes and a directed arc. An arc is attached with a symbol label, and a pair of nodes is given an arc. Since there are cases in which a static image appears in the middle of a gesture, a generation of a recurrent loop in the same input label is allowed. Thus, our strategy to construct a network architecture is described as follows:

1. When there is an arc corresponding to an input label, the transition follows the arc.
2. When an identical label continues, it forms a recurrent loop.
3. When there is no arc corresponding to an input label, a transition is made to a node which has an arc corresponding to the input symbol.

Self-Organizing of IPM Network

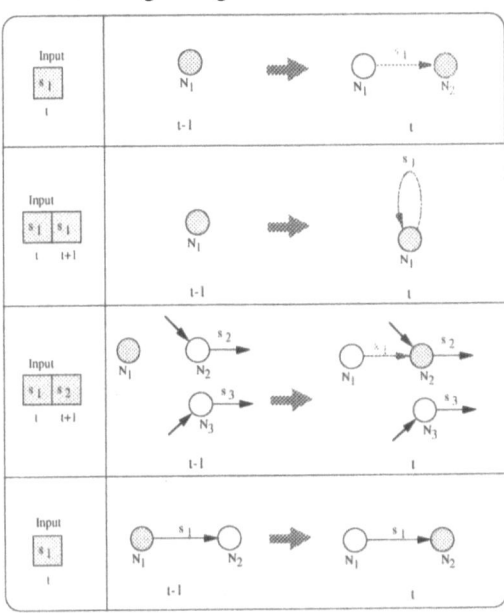

Fig. 11.2. Basic operations performed for self-organization by the IPM network

[Organizing algorithm for self-organizing IPM network]

N: set of nodes.

M: the number of nodes, $M = \|N\|$.

L: the maximum number of arcs held by a node.

$A_{i,j}$: a label associated with an arc from the "i"th node to the "j"th node.

P: the maximum number of labels read beforehand when generating a new arc.

K: a set of labels. $A_{i,j} \in K\phi$, $\% \in K$, $K \neq \phi$

ϕ: a null label

%: a skip label
u(t): input label at time t
l[x :] l[x]=l if x , % = 0 otherwise

  i. $t := 0$ and $\forall i, j \in N, A_{i,j} := \phi$
  ii. $i_0 := 1$
 iii. $t := t + 1$
 iv. $J \equiv \{j | A_{i_{t-1},j} = u(t)\}$ if $J = \phi$ then goto (vii) else goto (v)
  v. if $\exists j_t$ minimum of $j \in J$ and $\exists k$
     so that $A_{j_t,k} = u(t+1)$ and $\sum_{m=1}^{M} l(A_{k,m}) \leq L - 1$ then
     $i_t := j_t$ and goto (iii)
     otherwise goto (vi)
 vi. if $\exists j_t$ minimum of $j \in J$ so that $\sum_{m=1}^{M} l(A_{j,m}) \leq L - 1$
     then $i_t := j_t$ and goto (iii) otherwise goto (viii)
vii. if $\exists j_{new}$ minimum of $j \in N$ and $\exists p$ maximum of $1 < p < P$ and $\exists k_{1 \cdots p}$
     so that $A_{i_{t-1},j_{new}} = \phi$ and $\sum_{m=1}^{M} l(A_{j_{t-1},m}) \leq L - 1$,
     $k_0 := j_{new}, A_{k_0,k_1} = u(t+1), \cdots A_{k_{p-1},k_p} = u(t+p)$ and
     $\sum_{m=1}^{M} l(A_{k_p,m}) \leq L - 1$
     then $A_{i_{t-1},j_{new}} = u(t), i_t := j_{new}$ and goto (iii)
     otherwise goto (viii)
viii. if $\exists j_{new}$ minimum of $j \in N$ so that $A_{i_{t-1},j_{new}} := \phi$ and $A_{j_{new},k} = u(t)$
     and
     $\sum_{m=1}^{M} l(A_{k,m}) \leq L - 1$
     then $i_t := j_{new}$ and goto (iii)
     otherwise goto (ix)
 ix. if $\exists j_{new}$ minimum of $j \in N$ so that $A_{i_{t-1}j_{new}} := u(t)$ and $i_t := j_{new}$ and
     goto (iii)
     otherwise stop

11.6 A Proposal for an Automated Extraction Method of Elemental Motion Units

In order to segment elemental motion units, we use both topology and distance in the distance space arranged with nodes introduced for visualization purposes. As shown in Figure 11.3, a singular interval which is a collection of nodes without branches, other than a recurrent loop, represents a characteristic feature of a given type of gesture. This singular interval represents a characteristic feature of a given type of gesture and can be considered as an elemental motion unit. Furthermore, by considering each arc between nodes as an elemental motion unit, it can be used as an elemental motion unit of the IPM network when dealing with a type of gesture with an extensive vocabulary size.

11.7 Automated Extraction of Common Intervals

The IPM network has nodes with multiple arcs as well as arcs used in recurrent loops. Since not only singular intervals per se, but also singular intervals combined with common intervals are used to represent types of gestures, an automated extraction method for common intervals is needed as well.

The extraction method extracts all the arcs left unextracted through the extraction process of singular intervals. The extraction process of singular intervals will be introduced in the next section.

Automated extraction of singular intervals Using connection information of nodes in the IPM network, singular parts can be segmented as follows.

[Algorithm for automated extraction of elemental motion units]

i: node number
L: Length of a singular interval
N_i: number of arcs branching from the "i"th node
$A_i[x :]$ Arc number of the "i"th node
n: number of singular intervals

  i. i:=0,L:=0,n:=0
  ii. if $N_i = 1$ then goto (iii) else if $N_i = 2$ and $(A_i[0] = i$ or $A_i[1] = I)$ then goto (iii) otherwise goto (iv)
  iii. L:=L+1, i:=i+1 goto(ii)
  iv. if $i > I - 1$ then stop else if $L > 3$ n:=n+1 then goto (ii) ($\longrightarrow$ extraction of singular intervals) otherwise i:=i+1 goto (ii)

The above mentioned algorithm searches for nodes as shown in Figure 11.3, with only one arc (other than arcs used for recurrent loops) and extract nodes longer than the threshold level (set at 3 in this case) as singular intervals.

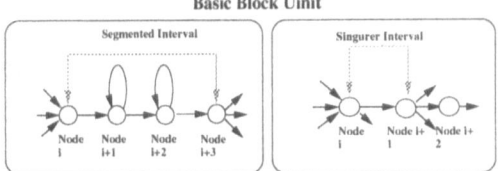

Basic Block Uinit

Fig. 11.3. Extraction of singular intervals

11.8 Experiment for Extraction of Singular Intervals

11.8.1 Input Data

As an experiment to investigate the usefulness of automated extraction of singular intervals in the IPM network, 3 types of time-varying motion image intervals are chosen from 5 types of gestures shown in Figure 11.4 (circle, x-shaped, square, right, and left) and connected to create one time-varying motion image sequence. There are 20 time-varying motion image sequences.

This collection of time-varying motion image sequences forms the IPM network and the comparison is made between extracted singular intervals and actual images. For any type of gesture a restriction is introduced to limit the movement starting from a knee and terminating at a knee. In the experiment, Indigo2 Impact from SGI corporation is used and the input is entered into a Workstation with a time resolution of 15 frames per second. Frames are 1420 movie frames with the size of 160x120.

Fig. 11.4. Types of gestures used in the experiment. (5 types: circle, x-shaped, square, right, and left)

The feature quantities used during vectorial quantization are created as follows. Each of the frame images in the movie is described as different levels of gray scale. Using the average gray level after the reduction of each frame into a 5x5 size, a 25th dimensional vector is constructed.

11.9 Vectorial Quantization of Images

Transformation from time-varying motion images of a gesture to a label sequence is accomplished by vectorial quantization. The generation method of centered vectors is such that the input vector is summed with a centered vector whenever the error of quantization becomes greater than a certain limit.

[Centered generation algorithm]

i. n:=0,t:=0
ii. if $\exists n$ minimum of $n \in N$ so that $\|I_i - C_n\| < d$ then goto (iv) else goto (iii)
iii. $C_N = I_t$, N:=N+1 goto (iv)
iv. t:=t+1 if $t < T$ then goto (ii) else stop

By using this method where a centered is incrementally generated, it is not necessary to prepare images of a gesture beforehand.

11.10 Generation of Label Sequence

Feature quantities of each frame of time-varying motion images of a gesture are defined as follows.

$$f(t) = [f_1(t), f_2(t), ..., f_n(t)] \tag{11.1}$$

The number of centurions closest to f(t) is chosen to determine u(t), where u(t) is the label for f(t).

11.11 Visualization of the IPM Network

A network is visualized through the mapping of nodes in the IPM network into a 3-dimensional space. Using the number of passages made through the arc when there is an arc and a negative number when there is no arc, the closeness between nodes is determined by the multivariate analysis to give node coordinates. As a result, the distance between nodes not connected by an arc becomes long, and the distance between frequently passed nodes becomes short.

11.12 Experiment Results

The number of centurions found from approximately 1400 frames of time-varying motion images of gestures processed through vectorial quantization with a quantization error rate of 50 turns out of 77. Based on the VQ codes, we construct the IPM network. This results in 70 generated nodes. Figure 11.5 shows the result in a 3-dimensional space.

Based on the connection between nodes in the network and the number of arcs branching out from each node, singular intervals are extracted. The results are presented in Figure 11.5. The neighborhood of the center region corresponds to common intervals in which nodes are passed through, even when other types of gestures have been performed. Considering the fact that this experiment deals with the complete movement of a given gesture, which starts from the hands and knees and terminates at the knees, it is a valid result to pass the same nodes around the region of starting and terminating points. Since the number of types of targeted gestures is small, the passage of corresponding lines can be used in gesture recognition.

Investigation of gesture recognition using an extensive vocabulary Pilot experiment and actual gestures representing extensive vocabulary used in the pilot experiment

We use sign language as input gesture motion images to inspect whether we can use this method for a practical gesture with a large vocabulary in future. The sign language is means conveying intention using a gesture, and

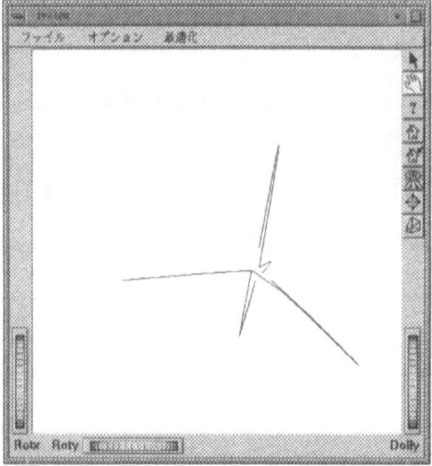

Fig. 11.5. Configuration of the IPM network in a 3-dimensional space

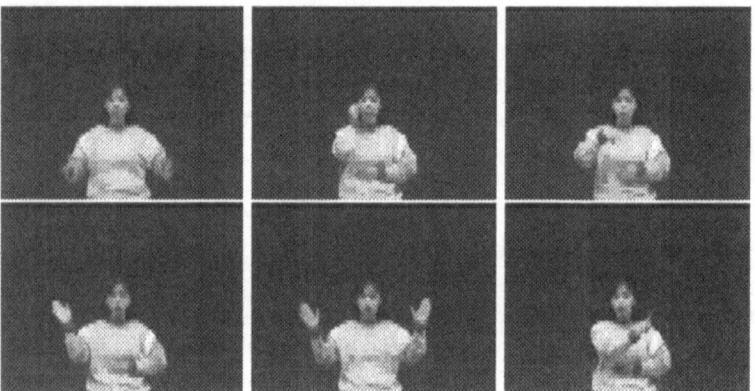

Fig. 11.6. Examples of input sign language images

the vocabulary is enormous. To apply this method in these sign language in the future, We select gestures with big movement in sign language, and we use them as gestures (shown Figure 11.5). We check whether automatic segmentation algorithm is well or not functions in case of gesture of large vocabulary moreover by inspection. The IPM network is generated using a subset of sign language. Figure 11.7 shows the projection of the generated network into a 3-dimensional space.

We show some segmentation results in Figure 11.7. Input motion images A,B,C and D in Figure 11.7 are not the same sign language word. The upper curette of Figure 11.7 shows a part of the IPM network in 3 dimensions space. The point shows a node, and the line is a arc for the input motion image. It consists of element movements from label a1 to a9 in case of input motion image A. It consists of element movements from label b1 to b4, a7 and b5 to b8 in case of input motion image B. Interval of label a7 is the common part

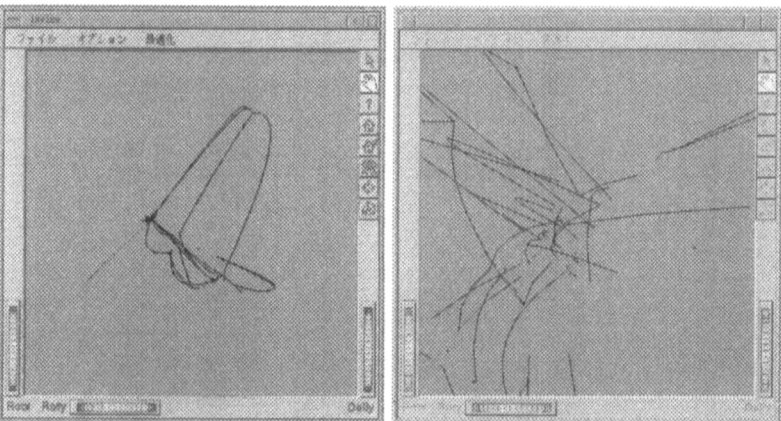

Fig. 11.7. IPM network projected into a 3-dimensional space

between input motion image A and B. We confirmed that those were almost same motion images about a part of label a7 manually. A part of label c7 was common about input motion image C and D, and it was almost same motion images at few different degree of hands.

11.13 Examination of Recognition Methods

We consider a recognition method when a gesture used as recognition target assumes an extensive vocabulary. Let us now define the variables used as follows:

$u(t)$: Input motion image of gesture
$G(t)$: A label sequence of elemental motion units added by the IPM network of $u(t)$
l_i: A label for an elemental motion unit
L: A set of labels for elemental motion units l1, l2, ..., lN
N: Total number of labels for elemental motion units

When the number of labels for elemental motion units becomes large, the mapping between gestures and elemental motion units does not necessarily follow a one-to-one mapping. To counter this problem, we use an extensive vocabulary word recognition method using demi-phoneme symbols by Nakazawa, et. al. [Nakazawa(1997)] to perform word-spotting recognition using $G(t)$. An example is presented in Figure 11.9. Given [BBBAAAAC-CCKK...] as an input elemental motion unit sequence, "*" indicates an elemental motion unit with a potential transition from the current state to another. Labels [C, E] show possible transition states in response to input A. When C enters as an input, K becomes the next candidate label for possible transition. When K enters as an input, [A-C-K] is recognized.

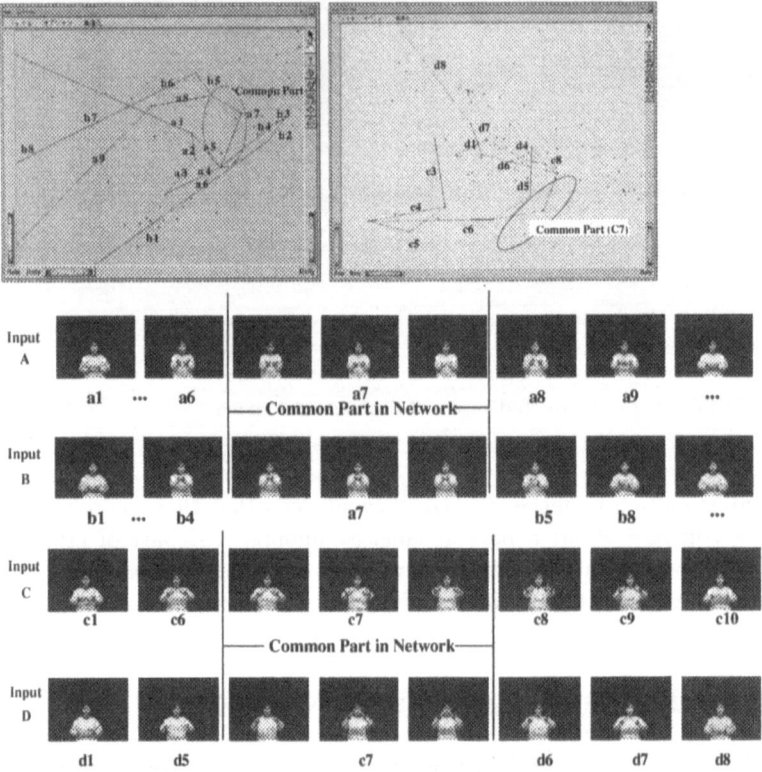

Fig. 11.8. Segmentation result at the IPM network

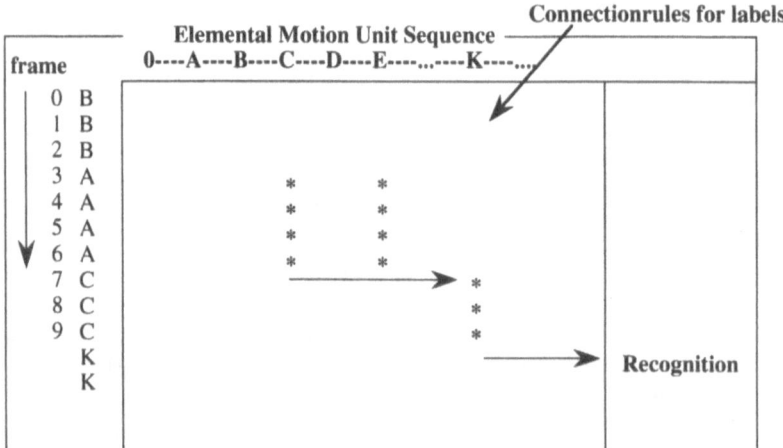

Fig. 11.9. Spotting recognition method for gestures with an extensive vocabulary (Example for a word: [A-C-K])

11.14 Summary

In this paper, we proposed a method to automatically segment a set of gesture motion images into so-called elemental units. We applied a method called the Incremental Path Method (already proposed by authors) for constructing a self-organized network to gesture motion images and extracted the elemental units consisting of both called common and distinguishable parts by analyzing the topological features of the network. these units should be useful to recognize a large amount of gesture categories because of the analogy of the role of phonemes in speech recognition.

Since 5 types of gestures whose starting and terminating points are similar were used in the experiment, these types of gestures pass through the same nodes at the starting and terminating points. And at the same time, we were able to extract characteristic parts of each type of gesture as singular intervals. Since the size of vocabulary used in this experiment was small, it was possible to recognize gestures with only singular intervals. However, as became clearer as a result of the pilot experiment in which gestures with an extensive vocabulary size were used, decisions based on singular intervals are not useful regarding gestures with an extensive vocabulary size. Rather, a method in which a set of arcs defined as elemental motion units consisting of arcs connecting common intervals between nodes and singular intervals, and recognition of a gesture performed at the level of elemental motion units is required. Future tasks involve expanding the vocabulary size of gestures (to the level of a few hundred) as well as furthering the investigation of automated extraction of a motion phrase from elemental motion units.

References

[Endo(1997)] T.Endo,H.Takahashi,J.Toyoura and R.Oka.:"Video image modeling based on a self-organizing network and visualization of dynamic features." Technical report of IEICE-PRMU, 97(78):49–54, July 1997.

[Toyoura(1997)] J.Toyoura and R.Oka. "Self-organizing network for transforming text into knowledge base." Technical report of IEICE-NLC, 59(96), March 1997.

[Oka(1995)] R.Oka, Y.Ito, J.Kiyama and J.X.Zhang. "Concept spotting by image automaton." Proc. of The Acoustical Society of Japan, pages 67–68, March,1995.

[Yamamoto(1992)] J.Yamato,J.Ohya and K.Ishii. "Recognizing human action in time-sequential images using hidden markov model." Proc. CVPR, pages 379–385, 1992.

[Nagaya(1995)] S.Nagaya, S.Seki and R.Oka. "A proposal of gesture trajectory feature for gesture spotting recognition."Technical report of IEICE-PRU, 95(142):45–50, October 1995.

[Ito(1995)] Y.Ito, J.Kiyama, H.Kojima, S.Seki and R.Oka. "Reference interval-free continuous dynamic programming(rifcdp) for spotting speech waves by arbitrary parts of a reference pattern."Technical report of IEICE-SP, 95(34):73–80, June 1995.

[Nakazawa(1997)] M.Nakazawa,T.Endo,K.Furukawa,J.Toyoura and R.Oka."A study on speech summary using demi-phoneme symbols generated from speech waves." Technical report of IPSJ-SLP, 97(15):119–124, 1997.

[Darell(1993)] T.J.Darell and A.P.Pentland. "Space-time gestures." Proc. of IJCAI '93 Looking at People Workshop, 1993.

[Ishii(1993)] H.Ishii, k.Mochizuki and F.Kishino"A Motion Recognition Method from Stereo Images for Human Image Synthesis." The Trans. of the EIC, vol.J76-D-II,no.8,pp1805-1812,1993.

[Takahasi(1994)] K.Takahashi, S,Seki, H.Kojima and R.Oka. "Spotting Recognition of Human Gesture from Time-varying motion images."Trans. of IEICE(D-II), J77-D-II,No.8,pp1552-1561,1994

[Seki(1995)] S.Seki, H.Kojima, S.Nagaya and R.Oka."Efficient gesture recognition algorithm based of Continuous Dynamic Programming." Proc. of RWC Symposium Technical Report,pp47-48,1995

[Sakaguchi(1995)] Sakaguchi, Ohya and Kishino."Facial Expression Recognition from Image Sequence Using Hidden Markov Model." The Journal of the institute of Television Engineers of Japan,49-8,pp1060-1067,1995

Index

CLARION 3
hybrid model 3,5
temporal difference 4
declarative knowledge 5,7
procedural skills 5
reactive sequential decision making .. 6
Q-learning algorithm 6
temporal difference rein forcement
  learning algorithm 6
extraction 9
expansion 9
shrinking 9
deletion 9
merge 10
navigation 11
maze 16
synergy 17
transfer 17
symbol grounding 17
dichotomy 18
integration 22
information-processing unit 22
IP-Unit 22,23
integrated IP-Unit 22
dynamic integration 22
independent IP-Unit 23
conceptual entity 24
classification structure 24
type 24
domain 24
granularity 24
direct serial concatenation 25
pivot variables 26,31
indirect serial integration 26
parallel integration 26
integration of alternative operations 27
integrator 28,33
procedural programming method ... 28
declarative knowledge-based method
  23,28,30

computational method 28,30
neural network 28,33
procedural processing 28,33
knowledge processing 28,33
symbol processing method 30
procedural method 30
declarative method 30
deductive inference engine 31
scope 31
symbolic form 33
non-symbolic form 34
logical inference 36
non-symbolic processor 36
granularity 36
deductive operation 36
state transition 36
transition matrix 36
imply 36
cubic matrix 36
symbol pattern integration 41
multilinear functions 41,45,50,66
pattern reasoning 41,43,67,68
logical reasoning 41,66,67
pattern 41
knowledge acquisition 43
LC 43,44,60,61,63,64,66
product logic 42,61
Lukasiewicz logic 43
multilinear function space 42,61,63
continuous Boolean functions .44,52,57
Euclidean space 44,48,49,57
multilinear function space . 44,48,49,57
Hasse diagram 44
linear space 46,57
atoms of Boolean algebra 46
Boolean functions 46
elementary algebra representations of
  logical operations 46
logical vectors 49,51
vector representations 49

252

neural networks 50,60,66,67
approximation of multilinear functions
    by Boolean functions 51
direct proportion 52
inverse proportion 52
elementary algebra model for classical
    logic 52
τ 53,54
L_1 54
calculation 54
continuously-valued logic 55
axioms of Boolean algebra 55
vector representation 59,60
interval $[0,1]$ 60,62,63
Lukasiewics logic 61
contraction 61
intuitionistic logic 61,62
heyting algebra 62,64
approximation 65
typical pattern 68
formal system 69
incompleteness 69
adaptive control 73
FYNESSE 73,75
GARIC 75,101
CLARION 75,86,96,101
autonomous learning 75
symbolic knowledge 75
subsymbolic knowledge 75
cart pole balancer 75
vague statement 76
symbolic fuzzy rules 77
approximate reasoning 77
possibility theory 77
interpolation 77
negative information 77
fuzzy numbers 77
B-spline-systems 78
fuzzy point 78
meta-rule 78,99
similarity 78
multistage reasoning 78
separable 81
reinforcement learning 81
neural critic 81
control policy 82
black-box simulation model 82
dynamic optimization problem 82
dynamic programming 82,83
local cost function 82
global cost function 82
value function 82
horizon 82

dynamic optimization 83
principle of optimality 83
value iteration method 83
greedy evaluation 83
real-time dynamic program-
    ming(RTDP) 84
fixed horizon algorithm 84
single step prediction 84
Q-learning 84
curse of dimensionality 85
function approximator 85
temporal difference (TD) learning ..85
reinforcement learning 85
backpropagation algorithm 85
constraints 86
local cost function 86
oprimality criterion 86
a priori knowledge 88
control characteristic 88
fuzzy control laws 88
linear control laws 88
linear quadratic regulator (LQR) design
    93
stability 94
positive knowledge 95
negative knowledge 95
possibility distributions 95
subsymbolic component 96
symbolic component 96
interpretation 98
rule extraction 99
least mean square algorithms 99
dynamic systems 104
fuzzy sequential knowledge 104
a priori knowledge 104,106
symbolic dynamic system (SDS)
    104,105,107
fuzzy symbolic sequences ..104,108,109
knowledge representation for dynamic
    characteristics 105
dynamic characteristics 105
symbolic sequential knowledge 105
state transitions 105
pendulum 105
seasonal adjustment model 106
SDS with fuzzy states 108
fuzzy granules 108
fuzzy state 108
discrete states 108
convex polyhedron 109
model identification 111
parameter estimation 112

expectation - maximization (EM)
  algorithm 113
prediction 117
hybrid system 122
incremental neuro-symbolic system
  (INSS) 122
SYNHESYS 122
KBANN 122
symbolic modules 122,125
connectionist modules 122
hybrid neuro-symbolic system 122
back-propagation algorithm 124
QuickProp 124
cascor 124
RProp 124
scaled conjugate gradient algorithm 124
cascade-correlation learning method
  124
incremental rule extraction 124
incremental rule extraction 124
NeuComp 125
NeuSim 125,128
extract 125,131
valid 125
c language integrated production
  system (CLIPS) 125
rule insertion 126
high level rules 126
sensibility 128
confidence 128
cascade-correlation learning algorithm
  128
network simplification 131
RBF networks 131
counterpropagation networks 131
grid partition 132
tree partition 132
linear partition 132
Mamdani fuzzy inference system .. 133
Sugeno fuzzy inference system 133
fuzzy automatically generated neural
  inferred system (FAGNIS) 135
mutual exclusiveness fuzzy sets 135
region of influence constraint 135
Monk's problem 137
medical diagnosis 139
multi-component 146
hybridization 146
fusion 146
complementary methods 146
neural network 147
learning 147
adaptation 147

a priori knowledge 147
connectionist paradigm 147
distributed knowledge representation
  147
fuzzy knowledge based systems 147
single component system 148
fusion based system 148
hierarchical system 148
single component system 148
ANFIS 148
NEFCON 148
FUN 148
FINEST 148
FLINS 148
hybrid system 148
ARIC 148
GARIC 148
FYNESSE 148
SHADE 148,166
fuzzy relation adaptation 148
learning agent architecture 149
performance element 150
critic 150
external reinforcement signal 150
credit assignment problem (CAP) . 150
temporal credit assignment 150
structural credit assignment 150
problem generator 150
reinforcement-driven fuzzy relation
  adaptation 151
rule-based fuzzy decision support
  system 151,165
adaptive critic 151,169
performance element 152
learning element 152
fuzzy relation calculus 152
max-min composition 153,154
cylindric extension 154
compositional rule of inference 154
fuzzy relation adaptation 156
action selection 156
knowledge update 156
defuzzification 156
maximum defuzzification 156
deterministic defuzzification 156
randomized defuzzification 157
knowledge update stage 157
reinforcement schemes 157
point-wise updates 157
neighborhood incorporating updates
  157,158
fuzzy set oriented updates 157,160
point-wise update 158

254

learning rate 158
function approximation 160
expert-guided hybrid neuro-fuzzy
    system 164
feed-forward neural network 165
fuzzy relations 166,167
aggregated fuzzy relation 167
fuzzy relation interpretation 168
decomposition problem 168
fuzzy relation decomposition problem
    169
adaptive discretization 169
sequential decision problem 169
deep fusion of computational and
    symbolic processing 173,184
virtual world-centered UI 174
real world-centered UI 174
intelligent UI 175
RVI-concept 175
RVI-desk 175
intelligent multi model agent 176
symbolic processing 177,186
computational processing 177,186
hybrid system 177
symbolic AI 178
computational AI 178
fusion of computational AI and
    symbolic AI 178
conceptual fuzzy set 178
logic on NN 178
combination of pattern and symbol 178
NN+attention 178
FINEST 178
FLINS 178,179,181
computational nature of fuzzy reasoning
    179
symbolic nature of fuzzy reasoning 179
extended aggregation function 179
extended implication function 180
extended combination function 180
fusion of symbolic AI and fuzzy theory
    181
basic inference layer 182
fuzzy inference layer 182
fuzzy CBR layer 182
learning without a priori knowledge 186
combined Q-learning and NN 186
Q-NN layer 187
Q-table 187
symbol-emergence layer 187
exploration process 188
extraction process 188
combination process 188

forced application process 189
meaning concept 200,208
conceptual fuzzy sets (CFS) 201
associative memory 201
bidirectional associative memories
    (BAMs) 203
long term memories 206
short term memories 206
inductive construction 206
hebbian learning 206
inductive learning 206
fusion of symbolic and quantitative
    processing 208
approximate reasoning 208
fusion of top-down and bottom-up
    processing 209
natural language processing 209
parsing 209
semantic analysis 209
context sensitive processing 210
recognition of "THE CAT" 211
recognition of facial expressions ... 212
multi-layer reasoning 214
semantic guide line 215
analogical reasoning system by
    association 220
area representation method 221
area representation (AR) 221,222
associative neural network 221
attribute 225
blackboard model 220
distributed feature map 221
distributed representation 220
efficiency for knowledge representation
    220
frame model 220
Hebb rule 226
inheritance learning 227
inclusion relation 222
interactive activation and competition
    (IAC) 220
inter-map weight learning 226
is-a relation 223
knowledge representation 220
Kohonen self-organizing feature map
    223,224
Kohonen feature map 221
local representation 220,221
lower level concepts 222
map formation 225
multidirectional associative memory
    221
neighborhood Hebb rule 226

neural networks 220
node 225
part/whole problem 221,223
PATON 221
recall process 230
relation 225
robustness 220
semantic map 221
semantic network 220,224
similarity of concepts 221
storage and recall of hierarchical
    knowledge 223
trace feature map 221
upper level concepts 222
demi-phonemes 238
elemental motion units 238,239,241
incremental path method (IPM) ...239
IPM network 239
label sequence 244
self-organizing IPM network 240
self-organizing network 238
topology of IPM network 239
vectorial quantization of images ...243
visualization of IPM network 244

Studies in Fuzziness and Soft Computing

Vol. 26. A. Yazici and R. George
Fuzzy Database Modeling, 1999
ISBN 3-7908-1171-8

Vol. 27. M. Zaus
*Crisp and Soft Computing with Hypercubical
Calculus, 1999*
ISBN 3-7908-1172-6

Vol. 28. R. A. Ribeiro,
H.-J. Zimmermann, R. R. Yager
and J. Kacprzyk (Eds.)
Soft Computing in Financial Engineering, 1999
ISBN 3-7908-1173-4

Vol. 29. H. Tanaka and P. Guo
*Possibilistic Data Analysis for Operations Research,
1999*
ISBN 3-7908-1183-1

Vol. 30. N. Kasabov and R. Kozma (Eds.)
*Neuro-Fuzzy Techniques for Intelligent Information
Systems, 1999*
ISBN 3-7908-1187-4

Vol. 31. B. Kostek
Soft Computing in Acoustics, 1999
ISBN 3-7908-1190-4

Vol. 32. K. Hirota and T. Fukuda
Soft Computing in Mechatronics, 1999
ISBN 3-7908-1212-9

Vol. 33. L. A. Zadeh and J. Kacprzyk (Eds.)
*Computing with Words in Information/
Intelligent Systems 1, 1999*
ISBN 3-7908-1217-X

Vol. 34. L. A. Zadeh and J. Kacprzyk (Eds.)
*Computing with Words in Information/
Intelligent Systems 2, 1999*
ISBN 3-7908-1218-8

Vol. 35. K. T. Atanassov
Intuitionistic Fuzzy Sets, 1999
ISBN 3-7908-1228-5

Vol. 36. L. C. Jain (Ed.)
Innovative Teaching and Learning, 2000
ISBN 3-7908-1246-3

Vol. 37. R. Słowiński and M. Hapke (Eds.)
Scheduling Under Fuzziness, 2000
ISBN 3-7908-1249-8

Vol. 38. D. Ruan (Ed.)
*Fuzzy Systems and Soft Computing
in Nuclear Engineering, 2000*
ISBN 3-7908-1251-X

Vol. 39. O. Pons, M. A. Vila and J. Kacprzyk (Eds.)
Knowledge Management in Fuzzy Databases, 2000
ISBN 3-7908-1255-2

Vol. 40. M. Grabisch, T. Murofushi and M. Sugeno
(Eds.)
Fuzzy Measures and Integrals, 2000
ISBN 3-7908-1255-2

Vol. 41. P. Szczepaniak, P. Lisboa and J. Kacprzyk
(Eds.)
Fuzzy Systems in Medicine, 2000
ISBN 3-7908-1263-4

Vol. 42. S. Pal, G. Ashish and M. Kundu (Eds.)
Soft Computing for Image Processing, 2000
ISBN 3-7908-1217-X

Vol. 43. L. C. Jain, B. Lazzerini and U. Halici (Eds.)
Innovations in ART Neural Networks, 2000
ISBN 3-7908-1270-6

Vol. 44. J. Aracil and F. Gordillo (Eds.)
Stability Issues in Fuzzy Control, 2000
ISBN 3-7908-1277-3

Vol. 45. N. Kasabov (Ed.)
*Future Directions for Intelligent Information Systems
on Information Sciences, 2000*
ISBN 3-7908-1276-5

Vol. 46. J. N. Mordeson and P. S. Nair
Fuzzy Graphs and Fuzzy Hypergraphs, 2000
ISBN 3-7908-1286-2

Vol. 47. E. Czogała† and J. Łęski
Fuzzy and Neuro-Fuzzy Intelligent Systems, 2000
ISBN 3-7908-1289-7

Vol. 48. M. Sakawa
*Large Scale Interactive Fuzzy Multiobjective
Programming, 2000*
ISBN 3-7908-1293-5

Vol. 49. L. I. Kuncheva
Fuzzy Classifier Design, 2000
ISBN 3-7908-1298-6

Vol. 50. F. Crestani and G. Pasi (Eds.)
Soft Computing in Information Retrieval, 2000
ISBN 3-7908-1299-4

Vol. 51. J. Fodor, B. De Baets and P. Perny (Eds.)
*Preferences and Decisions under Incomplete
Knowledge, 2000*
ISBN 3-7908-1303-6

Vol. 52. E. E. Kerre and M. Nachtegael (Eds.)
Fuzzy Techniques in Image Processing, 2000
ISBN 3-7908-1304-4

Vol. 53. G. Bordogna and G. Pasi (Eds.)
Recent Issues on Fuzzy Databases, 2001
ISBN 3-7908-1319-2

Studies in Fuzziness and Soft Computing

Vol. 54. P. Sinčák and J. Vaščák (Eds.)
Quo Vadis Computational Intelligence?, 2000
ISBN 3-7908-1324-9

Vol. 55. J.N. Mordeson, D.S. Malik
and S.-C. Cheng
Fuzzy Mathematics in Medicine, 2000
ISBN 3-7908-1325-7

Vol. 56. L. Polkowski, S. Tsumoto and T.Y. Lin
(Eds.)
Rough Set Methods and Applications, 2000
ISBN 3-7908-1328-1

Vol. 57. V. Novák and I. Perfilieva (Eds.)
Discovering the World with Fuzzy Logic, 2001
ISBN 3-7908-1330-3

Vol. 58. Davender S. Malik and John N. Mordeson
Fuzzy Discrete Structures, 2000
ISBN 3-7908-1335-4